japanese home cooking

japanese home cooking

Simple Meals, Authentic Flavors

SONOKO SAKAI

PHOTOGRAPHS BY RICK POON

Illustrations by Juliette Bellocq

ROOST BOOKS
Boulder 2019

contents

introduction

In ancient Japan, a small mound of salt was served at each table setting so diners could salt their own food. This notion of salting your own food—*teshio ni kakeru*—has evolved over time to mean "the act of nurturing," whether it is raising your child, making your own miso, or, as it applies to this book, cooking for the people you love.

This book is about Japanese cooking. It is also about home cooking. I was lucky to be raised with both. I was born in New York to Japanese parents and spent my childhood in Tokyo, San Francisco, Mexico City, Kamakura, and Los Angeles. While growing up, I had two wonderful teachers: my mother, Akiko Kondo, and my maternal grandmother, Hatsuko Ishikawa.

I watched my mother maintain a Japanese kitchen everywhere our family lived, which was often a challenge. She was an ingenious and resourceful cook who managed to make Japanese meals without always having access to Japanese ingredients. From my mother I inherited the arts of adaptability and flexibility. Shortly before I finished writing this book, my mother died at the age of eighty-nine. I was fortunate to have visited her in Tokyo just a few weeks before her passing. There is an old Japanese saying that when you really want to care for your parents, they are gone. So, care for your parents. My grandmother, who lived to the ripe old age of 102, was a *modan* (modern and open) person. She had a weekly regimen of baking bread, making pickles, practicing the tea ceremony, and going to church. Her baking ritual brought out the Westerner in her. She was one of the few people in Kamakura to own an oven, and she was still baking when she turned one hundred.

Her grandfather, or my great-great-grandfather, was Hermann Siber, a Swiss silk merchant who came to Yokohama in the 1870s looking for silk just after Japan opened its ports to the world. There he met Oshio, an accomplished geisha from Yoshiwara, the old geisha quarters in Edo (which is now Tokyo). My great-grandfather, Jiro Nakamura, was their mixed-blood illegitimate offspring, but that fact was shrouded in family secrecy. It was not until my grandmother was twenty years old that she learned of her ancestry after receiving a missive from Switzerland announcing Hermann's death. She learned that Oshio was not just a close family friend, as she had been told, but actually her grandmother. In my own relationship with my cherished grandmother, she related stories to explain what it meant to straddle two cultures.

As such, it is my hope that this cookbook reflects the values and practices of my mother and grandmother, as well as those skills I have developed in my own kitchen, an amalgam of today's contemporary cross-cultural experiences.

———

My father used to say that if you have a bottle of soy sauce, you can make Japanese food. He worked as an airline executive, and as one of the new generation of Japanese to live and work abroad after World War II, he was transferred from

Artisans making soy sauce in Noda, Chiba Prefecture. (Hiroshige III, Meiji Period)

Tokyo to New York in the early 1950s. My mother joined my father in New York a year later, with my brother Hiroshi in her arms. In her new kitchen in their tenement apartment in Queens, she took in with amused curiosity the world of midcentury American cooking. She found dozens of empty TV dinner trays stacked on top of the refrigerator (my father felt there *had* to be a use for the aluminum) and a bottle of soy sauce in the otherwise empty pantry. Not surprisingly, Japanese ingredients were not readily available back then, but my father was able to find soy sauce in New York City. In those postwar years in the United States, soy sauce gave my father some comfort, even though it was sprinkled on TV dinners.

I am my parents' first American-born child. At the time of my birth, anti-Japanese sentiments were still lingering in the United States. When my brother and I cried, the neighbor below us would hit the ceiling of his apartment with a broom and shout, "Remember Pearl Harbor!" My mother would take us out into the freezing cold New York winter to calm our nerves—and hers too. Soon we acclimated to our new life in the United States and our time here got better.

In my baby book, my mother pasted a letter from my grandmother that honored my birth and detailed the contents of the care package shipped to New York: tea, miso, wakame, and kombu—the staples necessary for a Japanese pantry. I developed a sense of Japan through the fragrance of the Japanese food sent in these care packages. My mother learned how to combine American and Japanese ingredients and turn them into

My father standing at the family dinner table playing a stacking game he invented called the Empire State Building.

hybrid dishes. She made fried rice with chopped onions and Birds Eye frozen peas and carrots. She stir-fried the vegetables in butter and garnished the dish with crispy flaked nori. (Being able to use butter was a dream come true for someone who had survived wartime hunger.) Mother whipped up the fried rice so quickly that my teeth would tingle from the still-frozen vegetables.

Every three to six years, my family moved back and forth between Japan and overseas because of my father's job, and with the moves came new aromas. My mother's repertoire of dishes grew, one of which was her flaky American apple pie that to date none of us—her five children—can replicate because she never followed a recipe. She also made honey-baked ham (which she only had to heat) on rice. Even after my parents moved back to Japan, my mother would always ask one of her children in America to bring back a large ham, so we always packed one in our suitcase.

———

I started elementary school in San Francisco, but right after I finished first grade we moved to Mexico City. My mother thought I would learn Spanish faster if I took guitar lessons, so she found a teacher for me. His name was Pancho and he was a mariachi. He wore pants with shiny silver eagle buttons running up the sides. When he took off his sombrero, I always caught a whiff of his hair tonic. He played the guitar beautifully, but he couldn't read music. So he dictated the lyrics of the songs to me, I wrote them down in my notebook, and we sang and played the guitar together. Our two housekeepers, Remedios and Celina, would interject *gritos* (shouts) and join joyously in the ranchera songs. I learned to play many love songs by heart and became fluent in Spanish. On Sundays, the two women would take me to church. If I sat through Mass quietly, I was treated to tamales and pan dulces. If I could just get my ears pierced, I thought I could turn into a Mexican girl. But my mother wouldn't allow that, and after six years of living abroad, it was time to move back to Japan.

We went to live with my maternal grandmother in Kamakura while we waited for our house in Tokyo to become available. Grandmother's house was a former Shinto shrine with a lotus bud on top of the patinated sloping roof. People would wander into her house, thinking it was a place of worship. In a way, it was.

Obachama (Grandmother) helped me with Japanese schoolwork (I had a lot of catching up to do), but what I enjoyed most was when she invited me to cook with her. We would talk about what we would eat, spending a great amount of energy on the subject until we decided on a menu. Often the discussions continued while we sourced the ingredients, which could all be had within walking distance. We would walk to the beach at dawn to buy fish directly from the fisherman's net, passing the various artisan shops in the neighborhood. Everyone was up working at the crack of dawn. The rice miller would be writing the haiku of the day on the chalkboard outside his shop. The tofu maker would be cutting the day's tofu into perfect squares. The aroma and warmth of the fresh soy milk were so enticing that I would beg Obachama to get us a block of tofu. We would take walks up the hill to forage bamboo shoots and wild herbs in the spring; we would pick ginkgo nuts from the old

Me as a baby eating *chirashi zushi*.

tree in town, roast them, and put them in the rice; we would work in her garden planting seeds and pulling weeds. A farm lady regularly visited us to sell her fresh vegetables, eggs, and natto (fermented soybeans) in rice straws. Those were special times.

My family left Kamakura for Tokyo, where we lived until the early 1970s, when my father was transferred to the United States again, this time to Los Angeles. I was a junior in high school at this time. My parents rented a big two-story house in Pasadena, with grapefruit, orange, and avocado trees in the backyard. Of all the places we lived overseas, we spent the longest stretch of time there and made many friends, among them Japanese Americans.

There was a relatively large Japanese American community on the Pacific Coast that had existed for more than a hundred years, as many had immigrated here. They helped construct the railroads, worked as fishermen and in the cannery, and established farms and nurseries—growing rice, vegetables, grapes, peaches, berries, and flowers. The elder *issei* (first generation of Japanese Americans) told us their immigrant stories. From them we learned about the internment camps during World War II, where *issei*, along with their American-born children (called *nisei*), were taken far away from home. They suffered serious financial and emotional losses, but they never lost their sense of community, mutual support, and pride in being Japanese Americans.

They invited us to their farms to pick strawberries and to participate in *nikkei* (Japanese American) potlucks. They offered *mochitsuki* (year's-end rice pounding) at the local Buddhist community center where people wished for good luck in the coming year. The children of *nisei* (called *sansei*) took me to parties where I learned to dance to Motown music. It was in Los Angeles that my mother started making miso (fermented rice and bean seasoning), natto, and *nukazuke* (fermented rice bran pickles) at home. My mother learned these disappearing Japanese food traditions from the *issei*. I would go into the garage where my mother stored the crock of miso to lick its dark, delicious miso tamari. Our life in California was bountiful, and we felt that our roots were growing in this land as our Japanese traditions were being reinvigorated. I wasn't an immigrant's child, but I began to feel a sense of permanence in America as a Japanese American for the first time in my life.

My parents moved back to Tokyo for the final time in 1980, but I decided to stay in California and go to college. I majored in international relations, thinking someday I would work in the foreign service, and then I went to graduate school with a major in education. But life has a way of leading you down different paths.

I ended up leaving graduate school and working in film, starting out as a production assistant and then working in the international market as a film seller and buyer. The job allowed me to broaden my appreciation for film, travel around the world, enrich my palate, and take regular trips to Japan, where I was able to see my family. The American economy was booming, and so was the newly discovered popularity of Japanese food—sushi was even becoming part of the global food scene. But I noticed that when it came to Japanese home cooking all the dishes and nuances I was used to experiencing were missing. So I decided to write a cookbook, *The Poetical Pursuit of Food: Japanese Recipes for American Cooks*, hoping not only to fill that gap but also to find my voice in English.

In hindsight, I realize I was perhaps ahead of the times. I remember appearing on a morning television show to make miso soup using bonito flakes and kombu; the TV host didn't seem particularly excited by the overwhelming smell of seaweed and dried fish so early in the day. How our senses change! Today my students respond with such joy when they smell the aroma of miso soup.

I met my future husband, Katsuhisa Sakai, in Los Angeles. He was born in Tateyama, Chiba Prefecture. The son of a fisherman, he worked hauling fish at the Tsukiji Fish Market in Tokyo while he pursued his dream of becoming an artist. He eventually came to the United States to go to art school. We carried on a bicultural tradition in our own family as we raised our son, Sakae. Every summer, my stepson, Tyler, would join us in California. We would go camping, clam digging, and fishing. While raising a family and continuing my work in the film industry, I began contributing stories and recipes about Japanese cooking to the food section of the *Los Angeles Times*, describing how I made Japanese and American dishes in my kitchen. Like my grandmother, I continued to pursue the taste of the seasons, visiting the farmers' markets and making trips to farms to pick strawberries and cherries.

In 2008, I left the film world after experiencing disappointing results with the film I had produced. It opened during the week of the stock market crash—and crashed as the market did. At this point I felt I needed to steer my life in a different direction. On a whim, I took a workshop in noodle making while I was in Tokyo. I liked eating noodles, but I also wanted to get my hands in flour to practice something tactile and restorative. The urge developed when the carpenter who had

worked on a film I produced in Nagano invited me to his house in the country for soba (buckwheat) noodles prepared by his eighty-three-year-old mother. He was very proud to tell me that she had grown the buckwheat, milled it in a stone mill, and made the noodles all by hand. I remember how the old woman sat on the hardwood floor in the kitchen, smiling while she watched her son and me eat the noodles in the tatami room. She was too humble to join us. I thought then that I would like to grow old like her, make food by hand, and share it with the people I love.

For the next few years, I returned to Japan to study noodle making; I didn't know where I was going with it, but I was loving the journey. My father thought I had lost my mind. "Why abandon a career in film for noodle making? I will take you to any noodle shop you want!" he protested. But I continued my education. One soba noodle master, Takashi Hosokawa of the restaurant Hosokawa in Tokyo, generously took me under his wing and taught me how to make soba noodles. I watched him mill the buckwheat in a stone mill, make dashi (stock), cook the bowls of noodles, and fuss over the quality of carrots or the oysters while I grated the fresh wasabi and daikon radish, washed dishes, vacuumed the buckwheat husks off the milling floor, and cleaned the windows until they sparkled every morning. He would let me taste the dashi, the tempura just out of the sizzling oil, and the freshly hand-cut soba. He explained the quality of these dishes every step of the way. It was an invaluable experience that gave me a profound appreciation and understanding of the fundamentals of Japanese cuisine inside the *shokunin* (artisan) world.

In 2009, I started teaching Japanese cooking out of my home in Los Angeles, learning as I taught and teaching as I learned. In a few years, I began teaching up and down the West Coast. I drove thousands of miles in my Prius loaded down with rice cookers, noodle knives, and pans; I crashed on my friends' couches and in their guest rooms; and I parked my car on country roads off the I-5 and

101 to take quick naps or pick up a bag of almonds, peaches, or strawberries from the roadside stands to keep me going. I took my workshops around the country. I was also invited to teach in Japan, France, China, Peru, and Mexico. I began meeting a wide range of people in the food world—farmers, chefs, scientists, bakers, millers, and students. I never imagined I would develop this kind of dialogue with people from around the world who share the common interest in good food and building a sustainable food system.

Although I have now lived in California for more than forty years, Japan will always be my home away from home, and it will always be my culinary home. I am now at the age my grandmother was when I first stepped into her kitchen in Kamakura. Obachama used to say, "I am living history," and I have come to understand what she meant by that. This book offers the sense of craft and reverence of three generations of women in my family: the wisdom, elegance, and independent spirit my grandmother shared with me; my mother's passion for life and people; and my own culinary discoveries.

—————

The book begins with an explanation of the principles that have guided me, my mother, and my grandmother. They are guidelines for Japanese cooking in general, and I first expressed them in my earlier cookbook, published more than thirty years ago. Revisiting them today leads me to think about how different things were thirty years ago. People today are more open-minded and curious about eating and cooking, and more mindful about health and sustainability. And I marvel at the diversity in my cooking classes—the way that flavors and cultures have started to blend and seep into our modern mind-set. I admire Mia Li, a chef from Austin, Texas, who was inspired by the miso her Laotian grandmother learned from a Japanese soldier during World War II; I think of the organic farmer Bill Keener of Sequatchie Cove Farm in

Tennessee, who went to school in Tokyo and fell in love with Japanese food and the Japanese ways of life. Now he wants to help his daughter and daughter-in-law farm grains and make soba noodles from the ground up. I consider the family stories of Miki and Mei Morioka, Peruvian Japanese siblings whose grandfather was deported from Peru to an internment camp in Texas during World War II because he was of Japanese descent; he died there. Two generations later, his grandchildren, proud of their Japanese ancestry, want to learn Japanese cooking. I admire Yolanda Burrell of Pollinate Farm and Garden in the Fruitvale district of Oakland's melting pot. She spent her girlhood on an Air Force base in Japan and still likes to hum the song "Sukiyaki" while tending her crops and flock of chickens. In her work she creates opportunities to advance the culture of urban farming by exploring diversity through food. In short, we have come a long way from my father and his solitary bottle of soy sauce. My Japanese kitchen now feels completely at home in America.

HOW TO USE THIS BOOK

Not only will your teachers appear, they will cook new foods for you.
—ALICE WALKER

When we step into someone's kitchen for the first time, it is always our sense of smell that tells us what is familiar or unfamiliar. In my kitchen, you probably would encounter many unfamiliar smells, such as kombu (seaweed), *umeboshi* (pickled *ume* plums), bonito flakes, dried shiitake mushrooms, and dried sardines. You probably would see many unfamiliar sights too—earthenware jars of fermenting foods such as miso and *nukamiso* (rice bran filled with vegetables for pickling) sitting next to kombucha and sourdough starter. My goal for this book is to make these unfamiliar smells and sights—those of Japanese cooking—familiar to you. As a cooking teacher, I am here to guide you. I want this book to be useful and joyful—both as a cookbook and as a means to expand your knowledge and experience of Japanese culinary culture and aspirations as a home cook.

For practical purposes, I have divided the book into two sections. Part one introduces the Japanese pantry and everyday *okazu* (dishes). Part two offers more involved *okazu*, as well as Japanese sweets, preserved fruits, and beverages including tea and sake. Every recipe will ask for your time in the kitchen, some more than others. Read each recipe from start to finish before you get started. Some of the recipes might look complicated and have a lot of ingredients. I want you to understand that Japanese food is made of components that are assembled into one—so everywhere there is dashi or *shoyu tare* (soy sauce-based seasoning). You can always make these staple recipes ahead, so you have them on hand to speed up your cooking time.

The parts and chapters in this book represent a progression, with part one, "The Japanese Pantry," perhaps the most important section and the one that deserves the most attention and time—from both you and me. This part introduces the ingredients unique to Japanese cooking and guides you in making some of the fundamental components of the dishes that appear in later chapters.

"Everyday *Okazu* (Pantry Recipes)" puts the ingredients and basic recipes of the Japanese pantry to work, with recipes that help you incorporate the flavors, seasonings, and cooking methods you've just learned into simple, everyday dishes. These are the recipes that I regularly prepare at home, and they are also the introductory recipes I teach to my beginning students. This chapter will make you more comfortable using the ingredients and basic flavors you've learned by translating them from the kitchen or pantry to the table.

Once you have understood the characteristics of the pantry ingredients and have made some of the pantry recipes, it is then time to move on to part two, "*Okazu*, Sweets, and Beverages." This part is a collection of more elaborate recipes, some of which can be made ahead of time and others that need to be assembled at the last minute. The recipes here will be more time-consuming but well worth the effort—they are Japanese cooking in full bloom. I have collected, adapted, and created these recipes over my decades in the kitchen. Some are family heirlooms, and some are my own inventions inspired by particular ingredients, places I have traveled, restaurants where I have eaten, and people I have met along the way.

Throughout the book you will find short reflections about various aspects of Japanese cuisine. You will participate in a seaweed harvest with Barbara Stephens and John Lewallen of the Mendecino Sea Vegetable Company; learn a few "good luck" culinary traditions in Japan; attend a rice harvest at Koda Farms with Robin Koda; take a fish lesson from Niki Nakayama and Carole Iida of n/naka in Los Angeles; walk in the wheat fields with farmer Alex Weiser of the Tehachapi Heritage Grain Project; and grate bonito flakes and learn about the tradition of *kanbutsu*—naturally preserved vegetables, seaweeds, and seafood—with Mamiko Nishiyama of Yagicho Honten, a three-hundred-year-old grocery shop in Tokyo. These essays are a tribute to those people and places cultivating good and sustainable food in my home state of California and in Japan, from whom I have benefited tremendously. The work of these colleagues, friends, and students continues to serve as an inspiration for my cooking.

My hope is that this cookbook will serve you as a guide and teach you enough to enable you to adapt the recipes here to your liking. Then you will have made Japanese cooking your own.

the principles of japanese cooking

There are five keys to Japanese cooking: freshness, seasonality, simplicity, beauty, and economy. At its most fundamental level, Japanese cooking, or *washoku*, is about respecting your ingredients and letting their natural flavor come through. Your ingredients should be as fresh and seasonal as possible. Relatedly, let the ingredients speak for themselves. I prefer not to fuss too much with the food. A fresh fish, simply salted and grilled over charcoal, can make a beautiful meal.

Although Japan is a small island country, its geographical diversity is similar to countries such as Italy, with long distances from its northern areas to its southern extremities. This diversity in the land lends itself to many regional specialties. Take noodles, for example: the ingredients for making the dashi (kombu, bonito flakes, shiitake, dried sardines, meat bones), the choice of seasonings (salt, soy sauce, miso), the variety of toppings (braised herring, stewed pork), and the style of noodles (soba, udon, *somen*, *kishimen*, ramen) can be fixed by regional traditions and ingredients that can be sourced locally. In this cookbook I will touch upon regionality when a recipe comes from a particular place in Japan.

There are traditional styles of Japanese cuisines such as *kaiseki ryori* (multicourse cuisine), sushi, *shojin ryori* (vegetarian cuisine), and other specialties that take years of discipline and artistry. Few Japanese home cooks attempt to make such restaurant food at home because it is too complicated or the ingredients are hard to source. You will not find a recipe for *nigiri*-style sushi in this book because it belongs in the realm of sushi bars, not home. But I offer you *Temaki Zushi* (Sushi Hand Rolls; page 203), *Mari Zushi* (page 205), and *Chirashi Zushi* (page 192), and *Inari Zushi* (page 131), the way I serve sushi at home. Of course, home cooking is the most essential cooking. Even the accomplished and revered Japanese chefs will tell you that they try to emulate *ofukuro-no-aji*, "a mother's palate."

You might find the experience of cooking Japanese food a little daunting at first, but there are some culinary ideas and menu compositions that you should be aware of. One is the *gogyosetsu*, the theory of five elements as applied to eating and cooking, and the second is *kondate*, Japanese menu composition. They will have practical applications in your kitchen when you are putting a meal together.

THE FIVE ELEMENTS OF COOKING AND EATING

Much of Japan's culture derives from ancient Chinese ideas, one of which is the five elements, which is *wu xing* in Chinese or *gogyosetsu* in Japanese. Broadly applied, it is a system of grouping things into fives to explain interactions and relationships in our world, some of which you are probably already familiar with.

THE FIVE FLAVORS

The five basic tastes are sweet, sour, salty, bitter, and umami. In parts of Asia, pungency (spiciness and hotness) is considered a fifth taste or sixth taste. What you should remember is these flavors are used to complement one another. No dish should have an overwhelming single flavor; rather, it should feature a balance of several.

THE FIVE SENSES

The five basic senses are taste, smell, touch, hearing, and sight. When you are cooking and eating, you want to use all your senses to "taste" the food. What aromas does it have? How does the dish look? Can you hear, for example, how a pan sizzles when it is hot enough?

THE FIVE COLORS

The five basic colors are white, yellow, red, green (blue), and black (brown, purple). Each color has a specific symbolism and function: white symbolizes purity; yellow and red increase appetite; green is comforting; and black adds contrast and tightens and balances the whole. Spreading colors around your plate or meal adds diversity to what and how you cook and also improves the nutritional quality of your meals.

THE FIVE COOKING TECHNIQUES

The five basic cooking techniques are *nama* (raw, sliced), which applies to dishes prepared without the application of heat, such as *sashimi*; *niru* (braised, simmered, or blanched); *yaku* (grilled); *musu* (steamed); and *ageru* (deep-fried or fried), which also applies to sautéed and stir-fried. These techniques involving oil were introduced to Japan from China. Later, the Portuguese introduced deep-fried technique, which has become part of Japanese cuisine: tempura. Each technique has both practical and artistic purposes. The variety of cooking techniques makes for interesting combinations in your meals. Since chopsticks are the basic tools for eating, many of the foods are served in bite-size morsels. At the same time, as a home cook you should not feel that you have to incorporate all of these techniques in a single meal.

THE FIVE ELEMENTS OF A MEAL

In a broader sense, the five elements that determine a successful meal are the skill of the cook; the quality of the ingredients; the temperature of the dishes (hot food should be hot, cold food should be cold); the size of the servings; and the aesthetics and mood of the dining space, including aspects such as the quality of the light, the choice of tableware, and the view out the window. These elements should complement one another and always be in balance—atmosphere should never overshadow a meal, a technique should never mask an ingredient, plates should never be piled high with food (which actually can be considered offensive in Japanese culture). A meal should be like a symphony, with all elements in harmony and working together to form a beautiful whole.

———

The ultimate goals of cooking and eating are health and pleasure. There is no greater joy than sharing good food with the people you love.

COMPOSING A JAPANESE MEAL

The basic ideas for composing a Japanese meal are helpful guides when planning a meal, as Japanese meals follow a particular structure. When I sit down to plan a Japanese meal, my first thought is *okazu*. This word is used by home cooks to describe the dish (or dishes) of the day, but not in the way that American cooks may think of it. In a traditional Japanese meal, there is no entrée or main dish in a Western sense, no big centerpiece of meat or fish (unless it is a special occasion such as New Year's, a birthday, or a wedding). Instead, a typical meal puts grains—namely rice—at the heart of a meal, accompanied by *okazu* (a number of dishes).

The most common configuration of a traditional Japanese meal is *ichiju sansai*, which means "one soup and three dishes." Yes, that's three dishes, or *okazu*—some kind of fish or meat dish and two vegetable dishes for balance, or three vegetable dishes if you prefer a vegetable-centered meal. These dishes can be prepared using a variety of techniques, from *nama* (raw) or *kiru* (slice), which is used for cutting and slicing fresh fish, meat, and vegetables such as sashimi and sushi, to *yaku* (grill), *musu* (steam), *niru* (braise or simmer), and *ageru* (deep-fry or stir-fry). In addition to a soup, three dishes, and the rice mentioned above, a typical Japanese meal will also include a small dish of pickles.

It's good to know that a traditional *ichiju sansai* place setting is designed to suit a right-handed person. The rice bowl is placed on the left side because in Japanese culture, the left side is considered more important than the right side. The rice bowl is held with your left hand and the chopsticks are held in your right hand to pick up the *okazu*. Chopsticks are placed horizontally to the place setting, with the tips pointing to the left. The soup bowl is placed on the right side, next to the rice bowl, because it's the other dish that you pick up with your hands and bring up to your mouth. The small plate of pickles is set in the middle. The fish, meat, and vegetable *okazu* are placed in the back of the place setting. If you have individual servings of a whole fish such as a grilled sardine, the head faces left. At home, you can relax and accommodate your left-handed person.

In the old days, Buddhist practitioners and the average person ate *soboku* (frugal and simple) meals composed around the concepts of *ichiju issai* (one soup and one dish) or *ichiju nisai* (one soup and two dishes), with pickles and a bowl of millet or barley (rice was reserved for special occasions). But people of higher social status could have elaborate, multicourse compositions, growing into two soups and five dishes (with a bowl of rice and pickles, of course!), or even more.

If you go to a *kaiseki*-style Japanese restaurant today, you can experience this multicourse feast, which is an elegant meal prepared by the chef with specifically chosen seasonal ingredients and elaborate presentations.

What I have described are traditional Japanese meals, but you should be aware that in the past century the Japanese diet and lifestyle have changed dramatically. While the simple and pure Japanese meal of *ichiju issai* (one soup and one dish), *ichiju nisai* (one soup and two dishes), or *ichiju sansai* (one soup and three dishes) is appreciated for its variety, deliciousness, and nutritional balance, the Japanese family table now features meat, bread, curry, pasta, and a variety of foods from around the world—including more processed and fast foods—all in much larger portions than traditional meals. In fact, the Japanese now eat, on average, more bread than rice.

This book focuses on Japanese home cooking, not restaurant foods, with the goal of offering you options for composing a nutritiously balanced meal made with fresh ingredients, preferably grown close to home, and using methods the home cook will find easy. While the expression of *okazu* can be simple or elaborate, we will understand it here to simply offer variety and a measure of informality; along these lines I follow the *ichiju sansai* (one soup and three dishes) concept loosely throughout this book. The soup and dishes can be served all at once or one after the next if you'd like to stretch out the evening.

If the soup is hearty enough to be a substantial part of the meal, I will base the meal around the soup, such as hot pot dishes (*nabemono*) that are often followed or finished by rice porridge or noodles. Noodle soups and grain bowls (*donburimono*) can be all-in-one meals; you can place your *okazu* right on top of the rice or noodles, and there you have two dishes in one. Finally, there is the bento box, the ingenious portable meal that contains a variety of *okazu* and grains or noodles (and, nowadays, also sandwiches and pasta).

the principles of japanese cooking

After reading about the number of dishes included in a meal, you may be wondering if this kind of cooking will mean more work in the kitchen. Not necessarily! I make some of the dishes ahead of time and then serve them over several days, either reheating them or presenting them at room temperature. Sometimes I will mix Japanese dishes with Western dishes. To me, they are all *okazu*. I also like to serve dishes family-style, on a large platter at the center of the table where people can help themselves (serving on large platters minimizes both my trips to the kitchen and the dishes to wash after the meal).

———

Understanding the principles of Japanese cooking may feel challenging at first, but once you get the hang of it, these guidelines simplify the process of creating wonderfully delicious and versatile meals.

kitchen equipment and tableware

When it comes to the tools you need for Japanese cooking at home, I believe in two fundamental principles. First, your hands are the best tools. Second, you probably already have the equipment you need to prepare Japanese dishes: knives, cast-iron pots, skillets, ladles, strainers, cutting boards, vegetable peelers, graters, measuring cups, digital scales, and spoons. The basic tools of any home kitchen are appropriate for the Japanese kitchen. There are, of course, a few items that are especially useful; they are listed below. Go to Resources (page 291) for Japanese kitchen equipment and tableware.

KITCHEN EQUIPMENT

KNIVES (HOCHO)

Perhaps the most important piece of equipment is a sharp knife. Since ancient times, the Japanese have preferred to eat their fresh fish and vegetables in season, preferably as sashimi, sliced raw and thin. A sharp knife is a must for making sashimi. The Japanese say that a person with a rusty knife can never be a good cook. My sculptor husband is an expert knife sharpener. He sharpens all my kitchen knives and instructs me to wash the knife after each use, wipe it completely dry with a clean cloth, and sharpen when needed (probably more often than you would think). I have Japanese knives that I have treasured for a couple of decades: an all-purpose knife (*santoku bocho*) for cutting meat, seafood, and vegetables; a vegetable knife (*nakiri bocho*), which has a broad, rectangular blade; a paring knife for peeling fruit; and a long, narrow knife (*yanagi bocho*) for cutting fish. The last is about ten inches long and is primarily used for slicing sashimi; the length of the blade allows you to slice a fillet of fish with a single continuous stroke. I also have a *deba bocho*, a thick knife primarily used for cutting through tougher matter such as fish and meat bones, squash, or pumpkin. You don't have to invest in Japanese knives specifically if you already have a good selection.

BAMBOO MAT (MAKISU)

This mat is for rolling sushi and shaping omelets and vegetables. The loosely woven texture of the mat drains water and other liquids well.

CHOPSTICKS (OHASHI OR HASHI)

I use a pair of long (fourteen inches) wooden chopsticks for cooking. I prefer them to tongs, which I often find rough for handling vegetables. It takes a little practice to learn to manipulate the chopsticks, but once you get used to them, they become extensions of your hands. Long chopsticks can also be made of metal: thin metal chopsticks are used like pincers to move delicate food around, while thick metal chopsticks are used mostly for tempura or for moving foods in and out of hot oil.

COTTON AND HEMP BAGS AND CHEESECLOTH

Bags for straining are very helpful in the kitchen. Of these, cotton is thicker, and I use a cotton bag for straining dashi. If you want to get really specific, the Japanese make a reusuable, dedicated bag for this purpose called *dashi koshi bukuro* that I cannot live without. I use the thinner hemp bags for straining soy milk. I use cheesecloth to line strainers and tofu molds. I wash and reuse all bags and cheesecloth multiple times.

DIGITAL SCALE

A digital scale is essential in my kitchen. I use a scale that measures in both imperial and metric (ounces and grams) units, and I use the metric units for all of my noodle and baking ingredients.

DONABE

A *donabe* is a clay pot used for cooking on the stove or the tabletop. It is indispensable for *nabe-mono* (hot pot dishes) such as *Oden* (Vegetable, Seafood, and Meat Hot Pot; page 217) and Pork and Vegetable *Mizore Nabe* (page 235). I also use a *donabe* rice cooker that is designed specifically for that purpose. Sitting around the *donabe* is intrinsic to Japanese culture. *Donabe* are durable but need to be seasoned and handled carefully so they don't crack or chip.

GRATER (*OROSHI-KI* AND *OROSHIGANE*)

The grater is a necessary tool in Japanese cooking. Grated daikon radish and ginger, for example, appear regularly in the Japanese meal as a garnish for many dishes. Most Japanese graters have a detachable container under the grater to catch the juices; this container is the difference between the *oroshi-ki* and the more common Microplanes and zesters that you may already have. The latter two don't quite do the same job as a Japanese grater but will work if you don't want to invest in a Japanese grater.

MORTAR AND PESTLE (*SURIBACHI* AND *SURIGOKI*)

The ridged interior of a Japanese mortar and pestle works efficiently to grind, crush, and mash sesame seeds for sesame paste. After use, soak the mortar in water and then scrub to remove all the paste that has collected in the grooves. Then turn it over to dry completely.

PRESSURE COOKER

I use my pressure cooker to make brown rice, beans, and *yakibuta* (braised meat). It's possible to make all of this in a regular pot, of course, but a pressure cooker saves time and produces food that is nice and tender. If you plan to use a pressure cooker, carefully read the manufacturer's instructions.

RICE COOKER

If you are cooking a lot of grains, an electric rice cooker is a very wise investment. It's one of the most useful pieces of equipment in the Asian kitchen. The Japanese rice cookers such as Tiger, Zojirushi, and Panasonic are reliable.

RICE PADDLE (*SHAMOJI* OR *OSHAMOJI*)

A rice paddle has a flat, wide surface that makes it easy to scoop rice. Wet it a little before use so the grains do not stick to the paddle.

RICE TUB (*HANGIRI* OR *HANDAI*)

A rice tub is a big, shallow wooden tub designed for preparing rice. The flat surface of the tub allows for the moisture in the rice to evaporate quickly so the rice doesn't get mushy when it is tossed or scooped with a rice paddle.

SCRUB BRUSH (*TAWASHI*)

There are certain tools that I can't live without, and a *tawashi* is one of them. This Japanese scrub brush is made of hemp, and it is extremely durable for scrubbing pots and pans.

STAINLESS STEEL STEAMER

I have a steamer that has three stackable units. Unlike bamboo, stainless steel does not wear out.

TABLETOP BUTANE STOVE

The portable butane stove is used for cooking at the table or outdoors. It is indispensable for *nabe-mono* (hot pot dishes) that are cooked at the table. When using the unit indoors, read the manufacturer's instructions and always leave a window open for ventilation.

COTTON TOWEL (*TENUGUI*)

This is a thin, all-purpose cotton cloth measuring about 10 x 16 inches (25 x 40 cm). It can be used as a washcloth, dishcloth, head wrap, or placemat—it is truly used for all purposes, and once you have a few you'll wonder how you ever lived without them. A *tenugui* can also have several lives. When I was a child, my grandmother would use worn *tenugui* to teach me how to sew.

VEGETABLE SLICER

A Japanese vegetable slicer or a mandoline is very practical for slicing vegetables that range in size and thickness. Make sure to use the hand guard.

TABLEWARE

Tableware plays an important role in the presentation of the meal. It is so important, in fact, that it can even influence the meal itself. When I see a beautiful bowl, for example, I become inspired to cook something to complement it. Just as the Japanese meal is composed of a variety of dishes, so should your table be composed of a variety of plates and bowls in all sizes, shapes, and colors.

Variety is a key concept that can be applied to all aspects of tableware: color, texture, size, shape, and even material. My mother would serve our everyday meals in Melmac dishes, which are made of melamine resin and are hard to break. This was smart of her, considering she had five children at the table. But she would bring out the good Japanese ceramics and pottery on special occasions, taking time to teach us to appreciate the value of objects.

One of the mainstays of a Japanese meal is soup, which is generally served in lacquerware, but here too you can explore other options.

Seasonality can be reflected in your choice of tableware. Think of color, tone, and weight when selecting plates and bowls for your meal. I like to serve food in glassware in the summertime to bring coolness and lightness to the table. I personally prefer pottery with neutral and subdued colors accented by bright colors and designs. On my table, these accents come in the form of small condiment dishes and chopstick rests. You can even get creative and use twigs, rocks, or seashells for your chopstick rests; all you need is enough height to keep the tips of the chopsticks off the table.

You can explore this component of Japanese cooking without spending a lot of money. Keep your eye out for interesting tableware wherever you go—flea markets, local markets, or craft fairs that may offer the work of local potters, ceramics galleries, even garage sales. Pick up chopstick rests on the beach or in the woods. Don't be afraid to mix and match—it's the guiding principle of the Japanese table.

PART ONE

the japanese pantry

Like an orchestra, Japanese cooking is a melding of components. Ingredients in a dish build flavors, and flavors within a dish build on one another. Same thing in a meal—all the dishes build on one another for a resulting symphony of tastes and sensations.

In this section we will consider the "instruments" of our orchestra and begin to build Japanese flavors. The instruments are our ingredients, some of which will be very familiar to you (eggs, flour) and others perhaps less familiar (bonito flakes, seaweeds). As our starting point, I offer you the ingredients and some basic recipes that are essential to Japanese cooking and that will be built on throughout the book. Rice, for example, is a staple in Japanese meals, and you will learn here basic cooking instructions and variations that will serve you in your journey into Japanese home cooking. And the dashi that you will learn to make in this section will show up as a base or seasoning in many recipes later in this book. By the end of this section, you will have a fully stocked Japanese kitchen—from grocery store shelves to the garden, and from the stovetop to the refrigerator—and an understanding of how to use and cook the ingredients in that kitchen.

dashi
the fragrant broth

At the heart of so many Japanese soups and dishes is an incredibly versatile broth called dashi, which serves as a base for many components of Japanese cooking—soups, of course, but also sauces and seasonings. The most popular dashi is made with bonito flakes and kombu (see Bonito and Kombu Dashi, page 27), which is what I use for everyday cooking.

Dashi gives aroma and flavor to the dishes it is intended to enhance without overwhelming them and is considered a showcase for a pleasant flavor called umami, which is now recognized as the fifth taste, along with the four more familiar tastes: sweet, sour, salty, and bitter. Umami was discovered by Kikunae Ikeda, a Japanese college professor who, in the early 1900s, scientifically linked the amino acid glutamate to the distinctive flavor of dashi made from kombu seaweed. The umami flavor in dashi is created with one or more specific amino acids in combination: glutamic acid (from kombu, soy sauce, or miso) and inosinic acid (from bonito flakes, dried sardines, chicken broth, pork broth, or shellfish) or guanylic acid (from dried shiitake mushrooms). The synergy of these amino acids (the building blocks of protein) creates an even deeper umami, making the sum greater than its parts. "One plus one doesn't equal two but multiplies into seven or eight or more!" as Mamiko Nishiyama, proprietress of Yagicho Honten, explained to me.

There are actually many dashi ingredients to try—dried shrimp, dried scallops, adzuki beans, and even nori (seaweed) all make excellent dashi. Meat bones and vegetables slowly cooked in water to make a stock can also be considered dashi—think of creamy ramen soup laden with umami flavors from pork bones, onions, and other ingredients (see Ramen Broth, page 257). One of my favorite pastimes in Japan is to explore regional dashi ingredients, which can vary widely depending on what is locally available and abundant. On Sado Island, for example, dashi is commonly made with *ago* (dried flying fish), which fits into the general category of *niboshi* (dried sardines).

One of the first steps in cooking Japanese food is the ritual of making dashi. It fills the kitchen with warmth and a light fragrance; it gives me comfort to know that I have dashi ready because it is the foundation for so much of my daily meals. My husband, for example, can't imagine breakfast without miso soup, and to prepare the soup in the morning, all I need to do is heat up the already made dashi and add some seaweed, tofu, whatever vegetables I have, and miso paste. Almost instantly I have a nourishing, totally satisfying bowl of soup. I make a pot of dashi weekly and replenish it as needed.

Ingredients for making dashi can also vary according to the dish the dashi is intended for. Bonito and Kombu Dashi (page 27) is my everyday dashi, but I also make a light and subtly sweet kombu dashi for the simmered tofu hot pot known in Japan as *yudofu* (page 77) and, for some vegetable soups, a *Shojin* Dashi (page 30) that includes toasted soybeans, kombu, gourd strips, and shiitake mushrooms. When I am making udon noodle soup, I use a strong and savory dashi that combines kombu, shiitake mushrooms, and *niboshi* (dried sardines).

These days there are many factory-made dashi ingredients that come as powders and granules sold in tea bags. Many Japanese cooks depend on them for the sake of convenience, but I don't like to use them. They often contain preservatives and flavor enhancers that taste unnatural and very salty. To me, because dashi is so simple to prepare, it doesn't make sense to sacrifice flavor for convenience. So instead I recommend that you always make dashi from scratch, with whole and natural ingredients. It takes no more than ten or fifteen minutes, and you can refrigerate or freeze whatever you don't use for your next meal.

Even though dashi is as simple and as easy to make as steeped tea, it is nevertheless the foundation of Japanese cuisine. The success of a Japanese dish often lies in the flavor of the dashi. If you see Japanese people taste a dish and then exclaim "*Dashi ga kiiteru!*" that means they taste the good dashi in the dish. It is the highest compliment a chef or cook can receive.

Below I've listed several main dashi ingredients (bonito flakes, seaweed, dried fish, dried mushrooms, and soybeans) and offer recipes for each. You'll also find suggestions for what to do with the ingredients once they are used (or "spent").

KATSUOBUSHI (DRIED BONITO FLAKES)

Katsuobushi refers both to the wood-like block of dried bonito (also known as skipjack tuna) and the shaved bonito flakes. *Katsuobushi* is the hardest preserved food in the world. When my father served in World War II, his mother gave him a block of *katsuobushi* for good luck;

the pronunciation of the Chinese characters for *katsuobushi* rhymes with the Japanese words for "victorious samurai." Beyond being a good luck talisman, the well-preserved fish block also served as food in case of emergency.

Katsuobushi keeps well because it was invented before refrigeration. To make *katsuobushi*, the bonito, which weighs about ten pounds, is gutted, filleted, cooked, smoked, and dried. Most of the packaged bonito flakes you find in grocery stores are *arabushi*-style, the result of a relatively straightforward thirty-day process. But there is also another level of *katsuobushi*: the more mature and elegant *karebushi*- and *hongarebushi*-style *katsuobushi*, with ash-brown surfaces that are the result of sun-dried mold. To make this style of *katsuobushi*, the block of bonito is inoculated with a fungus called *Aspergillus glaucus* to reduce the moisture level of the fish, deepen the umami, and enhance the fragrance. It can take as long as five months for these blocks to reach full maturity.

If you have a block of *katsuobushi*, you will need to shave it with a *kezuribushi-ki*, a device

that looks like a plane used to shave wood. This tool used to be essential in every kitchen; I remember watching my grandmother use one to shave beautiful long petals of *katsuobushi* that she used as *furikake* (seasoning sprinkles) on *ohitashi* (blanched spinach salad). These days most people buy the shaved flakes in packages. Nothing compares to the flavor and fragrance of freshly shaved bonito flakes, but the packaged flakes are a reliable and decent alternative.

Shaved bonito flakes are available in several varieties. There are thin to thick grades of flakes, and some are blended with other ingredients such as mackerel and sardine flakes that are smokier and stronger in flavor than bonito alone; it's suitable for noodle and miso soups. For the standard bonito flakes, look for *katsuobushi* (bonito flakes),

hanakatsuo (flower bonito), and *kezuribushi* (shaved fish filet). *Itokezuri* (finely shredded bonito flakes) are used for *furikake*; they are not appropriate for making dashi.

How to Store Dried Bonito: For the best fragrance and flavor, store a *katsuobushi* block in the refrigerator and use it within one to two years. Store unopened bonito flakes in a cool place away from sunlight; once the package is opened, keep it in the refrigerator for 1 month or the freezer for about 6 months.

KOMBU (SEAWEED)

Like *katsuobushi* (bonito flakes), kombu is one of the essential ingredients in dashi. Read more about kombu on page 36.

kombu dashi

This is an easy cold-brew kombu dashi. It is a versatile vegan dashi that can be used as a base for *suimono* and *misoshiru* as well as any dishes that call for dashi or stock. You can also use it like wine—a dash here and there—to bring more flavor to your dishes and soups. The cold-brew method makes a mild dashi, but if you prefer it stronger, cook the soaked kombu in its liquid over low heat for ten minutes. Kombu comes in various sizes, precut or whole. If hydrated, it will double or more in size.

MAKES 4 CUPS (960 ML)

> **1 piece of kombu, about 4 x 4 inches (10 x 10 cm)**
> **4 cups (1 L) filtered water**

In a large bowl, soak the kombu in the filtered water for a minimum of 3 hours (to a maximum of 10 hours) at room temperature. Remove the kombu and use the liquid immediately, or store it in the refrigerator, where it will keep for up to 1 week. This piece of kombu can be reused one more time to make a secondary dashi (see page 30).

bonito and kombu dashi

This combination of bonito flakes and kombu makes the most popular and flavorful all-purpose dashi. The idea is to extract the flavors by steeping the ingredients for the first round of dashi, which is called *ichiban dashi*, or "number 1 dashi." The amount of bonito flakes I use for this recipe depends on how I will use the dashi. For everyday dashi, I make a medium-strength dashi using 3 cups (20 g) bonito flakes. When I make noodle soups, I want a stronger dashi, so I use 4 cups (30 g) bonito flakes. This dashi is enjoyed for its fragrance and is so flavorful on its own that you can drink it straight, like soup.

MAKES ABOUT 4 CUPS (960 ML)

> **5 cups (1.2 L) filtered water**
> **1 piece kombu, about 3 x 3 inches (7.5 x 7.5 cm)**
> **3 to 4 cups (20 to 30 g) bonito flakes**
>   (*see headnote*)

Combine the water and kombu in a medium saucepan. Heat over low heat until bubbles begin to form around the kombu, 5 to 10 minutes. Remove the piece of kombu before the water comes to a boil. Bring the water to a boil, turn off the heat. Add the bonito flakes. Let stand for 2 minutes, without stirring, to steep the bonito flakes.

To strain the dashi, pour the liquid through a fine-mesh sieve or a sieve lined with cheesecloth or a paper towel. Do not press the bonito flakes while straining, as it will cloud the dashi. Use immediately, or cool completely and refrigerate for up to 4 or 5 days or freeze up to 1 month.

Note: You can reuse the bonito flakes and kombu to make one more pot of dashi (see Secondary Dashi, page 30).

Ago-no-Yakiboshi (Toasted Dried Flying Fish)

NIBOSHI (DRIED SARDINES)

Niboshi includes sardines and other silvery skinned fish—such as *ago* (flying fish)—that have been cooked and then dried. These dried fish make for a strong, fragrant dashi that is best suited for miso, udon noodle, and ramen noodle soups. Look for dried sardines that are silvery and shiny rather than yellowish with an oily surface, which is an indication that the fish have oxidized. Dried sardines come in sizes ranging from small to large, about 2½ to 3 inches (6.5 to 7.5 cm) in length. You will need to adjust the amount of fish according to how strong you want your dashi. Try a few batches with different amounts of fish to find what suits your personal taste.

How to Store Dried Sardines: Store in the refridgerator after opening. For best flavor, use the *niboshi* within a year.

niboshi and kombu dashi

You can make a cold-brew dashi with *niboshi*, or you can cook the ingredients, which will give you a stronger dashi than the cold-brew method.

MAKES ABOUT 4 CUPS (960 ML)

> 1 ounce (28 g) *niboshi* (dried sardines), about 15 dried sardines
> 1 piece kombu, about 1½ x 3 inches (4 x 7.5 cm)
> 5 cups (1.2 L) filtered water

Snap off the heads and remove the insides of the sardines with your fingers. They will be dried and brittle, so they won't be hard to clean. You can also buy cleaned sardines without the head and entrails. Place the cleaned sardines in a bowl, add the kombu and filtered water, and place in the refrigerator, covered, overnight.

For a light cold-brew dashi, strain the liquid. You can use this dashi in your cooking. For a stronger dashi, transfer the liquid with the sardines and kombu to a medium saucepan and set it over high heat. When bubbles begin to form around the kombu, remove it from the liquid. Lower the heat to maintain a simmer and continue cooking for another 7 to 8 minutes. The liquid will turn a light amber color. Skim off any surface impurities, then strain the liquid through a sieve lined with cheesecloth or a paper towel. Discard the spent fish. You can reuse the kombu to make one more pot of dashi.

HOSHI SHIITAKE
(DRIED SHIITAKE MUSHROOMS)

Dried shiitake mushrooms, along with bonito flakes and kombu, are indispensable to the Japanese pantry. Shiitake has a woody taste and pungent smell, which might take some getting used to on your part, but it is well worth the effort. Shiitake have been treasured in Asia as both food and medicine; they are high in protein, minerals, and dietary fiber, and are full of vitamin B_{12}. *Donko* shiitake mushrooms, with their caps that curl under, are the most fragrant and meaty. You can also substitute maitake (hen-of-the-woods) mushrooms for shiitake; they are treasured in Japan for their medicinal properties and good flavor.

You can easily dry your own mushrooms by leaving fresh ones out in the sun for 3 to 5 days or by using a dehydrator. I store the dried shiitake in a glass jar next to the kombu jar, so I can always have both in sight when making dashi.

Shiitake dashi is easy to prepare. Just put 2 or 3 dried mushrooms in 2 cups (480 ml) cold water and let it stand, covered, in the refrigerator overnight. My students have asked me if fresh mushrooms can be substituted for dried shiitake mushrooms for making dashi. Fresh mushroom will not give you the concentrated flavors nor the fragrance that dried mushrooms can offer, so try to keep dried shiitake mushrooms in your pantry. I like to put mushroom stock in my noodle soups.

How to Store Dried Mushrooms: Keep dried mushrooms in a cool, dry place. They will keep for up to 2 years.

SOYBEANS

Soybeans, rich in umami, are an excellent base for vegan dashi. I toast them lightly for fragrance and then combine the beans with shiitake mushrooms, *kampyo* (dried gourd shavings), and kombu for a beautiful amber-colored dashi with a burst of flavors. Make sure your soybeans are non-GMO. I use Laura Soybeans from Iowa.

shojin dashi

This is an all-purpose vegan dashi that combines umami-rich soybeans, the sweetness of *kampyo* (dried gourd shavings), the savoriness of shiitake mushrooms, and the subtle tang of kombu. This dashi would be considered a *shojin* dashi, reflective of the ingredients and methods used for cooking by Buddhist practitioners.

MAKES ABOUT 4 CUPS (960 ML)

> 1 piece kombu, about 3 x 6 inches (7.5 x 15 cm)
>
> 3 dried shiitake mushrooms
>
> 2 tablespoons dried soybeans, lightly toasted in a dry skillet
>
> 1 strip *kampyo* (dried gourd shavings), about 5 inches (12 cm) long, cut in half
>
> 5 cups (1.4 L) filtered water

In a medium saucepan, combine the kombu, mushrooms, toasted dried soybeans, and *kampyo*. Add the filtered water, cover, and leave overnight at room temperature. The following day, put the pan over medium heat and bring to a boil. Boil for 1 minute, then lower the heat and simmer for 20 minutes. Strain the liquid to remove the solids. It is now ready to be used. Use immediately, or cool completely and refrigerate for up to 1 week.

You can reuse the spent ingredients to make one more pot of dashi or *Dashigara-no-Tsukudani* (Dashi Pickles; page 31).

secondary dashi

The spent dashi ingredients can be used again to make another batch of dashi. The idea is to extract the flavors further by cooking the ingredients for a second round, which is called *niban dashi*, or "number two dashi." This secondary dashi is light but still excellent for miso soups and for seasoning. For a stronger secondary dashi, add fresh bonito flakes after you lower the heat to a simmer. Strain as you would regular dashi.

MAKES ABOUT 2 CUPS (480 ML)

> 3 cups (720 L) water
>
> Spent kombu, bonito flakes, and/or mushrooms from 1 dashi recipe
>
> 1 cup (8 g) bonito flakes (optional; *see headnote*)

In a medium saucepan, bring the water and the spent dashi ingredients to a boil over medium heat for 1 minute. Lower the heat and add the bonito flakes, if using. Maintain a simmer until the dashi is reduced by two-thirds, about 5 minutes. Remove from heat. Add the bonito flakes, if using, and let steep for a couple of minutes. Strain the liquid through a sieve lined with cheesecloth or a paper towel. It is now ready for use. Use immediately, or cool completely and refrigerate for up to 1 week.

dashigara-no-tsukudani (dashi pickles)

This is a quick pickle that can be made with any combination of spent dashi ingredients—shiitake mushrooms, kombu, *katsuobushi* (bonito flakes), soybeans, *niboshi* (dried sardines), *kampyo* (dried gourd shavings)—together or separately. The spent dashi ingredients are seasoned with *shoyu tare*, *kokuto* sugar, and sake and turned into a moist sweet savory pickle. If you would like a dry *furi-kake*, simply keep cooking it in the pan or put it in the dehydrator until the texture turns flaky. You can enjoy *dashigara-no-tsukudani* with plain rice or as a filling in *onigiri* (rice balls) or on crackers or toast. For a spicy touch, add a pinch of *shichimi togarashi* or your favorite hot pepper. This *tsukudani* recipe uses spent bonito flakes and kombu. My chef friend Hannah Tierry said the flavor is akin to a smoky beef jerky.

MAKES ABOUT 1 CUP (65 G)

Spent bonito flakes (from 3 cups/20 g bonito flakes)

1 piece spent kombu, about 3 x 3 inches (7.5 x 7.5 cm)

2 teaspoons untoasted or toasted sesame oil, or olive olive oil

1 teaspoon ginger juice (from grated ginger)

1 tablespoon sake

1 tablespoon *kokuto* syrup (page 109) or dark brown sugar

1½ tablespoons *Shoyu Tare* (page 105)

1 teaspoon toasted white or black sesame seeds

¼ teaspoon *Shichimi Togarashi* (page 107)

Squeeze the excess liquid from the spent bonito flakes. Discard the liquid. Spread the flakes and spent kombu on a cutting board. Cut into rough ⅛-inch x ⅛-inch (3 mm x 3 mm) pieces.

Heat the oil in a medium skillet over medium heat. Add the chopped kombu and cook for 1 minute. Lower the heat and add the chopped bonito flakes, ginger juice, sake, syrup, and *shoyu tare* and continue to cook for about 3 to 4 minutes, until most of the liquid is absorbed but the mixture is still moist. Remove from heat. Taste and adjust the seasonings as you like. Garnish with sesame seeds and *shichimi togarashi*.

Serve at room temperature. It will keep covered for 4 to 5 days in the refrigerator.

preserving the dashi tradition with yagicho honten

A *kanbutsuya* is a traditional grocery store in Japan that sells natural and dried foods. My early education as a cook started at the local *kanbutsuya*, which had aromas of the sea from an array of dried fish and seaweeds, but also of the earth from the baskets full of colorful legumes, dried daikon radish, dried gourd shavings, and seasonings from around Japan. Surprisingly, even dried foods have their seasons. The shopkeeper was meticulous about announcing the seasons by writing with a brush and red ink when the dried fish, seaweeds, legumes, and vegetables arrived and where they had come from. I would run home to tell my grandmother that the *tamba* (black soybeans) were here!

Nearly fifty years later, I learned that family of my old schoolmate from Kamakura, Mamiko Nishiyama, had a *kanbutsuya*. Mamiko is the ninth-generation proprietress of Yagicho Honten, a nearly three-hundred-year-old *kanbutsuya* in the Nihonbashi district of Tokyo. Her shop sells premium kombu and bonito flakes shaved to order. Mamiko and I became reacquainted several years ago through our mutual interest in Japanese artisanal foods, in particular, dashi ingredients.

Every year, Mamiko visits the United States, bringing with her a big black suitcase packed with the wonders of dashi. We go on road trips up and down the coast of California—crashing on my friends' couches like college kids—doing dashi workshops at farmers' markets, cooking schools, and Japanese American community centers. We have been known to stop at wineries, farms, bakeries, markets, and cafés to taste some of what California offers.

I visit Mamiko's shop whenever I am in Tokyo and chat with her ninety-plus-year-old father,

Chobei, who still comes to work every day. Chobei used to be able to look at a block of dried bonito and identify by name the artisan from the Makurazaki area of Kagoshima Prefecture who made the block, just by looking at its shape. He laments that such careful and distinctive work is dwindling as artisans are replaced with factories and machines, resulting in dashi laden with artificial preservatives and flavor enhancers.

"There is nothing more flavorful than *tenboshi*," he says, referring to "food made under the sun." He has handed over the *kanbutsuya* business to Mamiko, who will become the first female in almost three hundred years to inherit the historical shop. She has recently restored the interior of the store as part of her pursuit to spread dashi domestically and internationally. Mamiko often brings out the *kezuribushi-ki* (tool to shave the *katsuobushi* block) and happily demonstrates how to shave the bonito flakes. She holds the fish block, the tail end (as opposed to the head end) of the block facing forward. Using her palm, she firmly presses the block against the blade of the device and pushes the block forward in repetitive motion. Unlike the beige outer appearance of the *katsuobushi*, when shaven it is a translucent and deep ruby color inside. Mamiko's petals are smooth, long, and incredibly fragrant. "This takes practice," she says, smiling. Dashi has reunited us.

seaweeds

For as far back as ten thousand years, the small island nation of Japan, with its limited land resources, has looked to its marine environment for food. The Japanese have eaten seaweed as an important and daily source of nourishment in the same way that those in the West have eaten vegetables.

With more minerals (potassium, iron, calcium, iodine, and magnesium) than any other kind of food, seaweed is also full of nutrients—vitamins A, B1, B2, B6, B12, C, niacin, and folic acid. It helps maintain gut flora and aids digestion; it lowers blood pressure and promotes healthy skin, nails, and hair (my mother used to make me eat kombu as a child so I could grow luscious black hair). I have always considered it a kind of miracle food and, as a cook, I want to throw seaweed in all my simmering pots, salads, and pickling jars.

There are countless varieties of edible seaweeds that can be enjoyed in multiple ways, fresh or dried, and have so many uses in the Japanese kitchen; I have highlighted several varieties below. Kombu is, of course, one of the fundamental ingredients in dashi (pages 25 to 31). It also makes *tsukudani*, a sweet and savory pickle (see *Dashigara-no-Tsukudani*, page 31). Nori is a great-tasting seaweed that serves multiple purposes: it can be used as a wrapper or as *furikake* (seasoning sprinkles), and I even cut sheets of nori into small rectangles and eat them like potato chips. The crispy rectangles appear on the breakfast table to serve on hot rice or buttered toast. My dog and cats love nori too

and beg for seconds. For salads and stir-fries, I use wakame and dulse, preferably fresh; these seaweeds can also be roasted and crumbled into *furikake* on various dishes. Always buy seaweed from a reputable company. In the United States, Mendocino Sea Vegetable Company, Ocean Harvest Sea Vegetable Company, Strong Arm Farm, and Maine Seaweed Council all have sustainable practices. They harvest the seaweed from clean waters and dry them properly. In Japan, Yagicho Honten offers premium-grade Japanese seaweeds.

Preparation: If it is dusty, dried seaweed needs to be wiped lightly with a well-wrung towel or cloth before it is hydrated. Be careful not to wipe away flavor particles on the surface of the kombu. As seaweed dries, it will exude the minerals and, in the case of kombu, mannitol sugar, according to John Lewallen of the Mendocino Sea Vegetable Company. It is also the flavor that enhances the umami.

To hydrate dried seaweed, I use the slow cold-brew method: soak the seaweed in water for at least 3 hours and as long as 10 hours. Remember that dried seaweed will usually double or triple in size when it is reconstituted.

Once you hydrate dried seaweed, drain the soaking water (unless you are using it for a broth) and then cook the seaweed immediately or refrigerate it for a couple of days. Refrigeration affects the flavor of seaweed. Once hydrated, it is best to eat the seaweed right away.

Fresh seaweed should be carefully cleaned before use. I once did a pop-up meal using lightly roasted wild nori to make *onigiri* (rice balls). During prep work for the meal, we found tiny pebbles and even clams lodged in the nori! We had to pick everything out by hand, but it was well worth the trouble.

How to Store Seaweed: Keep dried seaweed in a cool, dry place and use within 1 to 2 years of purchase. Fresh seaweed needs to be refrigerated and eaten in 1 month. If stored in the freezer, it will last for up to 3 months.

KOMBU

Kombu is a large seaweed that belongs to the family of brown algae, which is also referred to as kelp. Some people refer to kombu as the bay leaf of Asia, but it is much more than that. I use it to make broth and as a seasoning. I also use kombu as a wrapper (see Kombu Cured Thai Snapper Sashimi, page 127). I put kombu in my pickles to enhance the umami flavor. In fact, I keep cut pieces of kombu in a glass jar in my pantry and throw a piece into any dish that needs an umami boost. Nutritionally, kombu is loaded with essential minerals, vitamins, and glutamic salts, the naturally sweet flavor enhancer that creates umami.

Kombu can be either wild or farmed. It is harvested in Japan, Korea, Australia, South Africa, Canada, and on both the Pacific and Atlantic coasts of the United States. (See page 40 for my account of a trip to a seaweed farm on the Mendocino coast, "Harvesting Seaweed with Barbara Stephens and John Lewallen.") Most Japanese kombu comes from the island of Hokkaido, where the mineral-rich sea ice that drifts from Siberia to Hokkaido provides an ideal environment for growing kombu.

Harvested kombu is washed and then dried in the sun or by machine. As a last step, it is shaped and cut into various sizes. Kombu is labeled based on a number of characteristics: its specific variety, its origin, whether it is wild or farmed, and when it was harvested. All Japanese kombu undergoes

a rigorous quality-inspection process, resulting in grades from standard to premium. Premium-grade kombu is often aged for up to three years, which softens the seaweed and deepens the umami. Color is also an important key in the quality of kombu; dark amber-green kombu is generally considered good quality. It is common to find white specks and dust on the surface of kombu; don't wipe that off! Those white specks contain mannitol sugar, which naturally occurs during the drying process; mannitol sugar gives kombu its distinct sweetness and umami. Never rinse kombu with water because it will drain off the umami.

Here are five varieties of Japanese kombu to try in your cooking.

HIDAKA
A good dashi base. I also use this kombu as a wrapper for rolls stuffed with vegetables, meat, or seafood.

MAKOMBU

Considered the best kombu, it is used primarily for making dashi. It is thick and wide, with an elegant, subtle sweetness.

RAUSU

Slightly brown, with excellent fragrance, and soft and rich umami. It is used for dashi, pickles, and kombu sweets. This is my everyday kombu for making dashi.

RISHIRI

One of the premium types of kombu. It is highly fragrant and sweeter and saltier than *makombu*. It produces a rich, savory, and clear dashi.

TORORO AND OBORO

Tororo is made by stacking many kombu leaves into a block, seasoning it with rice vinegar, and then shaving it to create a fluffy thread. *Oboro* is the inner part of the kombu that is shaved by hand. Both *tororo* and *oboro* kombu are slightly sour in flavor and turn slimy when hydrated—but it is the sliminess that Japanese people love. Combine hot water with a tablespoon of *tororo* kombu, *umeboshi* (pickled *ume* plums), and some chopped scallions seasoned with a few drops of soy sauce to make a flavorful instant *suimono* (clear soup). You can also sprinkle *tororo* or *oboro* kombu on vegetables or noodles, or wrap it around *onigiri* (rice balls) to boost umami.

ARAME

Arame, also called sea oak, belongs to the same brown algae family that includes kombu. In the sea, arame is an important habitat for abalone, clams, and fish. The fronds are finely shredded. It has a mild flavor and texture. Arame is versatile; you can use it in soups, rice, salads, and braised dishes. Soak dried arame in water for 5 minutes before use; it reconstitutes quickly. (See Arame with Carrots and Ginger, page 128 and *Takikomi-Gohan* [Vegetables and Chicken Rice], page 137.)

KANTEN

Kanten is the Japanese name for agar. It is a vegetarian gelling agent obtained from *Tengusa*, a red algae used widely in both savory and sweet dishes. *Kanten* melts when cooked with water and gels at room temperature but is less quivery than gelatin. It is a good source of calcium and iron and is very high in fiber. *Kanten* is sold in a variety of forms: flakes, a powder, or a crispy light bar that easily tears apart. Read the manufacturer's instructions on how to use *kanten*.

I make *kanten* desserts using fruit juice or fruit puree as a base (see Berry *Kanten-Yose* and *Shiratama* Mochi with Ginger Syrup, page 274).

NORI

Nori belongs to the family of red algae. You are probably familiar with nori, which is the seaweed used to wrap sushi, served crumbled or sprinkled on noodle and rice dishes, or eaten as a snack on its own. Nori is high in protein and vitamins A, B, and C; it is also rich in calcium and iron. Nori has a natural grassy flavor and is sold both seasoned and unseasoned; I prefer unseasoned nori. Most nori is sold dried and roasted, but you can also find wild nori, both in the United States and Japan, in fresh or dried form. I harvested wild nori on the Mendocino coast in Northern California (page 40), and it was the tastiest wild nori I have ever had. Dried nori comes as bundles of large sheets; small, rectangular, bite-size pieces; shredded; or powdered. Not all nori is the same. You will find bundles of rejects that couldn't make it to the sushi counter but are good enough for home use all the way up to premium-grade nori from the bay of Ariake off the southernmost island of Kyushu. Good nori has a vibrant black color; it is aromatic and dissolves nicely in your mouth. Cheap nori is thin, dull, and purplish and tends to crumble and fall apart easily, which can be frustrating if it happens in the middle of rolling sushi.

Nori is an extremely versatile seaweed with lots of potential preparations and uses. If you have sheets of it, you can cut them in halves, eighths, or thirds, or cut them in a diagonal. Use the cut nori to wrap rice or crumble and sprinkle on foods. Or use a whole sheet to wrap *onigiri* (rice balls) like an envelope. The two sides of the sheets of nori are slightly different; one is glossier than the other. Remember to always wrap your *onigiri* with the shiny side down because you want your *onigiri* to shine.

Once you wrap anything with nori or sprinkle it on your vegetables or tofu, it will immediately pick up moisture from the food and go limp. For this reason, you should keep your nori separate from other foods for as long as possible and then wrap the *onigiri* just before you eat them. The same is true when you are using nori as a sprinkle or garnish; use the nori just before serving so it stays crisp.

Most nori comes toasted, but you can make even toasted nori crispier by waving each sheet over a medium-hot flame for a few seconds or laying it in a hot skillet. Be careful not to burn your hands.

WAKAME

Wakame is a brown algae. It is a tender, mild, and subtly sweet seaweed that has been widely cultivated in Japan and Korea since ancient times. In Korea, the soup *miyeok guk* is popularly consumed by women after giving birth because the wakame has a high content of calcium and iodine. Wakame has also been used for blood purification; intestinal, skin, hair, and reproductive organ health; and menstrual regularity. I treat wakame like a leafy green vegetable and use it in soups, stir-fries, and salads. Be careful not to hydrate or cook wakame for too long; it is delicate and will begin to disintegrate. If you can't find wakame, other seaweeds including dulse, sea palm fronds, and sea lettuce can be used in similar ways.

Fresh wakame is sometimes available at Japanese markets in the seafood section. It is tender and sweeter than dried wakame. Fresh wakame is salted for preservation, so make sure to rinse it under running water to remove the salt before cooking. Use fresh wakame as you would dried wakame; keep it refrigerated and use within 2 weeks.

harvesting seaweed with
barbara stephens and john lewallen

I know very few Americans who eat seaweed, let alone love it the way the Japanese do. Most Japanese eat seaweed every day. But the American interest in seaweed doesn't seem to move beyond nori—the sushi wrapper—to any of the other varieties that float in the ocean and hold on to the rocks near tidal pools. I never expected to find any decent edible seaweed in America.

That changed when I read a story by Tara Duggan in the *San Francisco Chronicle* about wild seaweeds being harvested in Mendocino, about three hours north of San Francisco. My research led me to Barbara Stephens and John Lewallen, proprietors of the Mendocino Sea Vegetable Company, who have been introducing people to the art of harvesting and cooking with a variety of seaweeds for decades. Their cottage industry has earned a cult status among local chefs and cooks for their wild-crafted seaweeds. Wanting to know more, I called them. John spoke eloquently about seaweeds—referring to the various species by their Latin names and Japanese counterparts, such as *Alaria* for wakame and *Laminaria* for kombu— and the dishes he and Barbara make with seaweed.

John and Barbara invited me to try wild seaweed harvesting. We met on a Sunday in August, when the tide was lowest, near Van Damme State Park on Highway 1. August is the tail end of the harvest season, but there was still plenty to see and taste. John and Barbara, wearing T-shirts with peace signs and anti-drilling messages, led us to their favorite rocky beach, where all of us bathed in the blurry and mysterious views of the bluffs along the coast. The sound of the crashing waves and the salty smell of the ocean had a restorative quality.

"There are hundreds of species that grow on the Mendocino coast," John explained as we walked along the beach. "That's walking kelp." He pointed with a stick. "Kombu grows in with that. In terms of the next five hundred years, it's the one that can be developed as a food value." John named the kelp colonies as we walked by on the slippery rocks and explained how these colonies are an extensive ecosystem for many organisms, providing food and habitat for unseen creatures and then in turn feeding other animals.

I watched my step as I marveled at the bounty at my feet, in particular a crop of nori draped over the rocks in a shallow area crowded with anemones, crabs, and huge abalones. I picked some nori and put it straight into my mouth. It was so delicious, definitely the best wild nori I had ever tasted.

Barbara waded deeper into the water to a colony of wakame and demonstrated how to harvest it: with leaves of four to five feet, wakame should be rolled before the ends are cut off, and

the roots should be left in the water so the plants can regenerate. "When I started harvesting up here, many folks rinsed the seaweed in fresh water before drying it, to clear it of the small shells and pebbles," said John, "but fresh water strips the rich flavor and texture of seaweed's natural habitat, so I tell people to rinse seaweed in ocean water." We gave the sea lettuce, wakame, and kombu that we harvested a good rinse in ocean water and packed it in our bags to go.

For lunch, I made a seaweed-themed meal: stir-fried sea palm fronds with zucchini; wakame soup with clams; kombu-infused yellowtail with salad greens and herbs; and rice with wild nori *furikake*, which we pan-fried the way the local Pomo Indian tribes have been cooking it for generations. It was a scrumptious meal that helped me consider the possibilities of seaweed not only as a source of nourishment but also as a remedy for our ailing oceans. It was a good feeling to bring home.

rice and other grains

Rice is at the heart of the Japanese meal. It is so fundamental to Japanese culture that I could have structured this whole book around a bowl of rice, with everything else around it enhancing this deeply revered grain. When you trace back the history of nearly three thousand years of rice cultivation in Japan, however, you will find that not everyone was eating rice on a regular basis, at least not until the eighteenth century. In fact, historically rice was considered rather precious. Instead, people ate millet, wheat, barley, and buckwheat—and made blends with rice.

Even though these other grains played second fiddle to rice, they were important sources of sustenance. They were so important that Japanese people still pray at harvest festivities not only for rice but for *gokokuhojo* (a good harvest of the five grains). The five basic grains are rice, barley, wheat, millet, and legumes, though these can be swapped according to what grows locally. Behind all of this is the idea of the five principles—*gogyosetsu* in Japanese or *wu xing* in Chinese; in the context of farming, the principle promotes planting a variety of grains and legumes in rotation to restore the soil and promote a healthy agrarian society.

There are countless varieties of grains, each with its own history, lore, quirks, and cooking methods. While the grain I consume the most is rice, I also adore other grains such as corn, barley, oats, rye, spelt, and pseudograins (seeds from shrubs and bushy plants) like amaranth, buckwheat, quinoa, and millet—either on their own or mixed with rice.

I prefer to cook with whole grains, which are richer in nutrients and flavor.

These days, blending rice with other grains and beans is making a comeback in Japan, because such blends are much healthier than plain white rice. In this book, you will see rice in many forms: plain; blended with a variety of other grains and beans; and cooked with seaweed, vegetables, and meat, which adds flavor and nourishment.

How to Buy and Store Grains: I like to buy new crop grains whenever possible; you can find them at farmers' markets or Japanese markets. Japanese rice gets a new crop sticker when the harvest comes in at the market, from late summer to early fall. I buy five to ten pounds of grains at a time and store them in the refrigerator or freezer. If you don't have space there, keep the grains in a cool place, away from light and critters, in a jar with a tight-fitting lid.

HOW TO COOK RICE

Every evening, my mother soaked rice in an electric rice cooker and then got up at dawn to switch it on. This was the most important chore of the day, as far as she was concerned, because it ensured that her children wouldn't go hungry. We would wake up to the sweet aroma of rice that permeated the house every morning. I don't know how she could have managed without the help of the electric rice cooker (which, incidentally, was invented in 1955, the year I was born). Our family was like

U.S. CUPS TO JAPANESE RICE COOKER CUP (*GO*) CONVERSION GUIDELINE	
Uncooked short or medium grain rice	Approximate yield of cooked rice
¾ cups (150 g) = 1 *go*	2¼ cups (300 g)
1½ cups (300 g) = 2 *go*	5 cups (600 g)
2¼ cups (450 g) = 3 *go*	7 cups (900 g)
3 cups (600 g) = 4 *go*	10 cups (1.2 kg)

most Asian families in that the rice cooker was the central appliance in the kitchen.

My grandmother, on the other hand, owned a rice cooker because someone gave it to her, but most of the time it stayed in its original box, as did most of her other appliances (she never threw boxes away). She preferred to cook rice in a small cast-iron pot that fit right into the hole of the wood-burning stove in the living room, where she would invite me to come and sit with her. I would patiently wait for the rice to cook while my grandmother tended the fire and told me stories. When she opened the lid of the pot, steam would rise and fog her glasses. The grains shimmered like pearls and filled the room with a smell like fresh grass. It is one of the most mesmerizing experiences I have had with food and one of my strongest memories. I don't have the same cast-iron pot as hers, but I have a cast-iron Dutch oven, a *donabe* (clay-pot rice cooker), and an electric rice cooker. I love them all, but the *donabe* has a beautiful aesthetic and makes the best-tasting rice, with a flavor comparable to the rice cooked in a cast-iron pot on the wood-burning stove. If cooking on the stovetop, use a heavy and deep pot with a tight-fitting lid. Adjust the size of the pot according to the volume of the rice you are cooking. Rice will expand nearly three times its original volume. As a general rule, use enough water to cover the rice by the guidelines mentioned below for white rice, brown rice, sprouted rice, and blended rice. My grandmother used her long finger (middle finger) for

measuring the water in the pot for cooking white or mixed-grain rice. She made sure that there was enough water to cover the first joint of her finger by about 1 inch (2.5 cm).

I offer these memories only to make the point that modern rice cookers and older methods of stovetop cooking are both good options. But if you really like to eat grains, you can't beat the convenience of a rice cooker.

Measuring Rice: The Japanese system for measuring rice is called *go*. Japanese rice cookers supply you with a rice-cooker cup that applies this system, which measures about ¾ of a cup (180 ml or 150 g) of uncooked rice. This can be somewhat confusing for Westerners. In my recipes, I use 1½ cups (2 *go*), 2¼ cups (3 *go*), and 3 cups (4 *go*) of uncooked rice. The amount of water needed for cooking rice differs between white and brown rice. White short and medium grain rice require an amount of water equal to about 1.1 times the volume of uncooked rice. Brown short and medium grain rice require an amount of water equal to about 1.6 times the volume of uncooked rice. Consult the package instructions for guidance, as variety, freshness, and milling quality can make a difference in how the rice will turn out.

RICE ETIQUETTE

Growing up, I was taught to eat every grain of rice in the bowl, because to leave rice uneaten would be rude to the farmer who expended such effort to grow it. To ensure a clean bowl, my grand-mother made a ritual at home of *ochazuke* (rice tea soup). At the end of every meal, she would simply pour hot tea over the remaining rice in the bowl. We would drink it like soup to give the bowl a rinse. Sometimes she would add an *umeboshi* (pickled *ume* plum) or a piece of leftover salmon for added flavor. In high-end restaurants, how-ever, *ochazuke* can be considered bad manners if it is initiated by the diner; it can be interpreted as dissatisfaction in amount of food on the table. But there are also plenty of restaurants that put *ochazuke* on the menu.

TYPES OF RICE

Rice can be categorized into three groups: long-grain, medium-grain, and short-grain, with short-grain rice being the most popular in Japan. Among the three hundred varieties of short-grain rice grown in Japan, *koshihikari* and *akitakomachi* are the varieties that are exported to the United States and also grown in California. They are enjoyed for their firmness, subtle sweetness, translucency, and stickiness, and they are suitable for making sushi and *onigiri* (rice balls) because they mold easily and taste good even at room temperature.

My preferred rice is a medium-grain heirloom rice grown by Koda Farms in Dos Palos, the oldest family-owned and family-operated rice farm in California (see page 52). This organic variety con-tains the sticky strains of Japonica rice that were bred specifically for the region. The rice is fluffy in texture with subtle floral aromas, and it can be used in the same way as short-grain rice. If there is such a thing as terroir of rice, you can taste it in this grain.

It is important to clarify here that brown rice and white rice are not different types of rice. All rice is brown rice until the husk is removed from the kernel, at which point it becomes white rice. Brown rice is unmilled rice in its whole-grain form. Rich in dietary fiber and vitamins B and E, brown

rice contains healthy oils that give it a rich flavor and nutty aroma—making it my family's preferred rice. It was my mother who turned me on to brown rice. It was around the same time that she took up yoga and started doing handstands in the living room. Brown rice needs to soak overnight, and it takes longer to cook (and chew!) than white rice. You can also sprout brown rice (page 47) so it will cook more quickly and digest more easily.

Between brown and white rice is *haiga* rice—partially milled short-grain brown rice. The bran is mostly polished but it retains the germ, which retains the oils, some of the fiber, vitamins, and GABA (gamma-aminobutyric acid). *Haiga* rice became popular in the 1920s in Japan as a cure for beriberi, a disease caused by a vitamin B defi-ciency that was in turn caused by the consumption of too much refined white rice. *Haiga* rice is beige in color with a slightly nutty flavor and tender texture. This rice cooks the same way as white rice, making it easier to use and easier to digest than brown rice.

When brown rice is fully milled, the bran and germ are scraped away, leaving the starchy endosperm. This is white rice. It is not the health-iest rice to eat, as most of its nutrients have been stripped out, but it is enjoyed for its mild sweet-ness, subtle aroma, translucency, and tender texture. It is the easiest rice to digest and is highly versatile. It also cooks in half the time of brown rice. You will see a lot of white rice in Japanese food, specifically in sushi.

Sweet rice (or short-grain glutinous rice) is used for making pounded rice cakes, Fresh Mochi (page 50), and *Chimaki* (Wrapped Steamed Rice Dumplings; page 194) with vegetables, seaweed, and meat wrapped in bamboo leaves. You can also add a tablespoon or two of sweet rice to short- or medium-grain white or brown rice to boost its flavor and sticky texture.

basic white rice

To cook basic short-grain or medium-grain white rice or *haiga* rice (or what is often called sushi rice in the United States), I measure enough water to equal the volume of the uncooked rice and then add 2 tablespoons to ¼ cup (60 ml) more water. The amount of water will depend on the variety and freshness of rice as well as how firm or soft you want the rice to be. The fresher the rice, the less water it needs for cooking. With so many variables, it is wise to read and follow what the manufacturer suggests. Soak white rice for at least 30 minutes (or up to overnight) in the measured water. Use filtered water, especially if you have hard water coming out of your faucets.

MAKES ABOUT 5 CUPS (600 G) COOKED RICE

> **1½ cups (300 g) medium-grain or short-grain white or *haiga* rice**
> **1¾ cups (400 ml) filtered water**

In a medium bowl, rinse the rice under cool running water for about 10 seconds, then drain the water completely. Gently stir the rice with your hand about 30 times and rinse again under cool running water. Drain the starchy water. Combine the measured filtered water and rice in a heavy-bottomed 2-quart (2 L) pot with a tight-fitting lid. Let the rice soak in the water for at least 30 minutes and up to overnight.

Put the same pot on the stovetop, uncovered, over medium heat and bring to a boil with the water bubbling vigorously around the rim of the pot. This will take about 8 minutes. Cover, decrease the heat to the lowest possible setting, and cook, without lifting the lid to peek, for about 18 minutes.

Remove from heat and, without opening the lid, let the rice rest for 10 minutes. Remove the lid and gently fluff rice with a rice paddle or wooden spoon. Replace the lid and allow rice to rest for another 5 minutes. The rice will keep fresh for 1 day. It will harden if you refrigerate or freeze it. Japanese use the microwave or a steamer to soften hardened rice. I like to make fried rice with hardened rice.

basic brown rice

There are many ways to cook brown rice, but in general it takes more water and time to cook than white rice because it is a whole grain with its bran and germ intact. And while white rice only needs to be soaked for about 30 minutes prior to cooking, brown rice must be soaked for 6 hours or up to overnight. I measure enough water to equal one and a half times the volume of the uncooked rice and then add 2 tablespoons to ¼ cup (60 ml) more water. As with white rice, the amount of water for cooking depends on the variety and freshness of the rice and how firm or soft you want it to be. Consult the package instructions for the best guidelines.

MAKES ABOUT 5 CUPS (636 G) COOKED BROWN RICE

> **1½ cups (300 g) medium-grain or short-grain brown rice**
> **2½ cups (600 ml) filtered water**
> **¼ teaspoon salt**

In a medium bowl, rinse the brown rice under cool running water and drain. Stir the rice with your hands for about 15 seconds. Rinse again under cool running water and drain. Combine the rice, filtered water, and salt in a heavy-bottomed 2-quart (2 L) pot with a tight-fitting lid. Let the rice soak at room temperature for 6 hours and up to overnight.

Put the same pot on the stovetop, uncovered, over medium heat and bring to a boil with the water bubbling around the rim of the pot. Cover, decrease the heat to the lowest possible setting, and cook, without lifting the lid to peek, for 40 minutes.

cooking brown rice with a pressure cooker

Pressure cookers such as the Instant Pot have become very popular kitchen appliances, and you can certainly use them to cook brown rice. If you use a pressure cooker, you can skip the soaking, and the rice will cook much more quickly. The result will be more tender and stickier than rice you'd get from cooking it on the stovetop or in a rice cooker.

Follow the manufacturer's guidelines for cooking brown rice in a pressure cooker.

Remove from heat and, without opening the lid, let the rice rest for 10 minutes. Uncover and fluff rice with a rice paddle or wooden spoon. Replace the lid and allow rice to rest for another 5 minutes.

The rice will keep fresh for 1 day. It will harden if you refrigerate or freeze it. Japanese use the microwave or a steamer to soften hardened rice. I like to make fried rice with hardened rice.

ADDING OTHER GRAINS TO RICE

To supplement the nutrients and flavor of rice, I blend it with a variety of other grains and legumes. The choices are wide open: amaranth, buckwheat, millet, quinoa, and barley are all good grains to start your mix. Adzuki beans and black soybeans also make good blends on their own or with other grains. Here are a few of the heirloom grains—other than rice—that I stock in my pantry.

AMARANTH

Amaranth technically is not a grain but rather a leafy green, similar to chard or spinach. It has a striking ruby color and shaggy heads that contain thousands of tiny seeds. It is high in protein, minerals, and fiber, and has a nutty flavor similar to brown rice. This sacred food of the Aztecs was a staple crop of the Americas—perhaps my childhood in Mexico City gave me an affinity for it.

sprouting brown rice

Sprouting brown rice is easy. Sprouted rice is lighter in texture and subtly sweeter than regular brown rice. It is a little more work than cooking regular rice, but it is totally worthwhile. When brown rice is sprouted, the outer bran layer of the rice kernel softens and wakes up the rich nutrients and makes them more available. These nutrients include GABA (gamma-aminobutryic acid), antioxidants, minerals, and vitamins. Sprouted brown rice is also rich in fiber, protein, and folate. You can sprout brown rice by soaking it for two days, changing the funky-smelling soaking water completely twice a day. The ideal temperature for sprouting is between 84°F and 104°F (30°C–40°C). Soak 1½ cups of brown rice in a bowl with 3 cups (710 ml) of water and let it soak overnight. After 6 hours of soaking, rinse and drain completely. Repeat rinsing and draining, two times a day. When you begin to see very tiny sprouts emerge from the end of the grains, stop the sprouting process and cook the grain for best flavor. Sprouted brown rice has absorbed a lot of water during soaking so it doesn't need as much water for cooking. Cook as you would Basic White Rice (page 46), using 1½ (360 ml) to 1¾ cups (420 ml) of cooking water and a pinch of salt.

I like mixing amaranth into rice, but you have to be careful not to rinse away the little seeds. Amaranth has a natural stickiness that adds texture to the rice.

BUCKWHEAT

Like amaranth, buckwheat also technically is not a grain but rather a plant related to the rhubarb family. The seed is believed to have originated in the highlands of China and Tibet and then spread to Europe and the Americas. Buckwheat was introduced to Japan by Buddhist monks, who used this seed as a source of nourishment during and after their long periods of meditation, which they still do.

Buckwheat is considered a medicinal food in Japan because it is full of protein, minerals, and fiber. In the United States, buckwheat is an underappreciated pseudograin, grown mostly as a cover crop and, if it makes it to the table, used for making pancakes. Americans are starting to discover the potential of buckwheat. Milled buckwheat makes beautiful bread, noodles, and pasta, and cooked groats (the hulled seeds of buckwheat) make a wonderful addition to rice or salads. I also put groats in my Homemade Granola with Lucky Beans (page 171) for a good crunch, and I even make a dumpling soup with the flour (see *Kenchin-jiru* [Hearty Vegetable Soup with *Sobagaki* Buckwheat Dumplings], page 183).

MILLET

Millet is one of the oldest staple seeds of Asia. My mother was born in Okayama Prefecture, which in ancient times was called Kibi-no-kuni, the "Land of Kibi," which rhymes with the Japanese word for millet. It is the source of one of my strongest memories. I once visited our family grave in Okayama with my grandmother. It was so long ago that we traveled in a steam engine train; the smoke of the train turned my face and hands black with soot. In the graveyard, mosquitoes ate me alive. But I vividly remember the sweet little *kibi* dumplings we picked up at the train station made with rice and millet flour—the saving grace of the trip.

Millet has a pleasant flavor and creamy color; it is high in protein and easy to digest. I blend millet with rice and porridge, and I also use millet in my pancakes and granola.

OATS

Oats might be one secret to longevity. My grandmother, who lived to be 102, ate a tablespoon of cooked oatmeal for breakfast everyday along with her toast with jam, soft-boiled egg, and tea with milk. She had a tiny pot in which to cook her oatmeal, and when she passed away I inherited that pot. It has become the pot I use when I make my oatmeal. I like to use steel-cut oats to make a savory porridge (see *Ojiya* [Porridge] with Kabocha Squash and Ginger, page 177), and I make granola with rolled oats as my standby snack (see Homemade Granola with Lucky Beans, page 171). I love blending a variety of grains, dried fruits, soybeans, and nuts with the oats.

basic multigrain rice

This recipe uses short-grain white rice as a base to make a multigrain dish. You can also blend grains with your brown rice. Be creative and make your own multigrain mix. I blend buckwheat, quinoa, millet, barley, amaranth, and adzuki beans or black soybeans. These colorful legumes add a tint of burgundy color and good flavor to the rice. I use a 3-quart (3 L) Dutch oven for making this recipe. If cooking in an electric rice cooker, a pressure cooker, or a *donabe* (clay pot), follow the manufacturer's instructions; the preparation below is for stovetop cooking.

MAKES ABOUT 5 CUPS (700 G)

> 1¼ cups (250 g) medium-grain or short-grain white rice or *haiga* rice
> ¼ cup (50 g) whole grains and/or beans (*see headnote*)
> 1¾ cups (420 ml) filtered water
> ¼ teaspoon salt

In a medium bowl, rinse the rice and other grains or beans under cool running water for about 20 seconds. Then drain the water completely using a fine-mesh strainer so you don't lose any small grains such as millet or amaranth, if using. Transfer the grains back to the bowl, gently stir them with your hand about 30 times, and rinse them again under cool running water. Then drain the starchy water completely. Combine the grains and the measured filtered water in a heavy-bottomed 3-quart (3 L) pot with a tight-fitting lid. Let the rice soak in the water for at least 3 hours and up to overnight.

Put the same pot on the stovetop, uncovered, over medium heat and bring to a boil with the water bubbling around the rim of the pot. This will take about 8 minutes. Cover, decrease the heat to the lowest possible setting, and cook, without lifting the lid to peek, for 18 minutes. Remove from heat and, without opening the lid, let the rice rest for 10 minutes. Remove the lid and gently fluff rice with a rice paddle or wooden spoon. Replace the lid and allow to rest for another 5 minutes. The rice will keep fresh for 1 day. It will harden if you refrigerate or freeze it. Japanese use the microwave or a steamer to soften hardened rice.

MOCHI

Mochi is a sticky, chewy rice cake made of *mochi-gome* (sweet rice, also called glutinous rice). Mochi has served as nourishment for the Japanese people since ancient times; the ritual of pounding sweet rice is a traditional event in preparation for the New Year. For that celebration I make *kagami mochi*—two round pieces of mochi, one stacked on top of the other—and decorate them with tangerine and ferns. I then place them in my house and make another set for my husband's studio. *Kagami mochi* is believed to contain Toshigami, a spirit that is said to visit during the New Year's period to bring a good harvest, the blessing of ancestors, and the power of life. We also eat a lot of mochi during this time of year to bring more good luck, including *Ozoni* (New Year's Good Luck Soup; page 245); the elastic nature of mochi represents flexibility and endurance.

Mochi is also enjoyed year-round prepared in a variety of ways. Some mochi contains sesame seeds, seaweed, beans, dried fruit, or herbs. My favorite way of eating mochi is toasted—puffed up like popcorn, wrapped in a crispy sheet of nori, and dipped in soy sauce. When mochi gets old and hardens, it can be deep-fried into crackers. There are also *mochiko* and *shiratamako* rice flours, made with sweet rice, which can also be used to make quick mochi, such as Strawberry *Daifuku* Mochi (page 269), Butter Mochi (page 273), and Berry *Kanten-Yose* and *Shiratama* Mochi with Ginger Syrup (page 274).

The traditional way of making mochi is to place hot steamed rice in an *usu*, a large hollowed-out wood stump or stone, and pound it into a mash with a *kine*, a large wooden mallet. My brother Hiroshi was always in charge of making mochi at my parents' house in Tokyo when we were all young, and when I got older I would often spend my holidays in Japan with my son, Sakae, so he could experience this ritual. Hiroshi would invite all the children to take turns pounding the mochi, and then we would mold them into round dumplings and eat them with a variety of savory and sweet toppings including fresh grated daikon radish, natto (fermented soybeans), nori, *kinako* (roasted soybean flour), and sugar. In the United States, Japanese Americans hold annual *mochitsuki* (mochi-making events) at Japanese cultural community centers and Buddhist temples in various cities in which everyone can participate. You can also buy fresh mochi at the Japanese market and now even at some Whole Foods grocery stores.

There are electric mochi-making machines you can buy for home use that steam and pound the rice, doing all the muscle work for you, though you still have to use your hands to mold the mochi into little dumplings. I've also tried making mochi in a stand mixer and it came out nicely, a little coarser than what would come out of a mochi maker but just as sticky and stretchy.

fresh mochi

You can easily make mochi at home using a stacking steamer and a stand mixer with a dough hook.

MAKES ABOUT 12 MOCHI CAKES

EQUIPMENT
    Stacking steamer (two-tier)
    Cheesecloth or thin muslin cloth
    Stand mixer with dough hook

    2 cups (400 g) sweet rice or brown sweet rice, soaked overnight in 1 quart (960 ml) of water, drained
    About 1 cup (128 g) cornstarch or rice starch

Line the steamer with a double layer of cheese-cloth or a muslin cloth so it covers the entire sur-face. Put the drained rice on the lined steamer in a large doughnut-like shape to allow the steam to escape through the middle. Set the steamer to high and steam the rice until thoroughly cooked, turn-ing it over with a paddle several times so the grains cook evenly, 45 to 60 minutes. Brown rice will take longer than white rice to cook. The rice will turn from opaque to slightly translucent when cooked. Taste it to make sure the rice is soft inside.

To knead the mochi, attach the dough hook to the mixer. Prepare a small bowl of water and get out a rice paddle or spatula, which you will

---

rice crackers

When the mochi dries up and turns brittle, break it into bite-size pieces with a mallet or hammer and allow the pieces to dry for 2 days on a baking sheet lined with parchment paper. If you see any mold growth on the mochi, scrape it off with a knife. To deep-fry the pieces to make rice crack-ers, fill a 3-quart (3 L) heavy-bottomed pot with about 4 cups (960 ml) of grapeseed oil. Heat the oil to 350°F (175°C) and drop the pieces of rice into the hot oil. Cook for 1 to 2 minutes, until they puff up and lightly brown. Take the crackers out of the oil using a slotted spoon and transfer to a wire rack. Sprinkle with sea salt and *shichimi togarashi*, cinnamon and sugar, or *kinako* (roasted soybean flour) and sugar. Serve immediately.

---

need to wet the bowl of the mixer to prevent the mochi from sticking. Transfer the hot steamed rice into the bowl and start kneading the rice on medium-high speed until it is mashed and gooey. Wet the spatula in the bowl of water and turn the mochi from the bottom of the bowl to prevent it from sticking. Repeat several times. After 10 to 15 minutes of kneading, the mochi will become smooth and stretchy.

Generously dust a baking sheet with about ½ cup (64 g) of the cornstarch. Transfer the mochi to the sheet and sprinkle another ½ cup (64 g) of the cornstarch on top of the mochi to make it easier to handle. Using your hands, flatten and stretch the mochi to 1-inch (2.5 cm) thickness. Tear off a 3-inch (7.5 cm) piece of the mochi with your hands and quickly mold it into a ball, tucking the edges under and pinching the ends. Sprinkle with corn-starch and then flatten it into a disk. Repeat until all the mochi on the baking sheet is gone. Mochi will harden with time, so work quickly.

To eat the mochi, line a baking sheet with alum-inum foil and broil it until it puffs up on all sides.

How to Store Mochi: Wrap the mochi in plastic wrap and store it in a container with a lid in the refrigerator for up to 1 week. It will harden as days pass, but you can toast or broil or boil it to restore its chewiness. Mold can easily grow on mochi, so don't leave it out. If you see any mold, slice it off with a knife. You can freeze mochi; it will keep frozen for 2 to 3 months.

my kinship with robin koda of koda farms

Koda Farms is the oldest family-owned and family-operated rice farm and mill in California, and although I met Robin Koda, the granddaughter of founder Keisaburo Koda, just five years ago, it feels as if I have known her a lifetime. Perhaps this sentiment reflects our shared lineage tracing back to a farming hamlet in Fukushima Prefecture in Japan.

As the story goes, in 1908, my paternal great-uncle (one of fourteen siblings and whose name escapes me) and Keisaburo Koda left their tiny village of Ogawa on the same boat to America. My homesick great-uncle returned to Japan, while Keisaburo stayed and began farming, even though the California Alien Land Law of 1913 prevented Asian immigrants from owning or leasing land. Keisaburo toiled on and eventually bought land under his American-born sons' names in the town of Dos Palos, where he successfully cultivated rice and became legendary in Japanese American culture as the "Rice King."

However, Keisaburo's life took a dark turn during World War II. Their entire family, including their American-born children, was shipped to an internment camp in Colorado because they were of Japanese descent. They lost nearly everything—several thousand acres of land, their farm headquarters encompassing homes, milling and processing facilities, all their best farming equipment and airplanes, and a hog farm. When the war ended, the Koda family drew on their internal strength to rebuild their operation. Over a span of a decade of dedicated rice breeding at their farm, they introduced Kokuho Rose rice in the early 1960s.

Post–World War II, in a gesture of goodwill relations, Keisaburo initiated the first agricultural exchange study program for Japanese farmers. Eventually, when my father was transferred to the United States to manage the new Japan Airlines office in San Francisco, he contacted Keisaburo,

and the two families whose roots originated in Ogawa reconnected.

My mother was a big fan of Kokuho Rose rice. Whenever she went back to Japan, she took this rice as a welcomed souvenir from California. A Laotian chef recollected how when her refugee parents landed in Denver, Colorado, where they found employment as janitors, they would save up just to be able to buy Kokuho Rose. And Robin related how in years past, customers from as far away as Seattle would pool their fall *shinmai* (newly harvested rice) orders and make the pilgrimage to the farm in central California, trailers in tow.

I often visit on my way from Los Angeles to the Bay Area, where I teach workshops, spending the night at the farm with Robin and her nonagenarian mother, Tama, who is prim and proper and much younger-looking than her age. I have been

there in June when the fields are a lush carpet of emerald green and white cranes and dark-hued ibis stroll the paddies looking for something to eat. In the fall, after the grains have matured to a golden ochre, most of the harvesting is done with modern combine harvesters, but when it comes to collecting the seed nursery's rice, only old-fashioned hand scythes and twine come into play.

It reminds me of how rice was harvested in Japan in the old days. The only difference is that the songs I hear in the background are ranchera songs sung by the Mexican workers whose families have been working for Koda Farms for multiple generations.

Kokuho means "national treasure" in Japanese, and Kokuho Rose rice, as named by Keisaburo Koda, is truly a treasure of the land.

noodles and bread

It has been almost ten years since I began making noodles by hand. My initial motivation was based on a persistent, chronic kind of hunger. I couldn't find any good noodles in the United States. For years, decades even, I lived in the shadow of compromise, eating mediocre store-bought noodles, and I would have to wait until I returned to Japan to get my "good noodle" fix. But I wanted to eat better noodles at home in Los Angeles, so I began studying noodle making whenever I was back in Japan. I am still on this pursuit.

When you start putting your hands in flour, your sense of time and space changes. You slow down. This deceleration was by far the best thing that happened to me—besides being able to eat better noodles, of course. The moment you begin mixing flour and water to make dough, you are at the beck and call of the dough. You begin a dialogue with the flour and water, and all the elements that seem to make up the universe will influence the completed dish—the quality of the ingredients, your skill, the temperature and humidity in the air, the volume, and how you feel. I am always seeking to work in harmony with these five elements.

Besides slowing down my pace in life, another good thing happened. I began thinking of flour as a living thing, not something white and processed that sits on a shelf for years but the actual grains that are milled to make flour and the quality of milling. I began to appreciate not only the countless varieties of heirloom grains (wheat, barley, oats, rye, rice) and pseudograins (amaranth, buckwheat, and quinoa) available to us and their flavor profiles and characteristics, but also their history and contribution to humankind.

Now I am on a mission to advocate growing and milling heritage grains, including buckwheat, in the United States for local consumption, with the goal of diversifying the way we eat and grow food and ultimately restoring the health of our soil by using grains as part of the crop rotation. I realized that home cooks could contribute to this movement by making noodles and baking bread at home. Heritage grains are producing some tasty noodles and bread. Start exploring what your local farmers are growing; you will be doing the soil a lot of good.

In addition to a variety of wheat flours and buckwheat flour, I also keep several types of rice flours for making Fresh Mochi (page 50), including *mochiko* and *shiratamako*, both of which are glutinous (sweet) rice flours. *Mochiko* is slightly coarser than *shiratamako*. Finally, I use *kinako* (roasted soybean flour), which is a nutty, fragrant flour used for sprinkling on mochi, ice cream, cookies, and yogurt. I consider it the cinnamon of Japan.

I also keep several starches in my kitchen: potato starch, tapioca starch, cornstarch, kudzu, and buckwheat. These starches are all used as thickening agents in sauces and as coatings on foods to be deep-fried. I use buckwheat, cornstarch, and tapioca starch for dusting handmade noodles.

How to Store Flour: Seal flour in an airtight bag or container to lengthen its shelf life and protect from insects and rodents. Stone-ground and whole-grain flours, which contain the germ and bran, can become rancid over time, lending an unpleasant flavor to the flour. The best way to store flours is in the refrigerator or in the freezer. I use my flours within 3 to 6 months.

TYPES OF NOODLES

Japanese noodles are made with a variety of flours and starches. The common varieties include somen, udon, soba, and ramen. There are regional noodle specialties that have distinct names, shapes, thicknesses, and binding agents, like seaweed. In this section, I will introduce you to the common varieties.

SOBA NOODLES

I am particularly fond of buckwheat and have loved soba (buckwheat noodles) since I was a child. Despite its name, buckwheat is not actually a wheat but rather a pseudograin related to the rhubarb plant. The seeds produce a creamy and hauntingly nutty flour that makes the most delicious noodles—and it is healthy too, as buckwheat has been considered medicinal food in Asia for centuries. It has many health benefits, including lowering cholesterol and blood pressure levels; it is packed with vitamins and minerals and provides a highly digestible protein and dietary fiber. The Japanese slurp soba noodles on New Year's Eve for a long and lean life. Soba is a buckwheat noodle that is available dried and fresh. Flour made with new crop buckwheat flour has a pale-green color and an incredible nutty flavor. If the store-bought soba noodle package lists wheat first, there is a good chance you will be eating noodles that contain as much as 70 percent wheat flour. If labeled *Juwari* soba, the noodle is made with 100 percent buckwheat.

SOMEN NOODLES

Somen noodles are available dried. They are made from wheat flour and are similar in flavor to udon but thin like angel hair pasta. The hand-pulled *somen* noodles by Handa Somen, made by the Moriwaki family in Tokushima Prefecture on the island of Shikoku, are addictively delicious. I love to serve these noodles chilled with a dipping sauce (see *Shoyu Tare*, page 105) or in Water Kimchi (page 187).

UDON NOODLES

Udon, a thick round noodle, is made from wheat flour and is chewy and filling. Sanuki udon, from Kagawa Prefecture, is a thick and chewy round noodle. Inaniwa udon, from the Akita Prefecture, are famously elegant flat udon noodles. Another flat noodle related to Udon is Kishimen, a typical noodle from Aichi Prefecture. See Udon Noodles (page 60) and Peddler's Udon (page 253).

RAMEN NOODLES

Ramen—thin, thick, or ribbonlike—is a noodle made of wheat flour, salt, water, and an alkaline solution of potassium carbonate and sodium bicarbonate that gives them a springy and chewy texture and a distinct yellow color. You can buy these noodles dried or fresh. My grandmother called these noodles *chuka soba* or *shina soba,* which means "Chinese-style noodles." Packaged, preseasoned ramen is a popular convenient food, but many are loaded with fat, sodium, and chemical additives.

HARUSAME NOODLES

Harusame is a dried vermicelli noodle, also called "glass noodles," made from mung bean and potato flour. It is a flavorless noodle that can be used in stir-fries, salads, and soups for added texture and volume. Before using, cover with boiling water and let stand until tender, about 3 to 5 minutes, then drain and add it to the dish.

KUZUKIRI NOODLES

Kudzu root has been treasured for its restorative qualities. It is used as a jellying and thickening agent to make sauces. Kudzu also makes an elegant noodle called *kuzukiri*, which is transparent like *harusame* noodles and sold fresh or dry. These noodles are used in hot pots or served as dessert with *kokuto* (Okinawa brown sugar) syrup.

SHIRATAKI NOODLES

Shirataki is a translucent noodle that is available water-packed. They are made from the fiber that comes from the root of the konjac plant. These noodles are related to *konnyaku*, a gelatinous block also made from the same plant and available water-packed in the refrigerated section. Both *shirataki* and *konnyaku* are considered to be food medicine for their high fiber content. They are very low in calories and low in carbs. These noodles have a good chew and take on flavor well, shown when they are simmered in umami-rich soups such as *Nikujaga* (Beef, *Shirataki*, and Potato Stew; page 151) or *Oden* (Vegetable, Seafood, and Meat Hot Pot; page 217).

soba noodles

Soba noodles are made with buckwheat flour and water, to which wheat flour can be added as a binder. This *nihachi*-style soba recipe uses 80 percent buckwheat flour and 20 percent wheat flour. It is a classic blend that works beautifully. The wheat acts as a binding agent and provides a good chew, while the buckwheat gives it the hauntingly nutty fragrance. You can make soba with 100 percent *sobakoh* (buckwheat flour), if the buckwheat is fresh and very slowly milled in a stone mill. Japanese artisan buckwheat miller Yoshitomo Arakawa has dedicated more than thirty years of his life to milling buckwheat flour. He directs the operation of more than one hundred stone mills, each producing as little as 5 pounds (2 kg) per hour—very slow compared to the stone mills in the United States that mill grains over ten times that speed. But this slow milling is a gentle process that ensures freshness and good flavor. Since buckwheat is grown in this country and there is a growing demand for good soba noodles, I hope to see a market for that kind of flour in the near future.

You will find that some special tools come in handy if you want to pursue the artisan style of noodle making, particularly a *soba bocho* (soba knife) for cutting the noodles long, a *memboh* (rolling pin), and a *koma-ita* (cutting guide), which works like a ruler. If you don't have these tools, you can use your kitchen knife and a ruler. The thickness will be different from authentic soba noodles, but the flavor will be there. *Sobakoh* and authentic tools for making noodles are available at Japanese markets and online (see Resources, page 291). You can also use a pasta machine, but I do encourage you to try making it by hand. Use the grams on the digital scale to measure the flour.

MAKES 3 TO 4 SERVINGS

EQUIPMENT
>   Rolling pin
>   *Koma-ita* (cutting guide) or ruler
>   *Soba bocho* (soba knife) or other large knife

>   3⅓ cups (400 g) soba-grade buckwheat flour (*sobakoh*)
>   ¾ cup (100 g) all-purpose flour or whole wheat flour (preferably Sonora wheat or Pasayten wheat varieties)
>   1¼ cup (260 ml) filtered water
>   1 cup (128 g) tapioca starch
>   2 quarts (2 L) ice water

Line the bottom of a large bowl with a damp paper towel so the bowl doesn't move. Sift the buckwheat and all-purpose flours into a large bowl. Set aside 2 tablespoons of the water and put the rest in the bowl. Work the water into the flour in a swirling pattern. Quickly toss together the flour and water, using your fingertips, until well combined. If you have any flour on your fingers, scrape it off and add it back into the dough. Continue to work the dough until it forms a crumbly mass.

Working quickly and using the palms of your hands in circular motion (Wax on! Wax off!), knead the dough until it becomes smooth, shiny, and with no visible cracks. If the dough feels dry, add a tablespoon of water, and continue kneading until the crumbly mass becomes little dough balls. Gather the small balls and shape them into one large ball. Knead the ball until it is semifirm and smooth (it should feel like your earlobe), not sticky. Press the ball into a disk about 1 inch (2.5 cm) thick. This will take about 5 minutes. If the dough still feels dry, add an additional tablespoon of water but don't be tempted to add any more. You don't want a wet dough.

Sprinkle the cutting board and the dough with a pinch of starch. Using a rolling pin, roll the disk

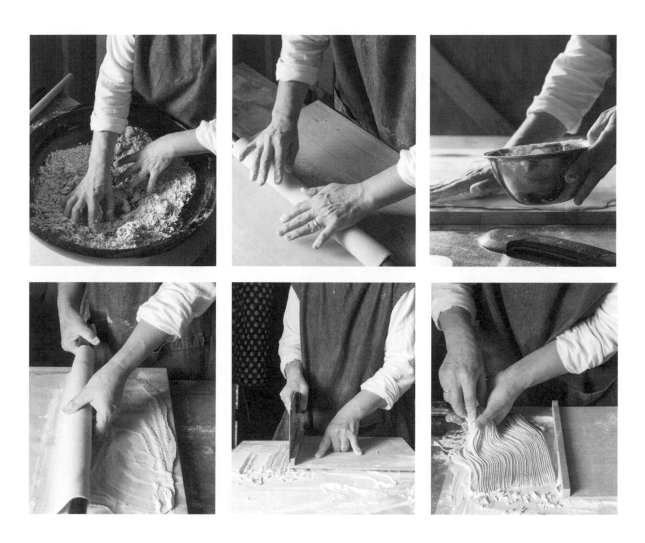

into a rectangle shape about 18 inches (45 cm) square and ⅛ inch (3 mm) thick. Feel the entire surface of the dough to check if there are any thick areas. Do not flip the dough while you are rolling it out. You want the dough to have an even thickness.

Generously sprinkle the tapioca starch over half of the dough and fold the other half on top of it (the dusting starch will keep the dough from sticking to itself). Generously dust another half of the dough, perpendicular to the rectangle you just folded, with tapioca starch and fold again. You will be shaking off the starch after the noodles are cut, so don't worry about overdusting.

You now have a "stack" of dough that is 4 layers deep. Starting along the short, folded side of the dough, use a ruler and knife (or cutting guide and

soba knife) to slice it into thin noodles that are even in size, about ⅛ inch (3 mm) thick (the thickness will vary from person to person). The idea is to handle the noodles gently (being careful not to squash them) and shake off the dusting starch by tapping the noodles on both ends. Transfer the noodles to a baking sheet, laying them flat. Do not bundle the noodles like you would with pasta or udon, or they will break. When the pan is full of noodles, cover it with a dish towel or plastic wrap and keep refrigerated until you are ready to cook the noodles. They are best made and eaten on the same day, but they will keep for up to 2 days in the refrigerator.

To cook the noodles, bring a stockpot of unsalted water to a rolling boil over high heat.

Gently drop the noodles into the boiling water, making sure the water stays vigorously boiling so the noodles don't stick together. Do not use ramen baskets. Cook only 2 servings at a time, so the noodles can swim in the pot, but do not stir. Cook the noodles until al dente, about 90 seconds (if they are thin like spaghetti) to 3 minutes (if they are thick like linguini). The timing will vary depending on the thickness of the noodles.

Scoop the noodles with a large sieve in one scoop. Transfer the noodles to a strainer that is set in the bowl of water to stop the cooking. Remove any surface starch by giving the noodles a vigorous rinse under cold running water. Drain and then rinse the noodles once more. Drain thoroughly by hitting the side and bottom of the strainer but don't toss the noodles. Serve immediately, in a soup (see Noodle Soup with Egg and Shiitake Mushrooms, page 149 or Spicy Duck Soba, page 251), or with dipping sauce (see Chilled Soba Noodles with Walnut Dipping Sauce, page 249), or in a salad (see Soba Salad with Kabocha Squash, page 143). The noodles are best eaten fresh. Cooked soba noodles do not hold up in the refrigerator very well.

udon noodles

Udon noodles are made with wheat flour, salt, and water. They are the most comforting Japanese noodle and the one that is made most often by home cooks because they are easy to make. Udon making is also a great way to entertain family and friends because it is traditionally made by stomping on the dough. You can use a stand mixer instead, but the stomping method is easier and the clean-up is faster. The noodles can be cut by hand with a kitchen knife, *menkiri bocho* (noodle knife), or *soba bocho* (soba knife) if you have one. You can also use a pasta machine to cut the noodles.

The standard amount of salt water used for making udon dough is around 50 percent of the weight of the flour. The salt adds *koshi*, structure, to the dough. The salt will get washed away when the noodles are cooked, so they won't taste salty. In Japan medium strength *Churikiko* wheat flour is traditionally used for making udon noodles. (Nisshin Komugiko is a popular brand.) Since *Churikiko* wheat flour is hard to find in the United States, I use Japanese *Hakurikiko*, an all-purpose flour available at the Japanese market. I also explore heirloom grain flours grown and milled in the United States such as Anson Mills' French Mediterranean white bread flour, Tehachapi Grain Projects' Sonora wheat flour, Blue Bird Grain Farms Pasayten hard white wheat flour. I also use a modern landrace wheat flour called Skagitt 1109 Hard Red Winter Wheat, which was bred by the WSU Bread Lab for the maritime climate of the coastal Pacific Northwest. These varieties bring a totally new slurping experience to the world of noodles. Use the grams on the digital scale to measure the flour.

MAKES 4 TO 6 SERVINGS

EQUIPMENT
  1 large mixing bowl
  1 gallon (3.75 L) heavy-duty zip-top plastic bag
  1 plastic garbage bag

Rolling pin

Koma-ita (cutting guide) or ruler

Soba bocho (soba knife) or other large knife

Manual pasta machine (if not rolling or
    cutting by hand)

1½ tablespoons (25 g) sea salt

Scant 1 cup (235 ml) water

3⅓ cups (500 g) *Hakurikiko* wheat flour
    (*see headnote*)

1 cup (128 g) tapioca starch, or cornstarch or
    potato starch for dusting the dough

Line the bottom of a large bowl with a damp towel. Add the flour into the large bowl. In a small bowl, dissolve the salt in the warm water and pour it over the flour. Using your fingertips, quickly and uniformly toss the flour and salt water, sweeping and scraping the sides and bottom of the bowl. The dough will look a bit shaggy. Put the dough in a 1-gallon (3.75 L) zip-top bag or wrap in a dish towel and let it rest for 30 minutes in the bag to activate the gluten.

Now it is time to knead the dough. Press out all the air from the zip-top bag. Then double-bag it with a plastic garbage bag (so you don't get dough all over your floor). Take off your shoes and stomp on the dough 100 times with clean socks or clean feet. Be careful not to rip the plastic bag. Take the dough out of the bag, place on a cutting board, and fold it into thirds like a letter. Put the folded dough back in the bag and repeat the stomp and fold action four more times. You can turn on some stomping music if you like. When it is fully kneaded, the dough will start to get smoother and easier to handle. Turn the dough out onto a cutting board and form it into a disk by tucking the edges under to meet in the center. Pinch the edges of the disk-shaped dough. Let the dough rest in a plastic bag or a well-wrung dish towel, pinched-side down, for at least 3 hours at room temperature or overnight in the fridge in its plastic zip bag. It can stay in the fridge for up to 2 days. The dough will relax and the surface will become silky.

To make your batch of udon noodles, bring the dough to room temperature. To roll out and cut the dough, you have two options. You can use a rolling pin and a knife or a pasta machine.

If using a rolling pin and a knife, flatten the disk with your hand into a larger shape. Then dust the dough with tapioca starch and roll it until it's about 3/16 inch (4 mm) to 1/8 inch (3 mm) thick. The dough will resist but keep rolling and pulling into shape with your hands until you reach the desired shape, about 18 inches (45 cm) square. To cut the dough, lay the dough lengthwise, then fold the dough accordion style back and forth into three folds. Slice into 1/8-inch (3 mm) or 3/16-inch (4 mm) wide noodles. The width is a matter of preference. Separate the cut noodles, bundle them up loosely, and put them on a baking sheet.

To make the dough into noodles with a pasta machine, cut the 18-inch (45 cm) square-shaped dough into 4 rectangular pieces. Feed each piece through the pasta machine, starting with the widest setting and moving to the narrower settings, until the dough is about 1/8-inch (3 mm) or 3/16-inch (4 mm) thick and a foot long. Dust each piece generously with tapioca flour and feed them one at a time through the linguini setting. Make sure the noodles are separated and not stuck together and place them on a baking sheet lined with starch in bundles.

The noodles will take about 10 to 12 minutes to cook in a large pot of rapidly boiling water. When cooked to desired doneness, scoop the noodles out of the pot and rinse under water. Serve the noodles with a sauce (see Peddler's Udon Noodles, page 253). Or, try them in a soup (see Noodle Soup with Egg and Shiitake Mushrooms, page 149) or with some noodle dipping sauce (see *Shoyu Tare*, page 105).

You can also freeze the uncooked udon noodles for later use. Just cook the noodles without defrosting them, giving them an extra minute of cooking time.

ramen noodles

Most Japanese people only eat ramen at ramen shops or buy store-bought ramen. It wouldn't dawn on any of my Japanese friends to make fresh ramen noodles at home because it is a lot of work. But I am surprised how popular ramen has become in the United States and how often I get asked to do workshops. Many people say that ramen is about the broth. As a noodle maker, I say the noodles are just as important. Ramen noodles are light yellow and springy. You achieve this by adding *kansui*, an alkaline solution (potassium carbonate and sodium bicarbonate) that regulates acidity and pigments the dough.

You can find bottled *kansui* water at Asian grocery stores, but I use baked baking soda, which can easily be made at home and has the same alkalinizing effect on the dough. I also add some heritage grain flour to the dough to make the noodles more flavorful.

Chef Ivan Orkin of Ivan Ramen makes ramen noodles with toasted rye. It adds good flavor and aroma. His recipe inspired me to try making ramen with ancient grains. I like making ramen noodles with spelt, rye, Pasayten wheat, and Sonora wheat flours. Use the grams on the digital scale to measure the flour.

EQUIPMENT
  Stand mixer
  Pasta machine

  ⅓ cup (50 g) Sonora wheat flour or
    other heritage grains
  2 cups (300 g) bread flour
  1 cup (150 g) cake flour
  2 teaspoons Baked Baking Soda (recipe follows)
  1½ teaspoons sea salt
  1 cup (240 ml) filtered water
  2 cups (256 g) cornstarch

In a small skillet, toast the Sonora wheat flour over low heat, stirring with a spatula, until fragrant, about 4 minutes. Transfer to a medium bowl and whisk in the bread flour and cake flour.

In a small bowl, whisk together the baked baking soda, salt, and the filtered water until the baking soda and salt are dissolved.

Add the baking soda solution to the blended flour in three equal additions. Once the dough resembles a shaggy ball, transfer it into a plastic bag and let stand at room temperature for 30 minutes. The dough will look a bit dry, but it will relax with time and take on moisture.

To knead the dough, place it in the stand mixer bowl and attach the dough hook to the mixer. Mix the dough at the lowest speed for 5 minutes, or until the dough is smooth. If the dough still feels dry and crumbly, add 1 to 2 tablespoons more water.

Turn the dough out onto a floured surface and shape into a disk by tucking the edges under with your hands. Allow the dough to rest for a minimum of 3 hours or up to overnight in the refrigerator.

To make the noodles, set up the pasta machine and a cutting board. Cut the dough into four pieces. Flatten each one with your hands and spread it wide enough so that it is slightly narrower than the pasta machine's width. Dust the dough evenly and generously with cornstarch on both sides to prevent it from sticking to the machine. Begin rolling the pasta through the pasta machine, 2 times per setting, starting with the widest setting and narrowing the dial until the width is at ⅛ inch (3 mm). The dough may feel dry and break apart in the beginning, but don't get discouraged. Simply fold it and start again. Cut each sheet of rolled dough into about 1-foot-long (30 cm) pieces.

Dust the dough again with a generous amount of cornstarch and run it through the spaghetti setting. Gently set the noodles on a baking sheet, sprinkling them with more cornstarch so they don't stick together.

To cook the noodles, fill a 6-quart (6 L) stockpot with water (do not salt it) and bring to a rapid boil over high heat. Working in two batches, boil the noodles until al dente, about 1 minute. Spread the noodles in the boiling water with tongs or chopsticks so they don't clump together.

Use a mesh strainer with a handle to scoop out the noodles. Drain the noodles. Transfer the noodles to the ramen bowls. Serve the noodles with Ramen Broth (page 257), *Yakibuta* Pork (Braised Pork Belly; page 258), and other toppings (see Ramen Bowls, page 255). The fresh uncooked noodles will keep in the fridge for 4 to 5 days. You can also make *Yakisoba* (Stir-Fried Noodles; page 254).

baked baking soda

This is the ingredient that gives ramen its bright yellow color and springiness. Note that when baked, the baking soda will look exactly the same.

MAKES 1 CUP (225 G)

  1 cup (255 g) baking soda

Preheat the oven to 250°F (120°C). Line a baking sheet with parchment paper.

Spread the baking soda on the prepared baking sheet in an even layer. Bake for 1 hour. Cool, then transfer the baked baking soda to a jar with a tight-fitting lid. It will keep in a cool place for up to 6 months.

dumpling wrappers

Fresh wrappers taste better than store-bought wrappers, which can sometimes be disappointingly dry. I learned how to make dumpling skins from my Chinese daughter-in-law Binah's mother, Laura Yeung, who makes really good dumplings. She boils her dumplings. I pan-fry mine. You can enjoy these dumplings either way. Laura turned me on to a short rolling pin, which you can find at Chinese markets.

MAKES ABOUT 50 TO 55 WRAPPERS, ABOUT 3½ INCHES (9 CM) IN DIAMETER

EQUIPMENT

3-inch (7.5 cm) cookie cutter or drinking glass with equivalent rim size

Stand mixer with dough hook

Pasta machine (optional)

1 cup (240 ml) filtered water, plus more as needed

½ teaspoon sea salt

1½ cups (180 g) all-purpose flour

1½ cups (270 g) bread flour

2 teaspoons light sesame oil or vegetable oil

1 cup (125 g) potato starch (or cornstarch) for dusting

Bring the filtered water to a boil in a small pot over medium heat and cook for 1 minute. Remove from heat. Dissolve the salt in the hot water.

Sift the all-purpose flour and bread flour into a medium bowl. Begin adding the flour to the salted water, ½ cup (120 g) at a time, stirring with a spoon or with your hands. Add the oil and mix to form a dough. Then shape the dough into a ball. If the dough feels dry, add another tablespoon of water. Let the dough rest for 15 minutes.

Place the dough in the bowl of a stand mixer fitted with a dough hook. Work the dough at medium speed for 8 to 10 minutes, until the dough is smooth and no longer sticky. Cut the dough in fourths and form 4 logs. Wrap the logs in plastic wrap and let them rest for 30 minutes on the kitchen counter. You can also prepare your filling while the dough is resting; see *Gyoza* (Fried Dumplings; page 145).

Line a baking sheet with parchment paper. Set aside. Unwrap the logs and slice each crosswise into approximately 14 pieces. Flatten each disk with a rolling pin so that it is paper thin, about 3 inches (7.5 cm) in diameter, then use the cookie cutter to make round wrappers. Use the rolling pin to flatten the wrappers again, so they are about 3½ inches (9 cm) in diameter, leaving the center a tad thicker than the edge. Alternatively, you can use a pasta machine to roll out the logs until they are paper thin and then use the cookie cutter to make round wrappers.

Sprinkle each wrapper with potato starch and put it on the parchment-lined baking sheet. Cover with another piece of parchment paper and roll out the next set of wrappers. Cover all the dough with a cloth while you are working to prevent it from drying out. Once the wrappers are done, wrap them in plastic and store in the refrigerator. Use them within 1 day for best results.

japanese milk bread

Milk bread is a popular yeasted bread in Japan. It is soft and chewy like mochi but light and airy. The lightness comes from an Asian technique involving a roux starter known as *tangzhong*. The roux is combined with the dough to produce a tender bread that doesn't dry out quickly like regular bread. I didn't have a chance to ask my grandmother for her milk bread recipe, so I looked to King Arthur Flour's baking school for help and inspiration. I have been teaching noodle making at their school for a few years. Whenever I am there, I come home with a few new tricks on baking. My sourdough is still in the works, but this milk bread recipe feels close to home. Milk bread can be used for toast, as sandwich bread, as buns to be filled with *Dashimaki Tamago* (Dashi-Flavored Omelet; page 82), to make *tamago sando* (Japanese egg sandwich), and more.

MAKES 1 LOAF

EQUIPMENT
    Stand mixer

FOR THE ROUX
    3 tablespoons whole milk
    2 tablespoons bread flour
    ¼ cup (60 ml) filtered water

FOR THE DOUGH
    2¼ cups (315 g) bread flour
    ¼ cup (30 g) buckwheat flour or other heirloom flour such as spelt, Sonora, rye
    2 tablespoons nonfat dry milk
    3 tablespoons cane sugar
    2¼ teaspoons active dry yeast
    1 teaspoon sea salt
    1 large egg
    ½ cup (120 ml) whole milk, heated to lukewarm temperature, plus 2 tablespoons for brushing on the loaf
    4 tablespoons (½ stick/60 g) unsalted butter, softened, plus 1 tablespoon for buttering the bowl and pan

To make the roux, combine the milk, flour, and filtered water in a small saucepan and whisk until visible lumps are gone. Bring to a boil over low heat, stirring vigorously with a whisk until the mixture thickens but is still pourable, about 3 to 5 minutes. Transfer the roux to a measuring cup and let it cool to room temperature.

To make the dough, combine the roux with the dough ingredients in the bowl of a stand mixer fitted with the dough hook and mix on low speed until an even, smooth, elastic dough forms, about 10 minutes.

Butter the inside of a nonreactive bowl. Take the dough out of the stand mixer bowl, shape into a ball, and place in the buttered bowl. Cover with a kitchen towel and let rise in a warm place for 60 to 90 minutes, until puffy but not necessarily doubled in size.

Punch down the dough and divide it in half. Sprinkle the surface of the cutting board with some dusting flour. Roll each dough ball into a diamond shape, about 8 x 8 inches (20 x 20 cm). Lift the left edge of the dough and fold it toward the center of the diamond. Do the same with the right side. Then lift the bottom edge near you and roll it into a log. Place the log in the loaf pan, seam-side down and crosswise at one end of the pan. Roll out the other ball, perform the same steps, and place it at the other end of the pan.

Cover the pan with a kitchen towel and let the dough rise for 40 to 50 minutes, until the log is puffy and has almost doubled in size and the two loaves touch at the center.

Preheat the oven to 350°F (175°C) and butter a 9 x 5 inch (23 x 12 cm) loaf pan. Brush the top of the log with milk and bake on the bottom shelf of the oven (about 4 inches/10 cm from the bottom), until golden brown, 35 to 40 minutes.

Let cool in the loaf pan for 10 minutes, then take the bread out of the pan, move to a wire rack, and allow to cool for at least 1 hour before slicing.

my adventures with bread and the heritage grain movement

When my family moved to Los Angeles in the 1970s, bread was at a low moment. My parents complained that American bread tasted bad, and Julia Child had said how can a nation be called great if its bread tastes like Kleenex? Every time my mother went back to Japan for a visit, she would return with a suitcase full of bread.

Japanese people eat more bread than people might imagine (these days, the Japanese consume more bread than rice). Back when I was young, my *obachama* in Kamakura baked bread regularly, and I helped her stomp the dough; it was through my feet that I first experienced the fun of playing with dough.

Serendipitously, my pursuit to find good buckwheat for my soba noodles connected me to the world of heirloom grains and artisan bread—and to a handful of mindful grain scientists, farmers, millers, and bakers.

Dr. Stephen Jones, who is a world-renowned wheat breeder and the director of the Bread Lab at Washington State University, organizes a grain gathering every year where you learn about the science of grains and flour and baking and can even take a lesson on the anatomy of a stone mill. The highlight of the gathering for me is Dr. Jones's crack-of-dawn lectures out in the fields. He has a ritual of reciting haiku; the flock of Canada geese that fly over the fields are one of his favorite poetic subjects. In his lectures, he talks about the varieties of heirloom and modern grains the Bread Lab breeds (over forty thousand was the last count) and what these grains can do to restore the health of our soils and the nutrition and flavor of our breads. Dr. Jones has invited me to teach noodle-making and tofu workshops, but one year

he also asked me to teach haiku. I know very little about haiku. I reluctantly accepted and crammed for the haiku lesson. (He also asked Nanna Meyer, a Swiss sports nutritionist at the University of Colorado in Colorado Springs and former Olympian downhill racer, to yodel. While Dr. Jones's requests may go beyond the realm of science, he offers us the chance to observe nature closely, including our own voices. Nanna and I both managed to rise to the occasion, and his audience—and even the good doctor himself—couldn't help but be moved.)

Glenn Roberts of Anson Mills in South Carolina, a miller and farmer with numerous other claims to fame, has been instrumental in restoring ingredients in the Southern larder including grits, cornmeal, Carolina Gold rice, and biscuit flour. But his heritage grain revival efforts go beyond that region. He donates heritage seeds and equipment to farmers around the country. He and I had an ongoing buckwheat dialogue that started in 2009 and eventually developed into the idea of planting heritage grains in Southern California. I know little about grains, but next thing I knew, I was meeting artisan bakers, such as Chad Robertson of Tartine Bakery in California, taking a seed-saving workshop at Native Seed Search in Arizona, and looking for organic farmers in Southern California who would take the donation of four tons of seeds and a vintage combine harvester from Glenn. The

goal was to bring back some of the heirloom varieties of grains in Southern California and thereby diversify the way we grow food and benefit the soil through crop rotation. But trying to convince a California farmer to plant obscure varieties of grains was not easy when fruits and vegetables are their main cash crops. Patience, passion, and persistence—and a lot of help from local chefs and LABB (Los Angeles Bread Bakers)—enabled us to eventually find a number of like-minded farmers who would give these heirloom grains a chance.

Alex Weiser, Jon Hammond, and Sherry Mandell in Kern Country, three of the founding members of the Tehachapi Heritage Grain Project, said yes to the experiment first. In Santa Barbara and Santa Inez, Nate Siemens of Fat Uncle Farms, Tom Shepherd of Shepard Farms, and Curtis Davenport of California Malting Company also came on

board. They started by planting a few rows or a few acres of heritage grains with which to experiment, working together and inviting others to join—local farmers, chefs, bakers, millers, and grain enthusiasts. Eight years later, more farmers in Southern California have joined in the endeavor and are growing over two hundred acres of heritage grains such as Sonora wheat, Abruzzi rye, Red Fife wheat, purple barley, and spelt. I am amazed that I can identify some of these grains by the shape of their spikes and florets and their exquisite flavors.

A single-minded obsession with buckwheat has helped me expand my universe of grains and discover how the way we grow and process food can improve the flavor of food and ultimately regenerate the health of our soil. And it turned me into a baker, though I still love my noodles.

beans and legumes

Beans are a powerhouse of nutrients and good flavor, and they are a fantastic soil amender. Your tomatoes are delicious because they were grown in soil amended by beans as a rotation crop. We should be eating more cover crops like beans.

The Japanese word for beans happens to rhyme with the Japanese word *mame*, meaning "diligence." During the New Year's celebrations, Japanese parents encourage their children to eat as many *kuromame-no-amani* (sweetened black soybeans) as their age to remind them to work hard, endure, and be diligent. It may sound a little Spartan, but to me these beans were the best part of the good luck foods of the New Year because they were sweet. The Japanese have a way with beans, enjoying them in both savory and sweet dishes. Be creative… how about adding some beans to your granola (see Homemade Granola with Lucky Beans, page 171) or tofu custard (see *Kinugoshi Dofu to Kuromame-no-Amani* [Homemade Tofu Custard with Sweetened Black Soybeans], page 272)? Or how about making Miso (page 101) and Tofu (page 75) from scratch? I will show you how.

How to Buy and Store Beans: Start with new crop beans, if at all possible. They will hold their shape together and hydrate faster than older beans, which will often split when cooked. Keep beans in a container with a tight-fitting lid, away from moisture. I try to use beans within 1 year of purchase.

TIPS FOR COOKING BEANS

Dried beans require rinsing and soaking. These steps help remove the dirt and some of the indigestible complex sugars that produce gas. Hydrated, beans will more than double in size, so soak them in three times their volume of fresh water for 12 to 18 hours, changing the water at least once. After soaking, drain and rinse the beans, then add them to a large pot. Cover the beans with three times their volume of fresh water. While the Western way of cooking beans can include adding an onion, bay leaf, carrots, bacon, and a variety of spices such as cumin and peppercorns to synergize flavors, the basic Japanese method is to add vegetables and proteins *after* the beans are cooked, not before.

Bring the beans to a boil, then reduce the heat and simmer very gently (no bubbling) until the beans are tender. Make sure the beans remain submerged in the cooking liquid to prevent them from being exposed to air, which will wrinkle them. An effective way to do this is to use *otoshi-buta*, the drop-lid method, which requires using a smaller lid, one that can fit *inside* the pot, that rests directly on top of the beans. Both wooden and metal drop lids are available in Japanese markets. Add more water to keep the beans from surfacing above the liquid and becoming dry.

Cooking time will vary depending on the type of bean, but start checking for tenderness after 45 minutes. The beans should be easily mashed between two fingers. Remove from heat.

SOYBEANS

Creamy and somewhat bland in flavor, soybeans
are called the meat of the fields, and rightly so.
They have served as a staple protein in Japan for
vegetarians and nonvegetarians alike for centuries. Soybeans have a wealth of health benefits,
including their ability to improve metabolism and
cardiovascular health, promote bone health, and
lower the risk of diabetes.

Edamame are young soybeans that are usually boiled and eaten fresh. Dried soybeans can
be roasted to make *iri-daizu* (crispy soybeans)
and can also be cooked and turned into soy milk
or made into tofu (see page 75). They are also
fermented to make soy sauce, Miso (page 101),
and Natto (see page 73). Though natto may be an
acquired taste for many Westerners—who find it
slimy, sticky like a gossamer web, and stinky—I

cooking beans with a pressure cooker

The best way to cook beans is with a pressure
cooker, which is becoming an increasingly popular
kitchen appliance (I have a very old kind of pressure cooker with a "jiggler" valve). Pressure cooking is so much quicker, and it results in plump and
tender beans. Some people don't soak the beans
when using a pressure cooker, but I still soak mine
overnight, changing the water at least once, to
make them more digestible. One cup of beans
will more than double in size when hydrated, so be
sure to soak in plenty of filtered water, about
4 cups (960 ml) of water for 1 cup (180 g) of
beans. When the beans are fully hydrated, transfer them to the pressure cooker with 4 cups
(960 ml) of fresh water. To be on the safe side,
don't fill up more than one-third of the pressure
cooker. Bring the water to a boil over high heat.
Once the water starts bubbling, skim off any foam
and then fasten the lid. Bring the pressure up to
high and cook for 7 minutes over medium heat.
The cooking time will depend on the type and
size of beans you are using and how fresh they are
(older beans may take longer). Turn off the heat
and release the pressure naturally. Open the lid
and check if the beans are cooked. If they need
more time, set the pressure cooker for another
5 minutes or so, and then check again. Read
the manufacturer's instructions before using a
pressure cooker.

encourage you to give it a chance because it is
delicious and very good for you. In fact, fermented
beans are probably the best kind to eat, because
the process of fermentation makes them easier to
digest while also increasing your body's ability to
absorb nutrients.

Most of the soybeans produced in the United
States are genetically modified, which is a problem
because we simply don't understand the long-term
effects on our health or soils. So look for non-GMO
soybeans; I prefer Laura Soybeans, from Iowa.

NATTO (FERMENTED SOYBEANS)

Traditionally, natto is made from whole cooked soybeans inoculated with *Bacillus natto*. The wild *Bacillus* live naturally in rice straw, so if you put warm cooked soybeans in a rice straw wrapper and keep it in a warm place, the bacteria will multiply and the beans will ferment and become natto. In Japan, you will find natto still sold in rice straws, but most are in little Styrofoam or plastic containers in the refrigerated or freezer section of Japanese markets.

Store-bought natto is usually labeled with an expiration date. If you keep natto past its prime, it will continue to ferment and develop a dry and shriveled appearance, sometimes with little white dots—which are amino acid crystals, not mold—on the surface. Natto at this stage is still edible, but for the best flavor it should be eaten fresh and by the expiration date of the manufacturer. If you freeze natto, it will keep for up to 3 months.

I like to eat natto for breakfast (see page 175); I think it is best straight with a little soy sauce and mustard. Another way to eat natto that is good for those new to the ingredient is to stuff a couple of tablespoons of seasoned natto into *abura-age* (deep-fried tofu pouches) with some chopped scallion. When the pouches are toasted on the grill or in the toaster oven, they come out crisp like a cracker while the natto inside stays soft and gooey. I serve them with soy sauce.

natto (fermented soybeans)

I learned this recipe from my chef friend Mutsuko Soma of Kamonegi, an artisan soba restaurant in Seattle. She serves a killer spicy natto soba composed of fresh soba noodles with natto, Korean nori flakes, crispy tempura batter flakes, garlic chile oil, and soft-boiled egg—all tossed together at the table to make a viscous bowl of deliciousness. I prefer to use Laura Soybeans from Iowa (see Resources, page 291).

EQUIPMENT

Pressure cooker

**One 2-quart (2 L) glass or food-safe plastic
container, with lid**

2 cups (300 g) soybeans

**One 1.6 oz (45 g) pack store-bought
organic natto**

12 cups (3 L) filtered water

Sterilize your tools. You will need a mesh strainer,
mixing bowl, ladle, and a spatula.

Rinse the soybeans in water and drain. In a
large bowl, soak the soybeans in 6 cups (1.4 L)
filtered water at room temperature for 18 to
24 hours; the soybeans should more than double
in size. Test the soybeans to see if they are fully
hydrated by splitting a bean in half. If you see a
white core in the middle, the soybeans need more
soaking time. When there is no white core, the
soybeans are fully hydrated. Drain the soaked
soybeans in a mesh strainer.

Place the soybeans in a pressure cooker and
cover with the remaining 6 cups (1.4 L) water. Bring
the pressure cooker to a boil over high heat. Fit the
lid and bring to full pressure (15 pounds [6.8 kg])
over medium-high heat according to the manufacturer's instructions, and then reduce heat to
medium-low and cook for 5 minutes. Do not walk
away from the pressure cooker while applying
pressure. If using a jiggler-style pressure cooker,
turn off the heat and transfer the cooker to the sink.
Run some cool water over the closed lid to cool
down the cooker. When the pressure is completely
gone, open the cooker and check the soybeans for
doneness. If a soybean is firm but squashes easily
between your fingers, it is cooked. If not, pressure cook for another 3 to 5 minutes, or until you
achieve that softness. Transfer the cooked beans to
a colander set over a pot and allow to drain. Transfer the beans to the sterilized mixing bowl.

Open the carton of store-bought natto, put ½ of
the whole carton in a sterilized cup, and add ½ cup
(120 ml) water. The water will turn opaque. This is
your starter. Save the remaining natto for eating.

Spread the starter over the hot steamed soybeans and mix well. Transfer the beans to 2 sterilized half-size baking sheets. Cover with a clean
dish towel. Leave the beans to ferment in a warm
room. The ideal temperature for fermenting natto
is between 86°F and 104°F (30°C–40°C). You can
put the natto in a dehydrator or in the oven if the
temperature setting goes that low. Let the natto
ferment for 24 hours in a warm space. When the
fermentation is complete, you will see a thin white
filament on the surface. The natto may not be
as sticky as the store-bought versions, but if you
whip it, it will gain stickiness. Cover and store in
the refrigerator in the sterilized container overnight. Keep in the fridge for up to 10 days or in the
freezer for 3 months.

soy milk

**Fresh soy milk tastes nothing like the store-
bought version. It is fragrant, creamy, and subtly
sweet. You can enjoy soy milk as a beverage on
its own; use its lees (curds) to make pancakes or
add them to your stir-fry; turn the whey (liquid)
into miso soup; or coagulate it to make tofu (see
below). Making soy milk is a two-day process,
which might seem like a long time, but it includes
the time it takes to soak the soybeans, which is
essential to making good soy milk. You just can't
rush this process; the results are worth the time.
Andrea Nguyen's *Asian Tofu* is an excellent book
on tofu. It eased me into the task of making soy
milk and tofu at home. If you are interested in
exploring the world of tofu, her book is a wonderful resource.**

EQUIPMENT
    1 extra-large nut milk bag (preferably
        100 percent hemp)
    Digital thermometer

2 cups (300 g) dried soybeans
14 cups (3.36 L) filtered water

Rinse the soybeans in water and drain. In a large bowl, soak the soybeans in about 6 cups (1.4 L) filtered water, enough to cover the beans, at room temperature for 18 to 24 hours; the soybeans should more than double in size. Test the soybeans to see if they are fully hydrated by splitting a soybean in half. If you see a white core in the middle, the soybeans need more soaking time. When there is no white core, the soybeans are fully hydrated. Drain the soaked soybeans in a mesh strainer.

Place 2 cups (480 ml) filtered water in a 4-quart (4L) pot and bring it to a boil over medium-high heat. While the water is being heated, start grinding the beans. Place 6 cups (1.4 L) filtered water in a pitcher. Combine 2 cups (480 ml) filtered water with half of the drained soybeans in a food processor and process at the highest speed for 2 minutes to yield a thick, smooth puree. Transfer the puree to the 4-quart (4 L) pot and stir with a spatula to prevent scorching on the bottom. Repeat this step with the remaining 2 cups (480 ml) filtered water and the remaining drained soybeans.

To rinse out the food processor, add the remaining 2 cups (480 ml) filtered water to the machine and process for about 10 seconds. Pour this liquid in the pot. You should now have a foamy soybean puree in the pot.

Heat the puree over medium-high heat, stirring frequently with a spatula to prevent scorching on the bottom, until the puree begins to rise and the temperature comes up to about 185°F (85°C), 8 to 10 minutes. Do not walk away from the pot, because the rise can happen rapidly and cause a spill.

Turn off the heat and let stand for 5 minutes to let the foam subside a little. When it does, turn the heat to low and cook the puree for another 10 minutes, again stirring to prevent burning or scorching. This extra cooking time will ensure that the soy milk is easily digestible.

To strain the soy milk, set the nut milk bag inside a 2-quart (2 L) pitcher and ladle the hot soybean puree into the bag while holding the bag with one hand. Gather up the nut milk bag and twist to extract the soy milk. To prevent burning your hands, you can wear rubber gloves, or let the puree cool off a little—but not too much. You need to strain the soybean puree while it is hot to ensure a maximum yield of soy milk. Discard the surface foam with a ladle. You should have about 7 cups (1.75 L) of soy milk. Cook the soy milk again for another 10 minutes over low heat while stirring constantly to prevent it from scorching. The final yield after simmering will be around 6½ cups. The *okara* (soy lees) will remain in the bag. You can use the lees to make *Okara* (Soy Lees) Pancakes with Blueberry Syrup (page 173). The soy milk is now ready to drink or to be used for making tofu (see below). Keep soy milk in the refrigerator and use within 3 to 4 days.

tofu (medium-firm)

Fresh tofu is one of the tastiest foods in the world. Like bread and noodles, however, most Japanese won't think of making tofu at home. It takes a lot of beans, coagulant, water, and patience to produce a little white block.

To make fresh medium-firm tofu, you start with making fresh soy milk as described above. The soy milk is reheated and a coagulant called *nigari* (magnesium chloride), a by-product of the production of sea salt, is added to extract the curds from the soy milk. In a sense, it is similar to making cheese. I like the subtly bitter flavor of *nigari* to make medium-firm tofu. I also use

gypsum as a coagulant to make creamy silken tofu (see *Kinugoshi Dofu to Kuromame-no-Amani* [Homemade Tofu Custard with Sweetened Black Soybeans], page 272). You can buy the coagulant and the wooden molds online from Hitachiya USA. I also use reusable aluminum pans and colanders for molds.

MAKES ABOUT 1 LB (566 G) TOFU BLOCK

EQUIPMENT

1 disposable aluminum pan with lid, about 6 x 4 x 2 inches (15 x 10 x 5 cm), or a Japanese wooden tofu mold

2 thin muslin cloth liners or a double layer of cheesecloth, about 6 x 12 inches (15 x 30 cm)

8-ounce (240 ml) mason jar with lid or a can equivalent in weight and size

Digital thermometer

4 cups (960 ml) Soy Milk (page 74)

4 cups (960 ml) filtered water, plus more as needed

2 teaspoons liquid *nigari* dissolved with ½ cup (120 ml) filtered water

If using an aluminum pan, pierce the bottom and sides with an ice pick or something similarly pointy. You will need 8 holes on the bottom and 2 on each side of the pan so the whey can escape from the pan. Then line the aluminum pan or wooden tofu mold with the muslin cloth liners or double-layer cheesecloth. Let the edge of the cloth hang over the pan or mold. If you want to reserve the whey, put the pan or mold into a large bowl to catch the whey as it leaves. The whey makes a delicious vegan dashi for miso soup.

Combine the soy milk and 4 cups (960 ml) filtered water in a 4-quart (4 L) pot and mix well. Heat the liquid over medium heat, stirring the bottom frequently with a wooden spoon to avoid scorching, until it comes to a gentle simmer. Simmer for 5 minutes, or until it reaches 175°F (80°C), and maintain that temperature until the coagulant is added.

In a small cup, combine the *nigari* with ½ cup (120 ml) filtered water. Stir it with a spoon until the coagulant dissolves.

Check the temperature of the soy milk. If it is 175°F (80°C), turn off the heat. Using a spatula, move the milk back and forth across the pot to create momentum. Pour two-thirds of the coagulant into the pot and stir a few times. Then remove the spatula, cover the pot, and wait for 5 minutes—no peeking! The soy milk should be curdling and forming light fluffy clouds, with the amber whey starting to separate. After 5 minutes, lift the lid and check the pot. If there is an opaque liquid at the edge that is not curdling, reheat the pot for a minute over medium heat until the temperature reaches 175°F (80°C). Replace the lid and wait for another 5 minutes for the curds to form. If the soy milk has not separated, add the remaining one-third of the coagulant on the surface of the tofu and mix lightly. You don't want to disturb the liquid that is forming into soft tofu clouds. Replace the lid and let stand for 10 minutes and check again.

Set the cloth-lined pan or mold in the sink or inside a large bowl. Carefully transfer the curds with a ladle to the cloth-lined pan or mold. Use a weight heavy enough to weigh down the tofu—a mason jar filled with water will work. Leave for 15 minutes for medium to firm tofu and 20 minutes for firm tofu. Then remove the weight and cotton cloth and transfer the tofu onto a plate.

To store, cover with plastic wrap and store in the refrigerator for 2 to 3 days.

---

how to eat very fresh tofu

You can make *yudofu* (tofu hot pot) or *hiyayakko* (tofu salad) using medium-firm or silken tofu; there is hardly any cooking involved in either dish. The less you fuss with fresh tofu, the more you can taste the nutty flavor of the bean.

To make *yudofu*, cut one block of tofu into smaller cubes, each about 3 inches (7.5 cm) in size. Set aside on a plate. Place a 2- or 3-inch (5 to 7.5 cm) piece of kombu in a medium pot, preferably a *donabe* (clay pot). Heat over medium heat until the water begins to simmer. Lower the heat and add the tofu; let it simmer for a couple of minutes, just to heat the tofu, not cook it. Each diner then scoops the tofu out into a bowl to eat with condiments, such as grated ginger, sliced scallions, sliced myoga, bonito flakes, and soy sauce. Chilled tofu can be served as *hiyayakko*, a salad. Instead of cooking the tofu as you do for *yudofu*, you serve it straight with the same condiments.

KUROMAME (BLACK SOYBEANS)

These round, black soybeans have a matte appearance. The *tamba* variety, grown in the Tamba region spread out over Kyoto and Hyogo prefectures, is especially prized for its large size, shiny skin, and silky texture. A bag of *tamba* black soybeans commands a high price. Black soybeans need to be cooked over a low temperature for 2 to 3 days to produce beans that are shiny and tender; rushing the cooking will produce hard and wrinkled beans.

These soybeans are eaten mainly during New Year's for good luck, but I enjoy them throughout the year. They are delicious mixed with yogurt or ice cream or used to top tofu custard (see *Kinugoshi Dofu to Kuromame-no-Amani* [Homemade Tofu Custard with Sweetened Black Soybeans], page 272) or as garnish for Berry *Kanten-Yose* and *Shiratama* Mochi with Ginger Syrup (page 274).

Black soybeans, including the *tamba* variety, and *kokuto*, brown sugar from Okinawa Prefecture, are available in Japanese markets and online.

kuromame-no-amani (sweetened black soybeans)

These sweetened black soybeans take 2 days to cook. Be patient—the reward is well worth the wait.

MAKES ABOUT 2 CUPS (350 G)

- 5 ounces (142 g) *kokuto* or muscovado sugar
- ¼ teaspoon sea salt
- 1 teaspoon soy sauce
- 4 cups (960 ml) water
- 5 ounces (142 g) black soybeans, preferably *tamba*, rinsed and drained

In a medium pot (preferably cast-iron), combine the sugar, salt, soy sauce, and water and bring to a boil over medium heat. Turn off the heat, add the black soybeans, and cover the pot. Let the beans soak in the liquid for 12 hours or overnight.

Bring the beans to a boil, uncovered, over medium heat. Skim the surface and turn the heat to the lowest setting to maintain a very gentle simmer. Rest a clean lid on the beans inside the pot to keep the beans submerged and to keep them from moving too much. Cook for at least 8 hours, until the beans are soft enough to squeeze with your fingers. Make sure the beans are always submerged in the liquid as they cook so they don't wrinkle; replenish with ½ cup (120 ml) or more water as needed.

Cook the liquid in the pot until it is reduced to half of its original volume and begins to look syrupy. Remove from heat and let cool. Store the beans with the syrup in a glass container with a tight-fitting lid in the refrigerator for up to 2 weeks.

Note: Alternatively, the beans along with the seasonings can be cooked in a pressure cooker, following Cooking Beans with a Pressure Cooker (page 72).

ADZUKI BEANS

These small burgundy beans are used in both savory dishes (such as *taiyaki*, fish-shaped pancakes that are a popular street food) and sweet dishes. Adzuki beans are also often cooked with sweet rice (*osekihan*) on festive occasions or mixed into Basic White Rice (page 46). The beans turn the rice red, the color of good luck.

ANKO (SWEETENED ADZUKI BEAN PASTE)

Adzuki beans are particularly enjoyed sweetened and made into the form of *anko* (bean paste). Though the idea of eating beans as part of dessert has not clicked with Westerners—not yet, anyhow—*anko* is used to make a variety of wonderful sweets. You will find *anko* in very delicate and hand-molded *wagashi*, confections that are shaped into seasonal themes and colors to complement tea. There are *wagashi* shops throughout Japan, where you will find artisans who have been making a variety of exquisite bean cakes for generations. Most are made fresh and must be eaten the same day lest they dry out. The closet equivalent to *anko* in the West is marzipan, the sweetened almond paste used in European confections as a filling or molded into small imitations of fruits and vegetables.

Anko is made with beans high in starch, including adzuki beans, white navy beans, and butter beans. Legumes that are low in starch such as peanuts or soybeans don't make *anko*. *Anko* can be "beany" and coarse (*tsubu-an*) or pureed and creamy (*koshi-an*). This is a very personal preference, akin to peanut butter. My father preferred *koshi-an*, my mother *tsubu-an*. I enjoy both and use a food processor when I want to achieve *koshi-an*, which is more time-consuming than making *tsubu-an*. You can also buy *anko* ready-made at Japanese markets.

How to Store Anko: Freeze what you don't use. It will keep for 3 months.

anko (sweetened adzuki bean paste)

This recipe is for *tsubu-an* (chunky) sweetened bean paste. You can puree it in the food processor and make it creamier if you like. Use *anko* to make Japanese sweets. I use it as a filling for Strawberry *Daifuku* Mochi (page 269) or Butter Mochi with Adzuki Beans and Walnuts (page 273). Serve it with Berry *Kanten-Yose* and *Shiratama* Mochi with Ginger Syrup (page 274). It is also delicious as an ice pop (see *Anko* [Sweetened Adzuki Bean Paste] Ice Pops, page 267).

MAKES ABOUT 3½ CUPS (875 G)

> 8¾ ounces (250 g) adzuki beans
> 1 cup (200 g) cane sugar
> Pinch of salt

Rinse the adzuki beans, then place them in a large pot and cover with filtered water to soak 8 to 12 hours. Once hydrated, the beans will more than double in size, so make sure the beans are submerged in water three times their volume.

Bring the pot of beans and the soaking water to a boil over medium heat. Then remove from heat and discard the broth. Refill the pot with enough fresh water to cover the beans and repeat the same step two more times. This helps remove the *aku* (bitterness) of the beans. Fill the pot with fresh water again and cook over medium-high heat and bring to a boil. Lower the heat and simmer until the beans are cooked, about 45 minutes. You should be able to smash them between your fingers.

Add ⅓ cup (65 g) of the sugar and continue cooking the beans over low heat; repeat this step twice more, stirring the beans to make sure nothing is sticking to the bottom of the pot.

Add the salt and continue to cook over low heat until all the liquid is absorbed, about 10 minutes. Then check the consistency; for the best and softest bean paste, the beans should leave a "tail" when you scoop up the paste and drop it back into the pot. If the bean paste falls in one lump (with no "tail" or thread), you've overcooked them and the bean paste will be on the tough side. So pay attention and don't walk away from the pot during these final minutes.

The bean paste should have a slightly lumpy texture. Remove the pot from the heat and spread the paste out on a baking sheet with a spatula to cool. Transfer the bean paste into a plastic or glass container with a lid and store in the refrigerator. It will keep for up to 10 days in the refrigerator or up to 3 months in the freezer.

eggs

Eggs are acknowledged as being packed with essential vitamins and nutrients and are one of the most beloved foods in the world. They certainly arc in my house, where my husband and I eat them almost every day.

Eggs should be fresh, of course, and laid by hens that get to spend their days outside on fresh pastures eating whatever their hearts desire—worms, insects, grass—instead of being cooped up in cramped cages or huddled by the thousands in barns eating industrially produced feed. With their creamy, bright orange yolks, eggs from pasture-raised and cage-free chickens taste better in every way.

There are a number of classic cooked egg dishes, such as egg custards, omelets, and rice dishes, that are central to Japanese cooking and distinctly Japanese in flavor and presentation. Recipes for two such classic treatments are in this section, and you will find even more in part two.

dashimaki tamago (dashi–flavored omelet)

Dashimaki tamago is a light and slightly sweet omelet with a rectangular shape. The rectangle is achieved by using a shaped pan called a *tamagoyaki-ki*, which can be found in Japanese markets or online. You can also use a well-seasoned 9-inch (23 cm) or 10-inch (25 cm) skillet.

The hidden flavor of *dashimaki tamago* is, as its name implies, dashi; here I am using Bonito and Kombu Dashi (page 00). [[ms 38]] If you don't have any dashi on hand, you can use chicken broth or milk as a substitute, but dashi is really preferred for the authentic flavor of the dish.

A distinguishing characteristic of the *dashimaki tamago* is its beautiful layers. The egg is not scrambled; instead, while the egg is cooking, a fork or pair of chopsticks is used to roll it, in stages, into a cylinder. You will start by using one-third of the egg batter to make the first layer, then adding half of the batter for the remaining two layers to accommodate the growing cylinder. When it is cut into slices, a pretty swirl pattern emerges. For more color and flavor, you can chop some wakame (seaweed) or chives and incorporate them into the egg batter.

In addition to eating this omelet on its own, you can make a *tamago sando* (Japanese egg sandwich) with it, put it in your bento box, or use it as a topping for your noodles (see Noodle Soup with Egg and Shiitake Mushrooms, page 000). [[ms 219]]

MAKES 4 SERVINGS

> 5 large pastured eggs
>
> 5 tablespoons Bonito and Kombu Dashi (page 27), milk, or chicken broth, at room temperature
>
> 2 teaspoons mirin
>
> 2 teaspoons cane sugar
>
> 2 teaspoons *usukuchi shoyu* (light-colored soy sauce)
>
> 1 tablespoon minced chives or hydrated wakame, drained and chopped (optional)

> 1½ tablespoons grapeseed or untoasted sesame oil
>
> 6 ounces (170 g) peeled and finely grated daikon radish (optional)
>
> Soy sauce for serving
>
> Microgreens for garnish

In a medium bowl, combine the eggs, dashi, mirin, sugar, and soy sauce. Whisk the eggs gently. Do not whip. Mix in the chives, if using.

Heat a skillet over medium-high heat. Soak a paper towel in the oil and use it to spread the oil evenly in the skillet, keeping the paper towel for later use. Test the pan by sticking the tips of your chopsticks or fork in the egg batter and putting a few drops into the pan; if the pan is hot enough, the batter will sizzle without burning. If the pan is too hot, lower the heat to let the pan cool a bit.

Pour one-third of the batter into the pan and cook the eggs, spreading the batter quickly and evenly. If you see any air bubbles form, use a fork or chopsticks to pierce them.

When the batter begins to set on the bottom, fold the omelet into thirds. Start by lifting the far end of the egg mixture and rolling it toward you. Let the rolled egg set for 30 seconds. Push the rolled egg into the corner on one edge of the pan. Regrease the pan with the paper towel, moving the egg roll around to ensure full coverage with the oil.

Now pour half of the egg batter into the pan, making sure to lift the egg roll with your chopsticks or fork so the batter gets underneath it. You are using more egg batter than the previous time to accommodate your growing cylinder.

Cook this second batch of batter until almost set, then roll the omelet again (essentially, you are rolling the egg omelet to make layers). Repeat this step one more time with the remaining batter, incorporating the first roll into the second and the second roll into the third.

Transfer the omelet onto a cutting board. You can use a bamboo mat to further shape the omelet, and then let the omelet rest, wrapped, for 3 minutes.

To serve, unwrap the omelet and slice it cross-wise into 1½- to 2-inch (4 cm to 5 cm) pieces. Serve warm or at room temperature with grated radish, soy sauce, and microgreens. The omelet will keep in the refrigerator for 2 to 3 days.

nitamago (marinated soft-boiled eggs)

This is the soft-boiled egg used to top ramen and other Japanese noodle soups; these eggs are hugely popular in my workshops, in part because they are so easy to make. The marinade is made with dashi and *shoyu tare*. When eggs are marinated in this medium for a day or two, the yolks become gelatinous and creamy. Serve these marinated eggs with your noodle soups or in a grain bowl. Or they can be the star of your bento box.

MAKES 6 EGGS

> 2 cups (480 ml) Bonito and Kombu Dashi (page 27)
> ½ cup (120 ml) *Shoyu Tare* (page 105)
> 6 large eggs, left out at room temperature for 1 hour

Combine the dashi and *shoyu tare* in a bowl or container that can hold all the eggs.

To cook the eggs, bring 2 quarts (2 L) of water to a boil in a medium saucepan over high heat. Using a slotted spoon, lower the eggs into the boiling water and continue cooking over high heat for 7 minutes, stirring the eggs gently with a wooden spatula once. Remove the pan from the heat and drain. Transfer eggs into a bowl of ice water and let them cool for 3 minutes.

Peel the eggs and place them in the bowl with the marinade. Leave the eggs in the marinade, covered, overnight or up to 3 days in the refrigerator. Slice them in half to serve.

pickles and ferments

*T*sukemono, or pickles, bring the season to the Japanese table and are an essential part of the Japanese meal, served in a small portion with rice at the end of the meal to clear the palate and aid digestion. At home, I do not wait till the end to serve pickles. I put them on the table with the other dishes. Another word for pickle is *oshinko*, which describes "new aromas." This alternate term is a subtler way to suggest what pickles bring to a meal: they are a hint, meant to be nibbled, not a course; they taste best when made in a timely way, using the best of the harvest. And these "new aromas" satisfy and complete a seasonal meal, just as a pleasant fragrance rounds out the experience of a certain food.

The practice of pickling in Japan is ancient. This preservation method is used to prolong the shelf life of vegetables, fruits, seafood, and meat, and it enhances flavors, tenderizes foods, and makes them more digestible and nutritious. Pickles can be made in a variety of flavors: sweet, sour, salty, umami, and bitter. It all depends on what you are pickling and what medium you are using. While you can pickle almost anything, here we will be looking mainly at vegetables; however, I have also included a recipe for *Umeboshi* (Pickled *Ume* Plums; page 00), **[[ms 129]]** the quintessential salty pickle of Japan.

There are countless varieties of Japanese pickles; you can even undertake a pickle tour of the country to taste regional varieties. There are many old shops in Japan that specialize in pickles, one of which is *tsukudani*, a type of pickle made with small seafood (such as baby sardines), meat, or seaweed that has been seasoned with soy sauce, sake, mirin, salt, vinegar, and spices. Like most pickles, *tsukudani* are eaten with rice. I make my own *tsukudani*, using repurposed dashi ingredients such as shiitake mushrooms, bonito flakes, kombu, and soybeans (see *Dashigara-no-Tsukudani* [Dashi Pickles], page 31).

Japanese pickles are made in vinegar and brine solutions as well as other pickling mediums such as soy sauce, miso, *sake kasu* (sake lees), and *shio koji* (fermented koji salt). Don't be afraid to try your own pickling, even though most Americans are used to buying pickles—well, pickled cucumbers—in a jar in the grocery store. In this section I will introduce you to a few different pickling mediums and some of my favorite pickles. We will start with *amazuzuke* (quick vinegar pickles) and *amazu shoga* (pickled ginger), which you probably have eaten at a sushi bar and wished you could make at home because of its freshness and brightness. We'll then explore pickling with *nuka* and *shio koji*.

amazuzuke
(quick vinegar pickles)

I have a basic and universal pickling medium—vinegar, water, salt, and sugar—that works with almost any vegetable. It is best to use a hearty vegetable for these pickles, such as cauliflower, green beans, asparagus, okra, radishes, lotus root, red onion, squash, peppers, carrots, and/or cucumbers; leafy greens won't work well. I serve these pickles like a salad as a side with ramen noodles, *gyoza* (fried dumplings), or *shumai* (steamed dumplings), or with a sandwich. I like to add kombu to enhance the umami. Soy sauce also works as a flavor enhancer, especially with cucumbers; simply add a few teaspoons of light-colored soy sauce and a squeeze of lemon to the pickling medium. Spices such as chiles, bay leaf, peppercorns, garlic, and ginger also can brighten pickles, but I use them sparingly. If you want sweeter pickles, add a tablespoon or more of cane sugar to the pickling medium.

This recipe was inspired by my chef friend Minh Phan of Porridges and Puffs in Los Angeles, who makes a heavenly rice porridge and accents it with a pinch of her savory jams and, yes, pickles.

MAKES EIGHT ½-PINT (240 ML) MASON JARS

2½ pounds (1.2 kg) assorted seasonal vegetables, trimmed and peeled (*see headnote*)

6 *shiso* (perilla) leaves

3 sprigs each thyme, dill, and parsley

1½ ounces (40 g) ginger, peeled and sliced

2 cloves garlic, peeled and sliced in halves

1 teaspoon peppercorns (black or pink) or seeds (cumin, coriander, fennel, or mustard)

4 dried red chiles or 1 jalapeno pepper, sliced crosswise and seeds removed

2 cups (480 ml) rice vinegar

2 cups (480 ml) filtered water

1 piece of kombu, 1 x 6 inches (2.5 x 15 cm), cut into 12 pieces

½ cup (100 g) cane sugar

3 tablespoons sea salt

1 tablespoon julienned orange or lemon peel

Sterilize eight ½-pint (240 ml) mason jars.

Slice the vegetables into bite-size pieces, about ¼ inch (6 mm) thick. If skinny like asparagus and green beans, leave them whole or cut them in half crosswise. Root vegetables should be blanched first for 1 minute in a pot of boiling water and strained before adding to the jars. Pack the vegetables, *shiso*, thyme, dill, and parsley in the sterilized jars tightly.

Combine the ginger, garlic, peppercorns, chiles, rice vinegar, filtered water, kombu, sugar, salt, and citrus peel in a medium saucepan and bring to a boil over high heat. Remove from heat and pour the hot brine over the vegetables in the sterilized jars. Let cool, then seal the jars and refrigerate. You can start eating the pickles after 1 day. The pickles will keep in the refrigerator for up to 3 weeks.

amazu shoga (pickled ginger)

Make this pickle—the kind you enjoy at the sushi bar—if you can find fresh young ginger at a farmers' market or Asian market. Young ginger is fragrant, tender, and not as spicy or fibrous as old ginger. You can tint the pickled ginger naturally using the red tip of the ginger root or a red beet. (If you use a beet, peel it and cut it into thin, ⅛-inch-thick [3 mm] slices before adding it to the ginger. The beet will turn the ginger a darker red.) I serve this pickle with *Chirashi Zushi* (page 192), *Mari Zushi* (page 205), *Okonomiyaki* Pancakes (page 261), and grilled fish.

4 cups (960 ml) filtered water

1 pound (455 g) young ginger

1 scant teaspoon sea salt

FOR THE PICKLING SOLUTION

1½ cups (360 ml) Kombu Dashi (page 27)

1 cup (240 ml) rice vinegar

⅔ cup (130 g) cane sugar

1 teaspoon sea salt

Bring 4 cups of water to a boil in a medium pot over medium-high heat. Meanwhile, peel the ginger with a spoon, reserving the red tip, if there is any. The red skin will naturally tint the ginger pink. Cut the ginger along the grain into very thin slices (about 1/16 inch [2 mm]). Toss the sliced ginger with 1 scant teaspoon of the salt. Let it stand for 5 minutes. Rinse it under running water and then blanch the ginger in the boiling water for 1 minute. Drain and let cool to room temperature.

To make the marinade, combine the Kombu Dashi, rice vinegar, sugar, and remaining sea salt in a small saucepan. Set the pan over medium heat and warm until the sugar is dissolved. Stir in the ginger. Remove the pan from heat. Marinate the ginger in the liquid for at least 2 hours before eating. Store the cooled pickled ginger in the refrigerator, where it will keep for up to 1 month.

namasu (daikon radish and carrot salad)

Many Japanese salads fall somewhere between a salad and a pickle. I make this salad, and the recipe that follows, regularly and keep them in the refrigerator to serve over the week. They are meant to be served in small portions as a nibble.

This salad is a good luck food eaten during New Year's, but I like to serve it all year round. The red of the carrot symbolizes fire and the white radish symbolizes purity. It is best to use a Japanese mortar and pestle to grind the sesame seeds, but if you don't have one, a food processor will work just fine. This salad pairs nicely with grilled meats and vegetables.

MAKES 4 SERVINGS

1 pound (455 g) daikon radish, peeled and julienned into 2-inch (5 cm) matchsticks

1 medium carrot, julienned into 2-inch (5 cm) matchsticks

1¼ teaspoons sea salt

FOR THE PICKLING SOLUTION

¾ cup (180 ml) rice vinegar

¼ cup (50 g) cane sugar

¾ teaspoon salt

¾ cup (180 ml) Kombu Dashi (page 27) or water

FOR THE GARNISH

1 tablespoon toasted sesame seeds, coarsely ground with mortar and pestle

½ dried red chile, seeded and chopped

1 teaspoon lemon, yuzu, or *sudachi* (Japanese lime) zest

¼ cup (20 g) dried persimmon or apricot, seeded and julienned (optional)

In a large bowl, combine the daikon and carrots. Add the salt and massage it into the vegetables for 2 to 3 minutes. Let stand for 5 minutes then squeeze the vegetables to remove any excess water.

In a small bowl, whisk together the vinegar, sugar, salt, and dashi. Add the dressing to the daikon and carrots and toss gently. Cover and let marinate in the refrigerator for 4 hours.

Serve the salad garnished with the sesame seeds, chile, lemon zest, and dried persimmon, if using. The salad will keep in the refrigerator for 1 week before garnishing.

sun-dried *kiriboshi* daikon radish salad with tofu, carrots, and peppers

Kiriboshi daikon radish is daikon radish strips that have been dried in the sun or a dehydrator. The semi-strips have a distinctive crunch, umami, and sweetness that are perfect for a picklish salad. You can semi-dry other vegetables like cucumber, eggplant, zucchini, Napa cabbage, and of course, tomato. Hydrated, *kiriboshi* daikon radish will expand three to four times its size. Allow 2 days to make this pickle. In this recipe, I combine the *kiriboshi* daikon with other vegetables for additional color, texture, and flavor, but you can stick to just the *kiriboshi* daikon if you like. You can also buy *kiriboshi* daikon at a Japanese market. If using store-bought *kiriboshi* daikon, soak in water for about 15 minutes before use to soften. The soaking liquid makes good dashi for *Nishime* (page 129). (Pictured at top.)

EQUIPMENT
Dehydrator (optional)

8 ounces (230 g) daikon radish, peeled and
julienned into 4-inch (10 cm) strips

2 tablespoons toasted sesame oil, or grapeseed
or olive oil

Two 2¾ x 2¾ inch (7 x 7 cm) *abura-age*
(deep-fried tofu pouches), sliced in half
crosswise, then julienned into ¼-inch (6 mm)
strips (optional)

1 medium carrot, julienned into ¼-inch x 3-inch
(6 mm x 7.5 cm) strips

½ green bell pepper, julienned into
¼-inch x 3-inch (6 mm x 7.5 cm) strips

2 tablespoons sake

2 tablespoons mirin

1 tablespoon *usukuchi shoyu* (light-colored
soy sauce)

To make the dried daikon radish, put the strips on
a baking sheet, cover it with a screen to keep out
insects, and leave it out in the sun to dry for 4 to
5 hours. Alternatively, place the strips in a dehydrator, turn it to the vegetable setting, and leave
for 2 hours, or until semi-dry or dry.

Heat the oil in a wok or well-seasoned cast-iron
skillet over medium heat. Add the dried daikon
strips, *abura-age*, if using, carrots, and bell pepper
and cook, stirring, for 3 to 4 minutes, until the
carrots and bell pepper are slightly tender. Add the
sake, mirin, and soy sauce and cook, stirring, for
3 to 4 minutes, until most of the liquid is absorbed.
Serve immediately hot or at room temperature or
let cool and store in the refrigerator for 3 days.

fukujinzuke (relish of the seven lucky gods)

Fukujinzuke are tangy and crunchy pickles that
match perfectly with Japanese curry but also are
delicious with plain rice. This pickle consists of
seven vegetables—daikon radish, carrot, cucumber, eggplant, burdock, lotus, and ginger—but
you don't have to make this pickle with all seven
if you have trouble finding any of them. You can
use mushrooms and other vegetables if you like
(but no leafy greens). The tanginess comes from a
sweet-and-sour vinegar sauce. Allow these pickles
to marinate in this sauce for 1 or 2 days for best flavor. The name *fukujin* is derived from the Seven
Lucky Gods of prosperity, abundance, dignity,
beauty, wisdom, longevity, and protection.

MAKES 4 TO 6 SERVINGS

FOR THE SAUCE
1 dried Japanese or Italian (Calabrian) red chile,
seeded and chopped

½ cup (120 ml) soy sauce

3 tablespoons rice vinegar

¼ cup (60 ml) mirin

1 tablespoon cane sugar

2 tablespoons sake

8 ounces (230 g) daikon radish, peeled and
quartered lengthwise, then diced ¼ inch
(6 mm) thick

4 ounces (115 g) lotus root, peeled and
coarsely chopped

1 small carrot, peeled and quartered lengthwise,
then diced ¼ inch (6 mm) thick

2 fresh or dried shiitake mushrooms (soaked
in 1 cup of water overnight in the refrigerator,
if using dried shiitakes), sliced ⅛ inch
(3 mm) thick

1 Japanese eggplant, sliced lengthwise, then
diced ¼-inch (6 mm) thick

1 tablespoon peeled and minced ginger

1 Japanese or Persian cucumber, diced ¼ inch
(6 mm) thick

In a medium saucepan, combine the chile, soy sauce, vinegar, mirin, sugar, and sake and bring to a boil over medium heat. Add the daikon radish, lotus root, carrot, mushrooms, eggplant, and ginger and bring to a second boil over medium heat; boil for 2 minutes. Turn off the heat and add the cucumbers. Let stand for 2 minutes, then strain the vegetables through a fine-mesh strainer into a bowl, reserving the liquid. Return the liquid to the pot and bring it to a third boil over medium heat. Remove from heat and let cool.

Transfer the pickled vegetables into a glass jar with a lid and pour the liquid over the vegetables. Stir with a spoon. Bring to room temperature then cover with a lid and let the vegetables pickle in the liquid in the refrigerator for 1 to 2 days before using. Store in the refrigerator, where your Seven Lucky Gods will keep for up to 2 weeks.

umeboshi
(pickled *ume* plums)

Umeboshi is a quintessential Japanese pickle, mouth-puckeringly sour and salty. Like all pickles, it serves as a palate cleanser and aids digestion, but it is also said to cure colds and hangovers.

My grandmother had an *ume* plum tree in her garden that probably was as old as she was. We would always look to the plums and the nightingales as the first signs of spring. The plum blossoms are very hardy and are known to hold up even in the snow. Grandmother preferred them over cherry blossoms, which she said were beautiful but ephemeral. She also was known to say that a woman should have dignity, like a plum blossom.

During the *ume* pickling season, I helped my grandmother make *umeboshi*. We sorted the plums by size, cleaned and rubbed them with sea salt, and placed them in a jar with red *shiso* (perilla) leaves. About a month later, when the rainy season was over, Grandmother took the plums out of the jars and laid them out in the sun

to dry for three days in a row, then returned them back to the jar. She would leave some jars alone for more than six months, so I got to taste different vintages of *umeboshi*. As a special treat, she would occasionally allow me a sip of the sweet and fragrant *Umeshu* (Plum Wine; page 287).

Fresh *ume* plums are available in late spring between May and June in Japanese and Korean markets.

MAKES ABOUT 2 DOZEN

EQUIPMENT

Small spray bottle

Ceramic, enamelware, plastic, or glass container, sterilized

Drop lid, sterilized

5-pound (2.5 kg) stone (or can) that fits on top

2½ pounds (1.2 kg) ripe but firm unbruised *ume* (preferably *Kaga ume*)

1 to 2 tablespoons *shochu* (Japanese grain liquor) or clear distilled spirit (35 percent alcohol)

½ cup (120 g) sea salt

½ cup (113 g) cane sugar (optional)

Using a toothpick or the point of a sharp knife, remove the small brown stems from the *ume*. Rinse the *ume* and set aside any unripe fruit. Also discard any bruised or blemished *ume*, as they can start to grow mold.

Soak the *ume* in water overnight to remove bitterness. The next day, drain the *ume* and pat dry with a towel. Place the *ume* in a large bowl and spray them with the *shochu*, using the small spray bottle. Sprinkle and gently rub the salt over the *ume* using your hands. Repeat until you use up all the *ume*. Reserve the remaining salt for the *shiso* leaves (see note).

Place salted *ume* in the container. Put a sterilized wooden lid or a sterilized plate on top of the *ume*. Place a sterilized weight directly on the top of the lid. The weight will press the plums and extract the brine. Cover the container with cloth or paper and tie a string around the container to hold the

cloth or paper cover in place. Leave it in a cool, dark place.

After a few days, check the container. You should start to see the brine that is being extracted from the *ume*. The brine (*umezu* or plum vinegar) should cover the *ume*. If you don't see any brine, you may need to add 2.5 to 5 percent more salt and 5 pounds more weight. You can also sprinkle sugar on top at this stage for a sweeter *umeboshi*. Gently turn the *ume* in the container so they get an even coating of brine, replace the lid and weight, and leave the *ume* for 4 weeks in a cool place.

After the 4 weeks, take the *ume* out of the container and reserve the vinegar in the container. Spread the *ume* on bamboo mats or baskets and place them in the sun. You can cover with a screen

to keep the bugs out. Dry them for 3 days, or until the surface of the fruit turns slightly white. The plum vinegar in the pickling container should also get time in the sun, about the same amount of time as the plums.

At the end of each day, place the sun-bathed *ume* back in the container with the sun-bathed plum vinegar, and bring the *ume* back out the next day. Repeat this for 3 days in a row. Then replace the plums one final time and store the *umeboshi* and the vinegar in separate containers in a cool, dark place. The plums can be eaten after 10 days or so, but it is good to wait for a few months to a year or longer for better flavor.

Note: You can enhance the color and flavor of *umeboshi* with red *shiso* leaves. You will need about 50 *shiso* leaves. Wash the leaves well and drain in a strainer. Weigh the *shiso* leaves. You will use sea salt to equal 10 percent of the weight of the leaves. For example, if you have 4 ounces (113 g), use 2½ teaspoons (13 g) of sea salt. To remove the bitterness of *shiso* leaves, rub the salt into the leaves, working them until a dark purple liquid is extracted. Discard the liquid. Once this dark purple liquid is extracted and discarded, you can add the *shiso* leaves into the *umeboshi* container. It will turn the *ume* brine red. This is the *umezu* (plum vinegar).

The red *shiso* makes an excellent *furikake* (seasoning sprinkles) called *yukari* for rice, meat, fish, and vegetables. For making *furikake*, dry the pickled red *shiso* leaves in the sun with the *ume* and vinegar. When the leaves are fully dried, finely grind them in a spice grinder or with a mortar and pestle. Store the *furikake* in a container with a tight-fitting lid, where it will keep for up to 3 months.

PICKLING WITH *NUKA* AND *SHIO KOJI*

The Japanese have a variety of pickles that use solid, rather than liquid, pickling mediums such as miso, sake lees, rice bran, and *shio koji* (fermented koji salt)—all of which undergo the process of lacto-fermentation. The result is a distinctly tangy, crunchy, and delicious assortment of pickles. Of this category, I am particularly fond of the nutty aroma and mild flavor of *nukazuke*, rice bran pickle. The pickling medium is made with *nuka* (rice bran), water, salt, and other umami-rich ingredients such as bonito flakes, *niboshi* (dried sardines), kombu, and dried shiitake mushrooms. Japanese use any type of firm vegetable, including carrots, cucumbers, cabbage, radishes, zucchini, kabocha squash, eggplant, and burdock to make *nukazuke*. The vegetables are buried in the fermented medium to pickle for just a few hours (or overnight) and are then removed. The medium is reused and replenished as needed. The vegetables become infused with the nutty *nuka*; the result is not as sour or spicy as kimchi or sauerkraut, but the health benefits are just as high.

In the old days, every family had its own version of *nukadoko*, the fermented rice bran mash. It was treated as a family heirloom and passed on from mothers to daughters as a wedding gift. My husband, Sakai, told me about how my late mother-in-law brought her *nukadoko* to the train station when she went to see off one of her daughters, who was moving to another city with her new husband. Every time this tender image comes to mind, it brings tears to my eyes, even though my mother-in-law passed away long before I met my husband. In those days it was not uncommon to find a *nukadoko* that was more than fifty years old. I'm sorry to say that this pickling method—and the tradition of passing it on from one generation to the next—is disappearing in Japan as convenience foods take over. People just don't want to stick their hands in a smelly pickling medium every day. At the same time, though, a movement to restore traditional foods, including here in the United States, is slowing growing, and I can report that I have Americans, including fourth- and fifth-generation Japanese Americans who come to my pickling workshops to learn how to make their grandmothers' *nukazuke*, as well as Americans

how to maintain the *nukadoko* medium

To maintain a healthy *nukadoko*, you will need to mix the base once a day with your hand; it needs the bacteria on your hand to thrive, so don't use a wooden spoon or rubber spatula. If it feels dry or grainy, add a little beer (flat beer works fine). You want the texture to feel like wet sand. If your most recent batch of pickles tastes too sour, add some fresh *nukadoko* medium. If the *nukadoko* becomes too wet, just add a little cooked rice or a piece of day-old bread. Replenish the *nukadoko* with some fresh *nukadoko* (about 2 cups) every 30 days.

You will notice that the medium has a distinct sour smell (which I actually find rather pleasant), which indicates the bacteria is actively working. I keep my *nukadoko* in the pantry, which makes the daily stirring an easy task, but some people prefer to keep it in the garage. When choosing a spot to keep it in, be sure it is a cool place. If you live in a very warm climate and don't have a garage or basement, you can keep the *nukadoko* in the refrigerator; it will stay alive, but the fermentation process will slow down.

The *nukadoko* base should be kept at room temperature, but if you are traveling out of town, you should move it to the refrigerator. The bacteria will go dormant there, but you can revitalize it by giving it a stir and leaving it out at room temperature when you return. If you see any green mold growing on the surface of the *nukadoko*, scrape it off and discard it. Smell the *nukadoko*. Taste it. It should have a pleasant nutty flavor.

who are curious about *nukazuke* and suggest making the pickling mash using other grain brans, such as wheat and barley. I am totally inspired by their pickling pursuits. One of these students commented that making *nukazuke* is a bit like making compost, and it is true.

As rice is grown widely in California, sourcing rice bran in the United States is not as difficult as it might seem. You can also buy rice bran at Japanese markets or online. Keep the bran in the refrigerator or freezer because it is highly perishable.

Shio koji is an ancient probiotic salt seasoning that is used to marinate, tenderize, and enhance the umami in foods. I use it like salt. It acts like miso but it is creamier, mellower, and easier to use. It is made with rice koji, rice that has been inoculated with strains of the beneficial mold *Aspergillus oryzae*. Don't let the word *mold* scare you! If you look inside any Japanese pantry, you will find so many seasonings made with rice koji, including miso, soy sauce, rice vinegar, sake, and mirin.

Shio koji has many health benefits; it contains a number of enzymes known to be beneficial for well-being, including amylase, which aids digestion and promotes a healthy gut. Two teaspoons of *shio koji* equals approximately 1 teaspoon of salt, and the amount of the pickling agent you will want to use is about 8 to 10 percent of the weight of the food that you are trying to season, marinate, or tenderize. For example, if you want to pickle 1 pound (455 g) of Napa cabbage, you should use about 2 to 3 tablespoons (36–45 g) of *shio koji* to rub all over the leaves. A digital scale will come in handy to do the math, but once you get used to using *shio koji*, you can trust your taste buds to do the measuring. I rub my seafood and meat with *shio koji* and use it like a marinade. I add *shio koji* to my salads, soups, stews, and even ice cream. It's my secret seasoning.

nukazuke (fermented rice bran pickles)

To make *nukazuke* you will need a clay jar, enameled pot, or glass bin; whatever you choose must have a lid. I use an enameled pickling jar that is about thirty years old, and it still works perfectly. The *nukadoko* (*nukamiso*) medium has a texture similar to wet sand or soft miso paste, and it takes about a week to prepare. Making *nukadoko* may seem a little tedious and time-consuming, but once you have trained the medium, you can keep it indefinitely and pass it on to friends and loved ones. The recipe below makes a good starter *nukadoko*. Use the full amounts here and do not try to cut the recipe in half; you will need it all to ensure the bacteria propagates effectively.

MAKES 1 BATCH OF *NUKADOKO*

- 2.2 pounds (1 kg) rice bran (*nuka*)
- ⅔ cup (130 g) sea salt (13 percent of the weight of the rice bran)
- 4½ cups (1 L) filtered water
- 3 dried Japanese red chiles, seeded, or dried Korean or Italian (Calabrian) chiles
- One 3-inch (7.5 cm) piece of kombu, cut into small pieces
- 2 ounces (57 g) ginger, sliced into ½-inch (12 mm) pieces
- 1 teaspoon *sansho* peppercorns (optional)
- 5 *niboshi* (optional)
- Peel from ½ lemon, cut into ¼-inch (6 mm) slices
- 2.2 pounds (1 kg) discarded ends and peels of vegetables (such as cabbage, eggplant, celery, carrots, cucumbers, bell pepper, and daikon radish, but not onions)

Place the rice bran in a dry, heavy, large cast-iron pan and toast it over low heat, stirring with a wooden spoon or spatula so it doesn't burn, for about 3 to 4 minutes. Remove from heat and let stand.

In a large pot, combine the salt and filtered water and bring to a simmer over medium heat. Stir to dissolve the salt and make a brine. Remove from heat.

Slowly add the brine to the toasted rice bran and mix it with a paddle until it reaches a consistency comparable to slightly moist sand. Add the chiles, kombu, ginger, and lemon peel.

To train the *nukadoko*, start by putting various vegetable scraps (try cabbage leaves, eggplant, celery, and carrots) into the rice bran bed and keeping them in a cool, dark place for about 2 days to allow them to lightly ferment.

Take the vegetable scraps out and discard them. Repeat this step 5 or 6 times, with the whole process taking about 10 to 12 days. You are training the *nukadoko* by replenishing it with new scraps every 2 days

After 10 to 12 days, the *nukadoko* will develop a unique aroma and look like moist sand. At this point, the *nukadoko* is vital and contains active organisms such as yeast and lactobacillus. Check the *nukadoko* for flavor and saltiness. It should taste pleasant and nutty. You can now start putting vegetables such as cucumber, eggplant, cabbage, carrot, cauliflower, and bell pepper into the *nukadoko* for fermenting. To speed the pickling process, rub a little salt on whole or large chunks of vegetables such as cucumber and carrots before you put them into the *nukadoko*. Do not let the vegetables touch each other in the *nukadoko*. Place fresh vegetables in the *nukadoko* for 1 to 2 days maximum. Cucumbers may only take 2 or

3 hours on a warm day or 4 to 6 hours on a cold day. The longer you keep the vegetables in the *nukadoko*, the saltier they will be.

To serve the *nukazuke*, simply take them out of the *nukadoko* and rinse them briefly under cold water to remove the *nuka*. Slice the vegetables and serve straight or with a sprinkle of bonito flakes, if you like. You can keep the *nukazuke* in the refrigerator for 2 to 3 days.

shio koji
(fermented koji salt)

Making *shio koji* at home is very easy. It involves simply mixing dried rice koji together with salt and water; the mixture will ferment at room temperature. You can find dried koji in the refrigerated section at Japanese markets or online. (I recommend Cold Mountain, South River Miso Company, and GEM Cultures.)

MAKES ABOUT 2½ POUNDS (1.2 KG)

> 1 pound (455 g) dried brown or white rice koji
> 8 tablespoons (145 g) sea salt (a Japanese sea salt such as *arajio* is preferred)
> 2½ cups (600 ml) hot water (140°F/60°C)

If the koji granules are whole, grind them with a mortar and pestle or in a food processor until they are about half their size.

In a large bowl, combine the rice koji with the salt and mix well.

Add the hot water and rub the granules with your hands. Transfer to a container with a lid to let it ferment at room temperature for 5 days. Stir with a spatula once a day. The *shio koji* will become thicker and creamier, and it will begin to smell sweet like miso from the fermentation process. You can make a creamy *shio koji* by putting the mixture through a food processor and processing it until smooth, or you can use it in its grainier form. It will keep in the refrigerator for up to 3 months.

quick *shio koji*–cured napa cabbage

I used to make these pickles with sea salt, but when I discovered *shio koji*, I switched. All you need to do to make these pickles is give the cabbage a good *shio koji* massage; it takes just a few minutes. This recipe is more like a salad than a pickle. You can use Savoy and green cabbage, radishes, squash, or carrots—if you can name it, you can pickle it with *shio koji*. The hidden umami agent is kombu, of course. I spice up this pickle with chiles and ginger and brighten it with lemon zest.

MAKES 6 TO 8 SERVINGS

> One 1 x 2 inch (2.5 x 5 cm) piece of kombu
> 1 pound (455 g) Napa cabbage, sliced crosswise into 2-inch (5 cm) pieces
> 2 to 2½ tablespoons *Shio Koji* (at left)
> 1 teaspoon lemon, *sudachi* (Japanese lime), or yuzu zest
> 1 Japanese chile, seeded and thinly sliced

Soak the kombu in 1 cup (240 ml) of water for 1 hour or up to overnight. Drain the kombu dashi, reserving it for other uses. Cut the kombu into matchsticks. Set aside.

Rub the cabbage with the *shio koji*. Mix in the lemon zest, chile, and kombu. Let the mixture rest in the refrigerator for 1 hour or up to overnight, then squeeze out the excess brine. The pickled cabbage will keep in the refrigerator for 2 to 3 days.

seasonings and condiments

Much of the flavor of Japanese cuisine comes from its distinctive fermented seasonings, which can be daunting to new cooks facing a store shelf holding an array of soy sauces or miso with barely translated labels. But don't be afraid! Japanese cuisine shares with others some basic essentials, such as salt. Here I share with you my five essential seasonings, as well as other staples that are good to have around, including nuts, sweeteners, oils, and spices.

MY FIVE ESSENTIAL SEASONINGS

The Japanese use a phonetic alphabet (*sa–shi–su–se–so*) to show the order in which seasonings are added:

sa (sugar) [*sato*]

shi (salt) [*shio*]

su (vinegar) [*su*]

se (soy sauce) [*shoyu*]

so (miso) [*miso*]

There is a logic to this order. Sugar doesn't dissolve easily, so it is added to the pot first, which gives it more time to blend into the dish. You also need to add sugar before strong seasonings such as soy sauce and salt, which can overwhelm the more delicate sweetness. Salt, the second addition, dissolves easily and draws out moisture from foods; it also concentrates flavors, so it is added early in the cooking process. Vinegar comes in

midway so it can retain its fragrance and acidity; it tends to overpower other flavors, so it is better to add it after salt, which concentrates them. Soy sauce and miso, enjoyed for their rich fragrances and umami flavors, burn easily, so they come last in the cooking process. Sometimes sake and mirin are added at the start of cooking to erase odor in foods, so there is flexibility to the phonetic system described here, but nonetheless, most Japanese cooks keep this little alphabet in mind for reference.

Over the years I have carved out my own version of this alphabet as I have tried to cut back on sugar in my cooking. So my alphabet starts with sake, which includes mirin, followed by salt, vinegar, soy sauce, and miso. I use sugar sparingly. I prefer the minerally rich Okinawa brown sugar, *kokuto*, in some recipes that call for sugar.

sa (sake, mirin)

shi (salt)

su (vinegar)

se (soy sauce)

so (miso)

SAKE AND MIRIN

Sake, made by fermenting rice, is the most important alcoholic beverage in Japan, and it is also used as a seasoning in many Japanese dishes, just as wine is used in European and American cooking.

Sake is a miracle elixir—it tenderizes, flavors, sweetens, acts as an antiseptic, removes odors of meat and seafood, and adds umami without coloring or overwhelming the natural flavor of the food it is intended to enhance.

While cooking sake is sold at the market, I use regular drinking sake. There is no need to buy an expensive bottle; there are reasonably priced sake brands such as Sho Chiku Bai, which is produced in California, that work well in the kitchen.

In addition to sake, there is mirin (also called *hon mirin*), which is made from naturally fermented sweet or glutinous rice. Mirin is used mostly as a cooking sake to sweeten foods. It is golden in color with a syrupy consistency but has no added sugar. Some mirin is aged for three years and thus has deep and developed umami and *amami* (savory and sweet flavors). Mirin has a lower glycemic index than cane sugar, honey, or maple syrup, making it a viable substitute for those looking to limit their sugar intake.

When buying mirin, avoid mirin that contains corn syrup as its sweetener. Look for mirin specifically labeled *hon mirin*, not mirin-type; the latter is not a true mirin. If you cannot find mirin at your market, you can substitute 1 tablespoon sake mixed with 1 teaspoon of sugar for each tablespoon of mirin. Brands of aged (about 3 years) Japanese *hon mirin* that can be found in Japanese markets include Sanshu Mirin and Fukuraijun Mirin. You can also buy America *hon mirin* brands such as Takara Mirin and Shiragiku Mirin.

How to Store Sake and Mirin: Keep the cap tightly closed to prevent oxidation. Store in a cool place, away from sunlight.

SHIO (SALT)

Salt is probably the most versatile and common seasoning known to humankind. Salt brings back good memories of Kamakura for me: swimming in the ocean; collecting seashells, sea glass, and little bits of broken pottery from shipwrecks that dated back to the Ming dynasty (or so I was told); and eating chilled watermelon that my grandmother would pull out of the well just as we came home from the beach, our skin tingly with sand and salt. We would sprinkle salt on the watermelon to boost its sweetness. My grandmother would also dab salt on her palms to make *onigiri* (rice balls).

Obachama also had other uses for salt. She would put a small mound of salt at the front door on special days to purify the house. And when she had unpleasant visitors, she would scatter salt after they left to shoo away bad spirits. I thought salt contained magical powers, and perhaps it does, when used sensibly. Being an island nation, Japan has always relied on seawater to make salt.

For my everyday cooking, I use *arajio*, a fine Japanese sea salt. I use it as a rub for meat and as a preservative for fermented pickles, and I put it in dough to give structure to my breads and noodles. *Arajio* is subtly moist to the touch, which makes it easier to handle than table salt. *Arajio* contains iodine, calcium, and magnesium chloride (*nigari*), which are all important minerals in our diet, and it offers a wide range of flavor profiles: umami as well a hint of *amami* (sweetness).

There are a number of artisan sea salt producers in Japan that produce small batches of high-quality sea salt, using traditional methods. In Nanaura Kaigan of Sado Island in Niigata Prefecture, Shio Kobo produces salt by boiling seawater in an iron pot over a wood-burning fire to extract the flaky salt crystals. The salt here is known to be significantly higher in magnesium, potassium, and calcium than industrial sea salt, because the seawater is collected where the cold and warm currents meet. This salt is delicate and subtly sweet. On Awaji Island in the inland sea of Hyogo Prefecture, producers at Amabito no Moshio use an ancient method to extract *moshio* (seaweed salt) that has been revived in the region. The seawater is boiled with seaweed in clay pots to produce salt crystals that contain seaweed ash. The beige mineral-rich salt-ash mixture is further sifted to make a finer salt. Some artisan Japanese salts are available in Japanese markets and online.

VINEGARS

SU (VINEGAR)

Vinegar, which brightens and balances flavors in foods, is one of humankind's oldest friends. I use it to season sushi rice and salads, marinate fish, braise meats, preserve vegetables and fruits, and drink as a tonic. Vinegar restores. It aids digestion, stimulates the appetite, improves blood circulation, lowers blood pressure, boosts energy, and more.

KOMEZU (RICE VINEGAR)

Light and mellow rice vinegar. I use it in both Japanese and Western cooking. Not all rice vinegars are alike, though. I prefer organic *seichihakko*, which is slowly brewed (like raising a child, one brewer said). This traditional method of making rice vinegar involves two steps: first, sake is brewed, using rice, water, and *Aspergillus* mold. Then the sake is turned into vinegar, a slow fermentation process that can take six months or longer. Today, more than two-thirds of Japanese rice vinegar producers skip the initial step of making their own sake and instead buy a concentrated vinegar base and dilute it with water to make vinegar.

The Japanese government requires rice vinegar to use a minimum of 1½ ounces of rice to 4½ cups (1 L) of vinegar in order to qualify as rice vinegar; this is a somewhat antiquated policy that was put in place during the rice shortage in Japan during World War II to ensure a measure of quality. Traditional rice vinegar, however, uses four to eight times more rice than that dictated by this policy. More rice translates into more amino acids and deeper umami flavors. Industrial producers use less rice and a rice vinegar base (rather than sake) for their vinegars, and they often also add alcohol (made from sugar cane or genetically modified corn) and other vinegars to speed up the fermentation process, which can take as little as

eight hours for some of these brands. Artisan rice vinegars such as Chidorisu and Fuji Junmaisu can be purchased at Japanese and specialty markets in the United States and online—but many smaller producers don't have wide overseas distribution networks, so you will have to hunt for them. But it is worth the effort.

How to Store Vinegar: Keep the cap tightly closed to prevent oxidation and deter fruit flies. Store in a cool place, away from sunlight.

GENMAIZU (BROWN RICE VINEGAR) AND KUROZU (AMBER RICE VINEGAR)

As its name suggests, brown rice vinegar is made from brown rice rather than white rice. It is amber in color and involves more rice in the brewing process than white rice vinegar. It is richer in amino acids, which provide deeper umami. It is my everyday vinegar. An even richer version is *kurozu* (amber rice vinegar), which is also made with brown rice but is darker, tangier, and thicker than regular rice vinegar or brown rice vinegar. *Kurozu* is produced primarily in southern Kyushu, where the brown rice mash is fermented in dark earthenware and allowed to *seichihakko*, or slowly ferment, for one to three years. The elements that make this dark-color vinegar with rich umami are said to be the heat of the sun and the wind from the sea of Kagoshima. I enjoy *kurozu* mostly as a tonic or I splash it in *Yakibuta* Pork (Braised Pork Belly; page 258) and *Gyoza* (Fried Dumplings; page 145). You can find brown rice vinegar in Japanese markets. Look also for Ohsawa, Eden, and Mitoku brands for brown rice vinegar (and a variety of traditional and natural Japanese foods) in stores and online.

UMEZU (PLUM VINEGAR)

This is the liquid that results from making *Umeboshi* (Pickled *Ume* Plums; page 90). It is a salty vinegar that is very refreshing and can be used as an all-purpose seasoning. Red *shiso* leaves turn the brine a deep ruby color and add a refreshing minty flavor to the vinegar (see page 92). Use sparingly. You can buy *umezu* at Japanese markets and online.

MISO

Miso is a highly nutritious fermented paste, high in protein, vitamins, and minerals. It is used to season soups and dishes and to tenderize and preserve foods. It is a living seasoning.

There are countless varieties of miso, made with a variety of grains and beans—including rice, barley, wheat, millet, adzuki beans, and garbanzo beans—that undergo fermentation with salt and koji (the mold *Aspergillus oryzae*). Miso is generally fermented for six months but can often be fermented for as long as three years. Depending on the type of grains, amount of salt (usually between 5 and 12 percent), and length of fermentation, miso can range in color from white to red (like wine) and in flavor from mildly sweet to savory (also like wine). There are, of course, regional differences as well. You should feel free to experiment and develop your own taste with both store-bought miso and your own homemade miso. If you are buying miso, look for pastes that are naturally fermented with no added alcohol or flavor additives such as dashi and amino acids or MSG. I make my own (see Miso, page 101) because I find the practice quite rewarding and worth the effort.

You may see miso labeled *inaka miso*, or "country-style" miso. *Inaka miso* can be red or white but is distinguished by being made with coarsely ground grains.

How to Use Miso: Miso varies in degrees of saltiness, so use it sparingly to season soups and stews, and taste as you go. Since miso is probiotic and heat sensitive, add it at the end of cooking. Once miso is added, turn off the heat. If you want to fully enjoy the live cultures of miso, eat it straight as a crudité dip, as a salad dressing (see First Garden Soba Salad with Lemon–White Miso Vinaigrette, page 247), or as a marinade (see *Kasuzuke* [Miso–Sake Lees Marinade] Mahi-Mahi, page 213).

How to Store Miso: Keep miso in the refrigerator or a cool place away from light.

SHIRO MISO (WHITE MISO)
Shiro miso is creamy and light in color with a mild and sweet flavor; it undergoes a fermentation period of about one year. *Saikyo miso*, from Kyoto, is among the lightest, least salty (5 percent), and sweetest of *shiro miso*, made with more fermented rice than soybeans, and some contain a sweetener such as mirin.

MUGI MISO (BARLEY SOY MISO)
Mugi miso is made mostly in the southern part of Japan, namely Yamaguchi and Ehime prefectures and throughout the Kyushu region. It uses barley koji as a base and is a fragrant miso and less salty than darker red miso.

SENDAI MISO
This is a typical red miso from Miyagi Prefecture. It is made of rice and soybeans. It undergoes a longer fermentation period than *shiro* (white) *miso*. It is saltier, darker, and stronger in flavor.

HATCHO MISO
Hatcho miso originated in Aichi Prefecture. It is made of 100 percent soybeans, including the bean koji. No grains are used in the fermentation process. It takes about two years to produce the miso, which results in a dark, robust, chunky, and strong flavor, but it is not as salty as some of the red miso varieties.

miso

Miso is easy to make at home, but it takes time—about six months to one and a half years, depending on how fermented you want it to be. The color and flavor of the miso will deepen with time and it will take on very complex flavors that make you feel grounded to the earth. Rice koji, soybeans, sea salt, and water are the main ingredients. You can also try blending other legumes such as chickpeas or adzuki beans or grains such as barley. The beans all need to be cooked and mixed with rice koji and brine while warm. The process is like making mud pies. Once you start making your own, it is hard to go back to store-bought miso. You can experiment with other grains and legumes. I use Laura Soybeans, which are non-GMO and grown in Iowa. You can buy fermented brown rice koji or barley koji online from GEM Cultures, Cultures for Health, and South River Miso Company.

MAKES 3 POUNDS (1.4 KG)

EQUIPMENT
 Pressure cooker
 3-quart (3 L) wide-mouth container
 2-pound (910 g) weight (such as stone or cans)

 2 cups (300 g) soybeans, preferably medium to large, rinsed
 14 cups (3.36 L) cups filtered water
 9 tablespoons sea salt
 3 cups (455 g) rice koji
 1 tablespoon raw miso (optional)
 ¼ cup (60 ml) *shochu* or other white liquor such as vodka, for sterilizing the container

Rinse the soybeans well to remove dirt and other foreign particles.

Place the soybeans in a medium bowl with 8 cups (scant 2 L) of water. Soak for 18 hours. The soybeans will more than double in size when fully hydrated. Split a soybean in half. If there is a white core, you need to soak it longer.

Drain the beans, transfer them to a pressure cooker, and cover with 6 cups (1.4 L) of water. (The amount of water should be about 1½ times the amount of soybeans.) Bring the pressure cooker to full pressure over medium heat according to the cooker's instructions, then reduce the heat to low and cook for 7 minutes. Do not walk away from the

pressure cooker while applying pressure. Remove from heat and take the pressure cooker from the stove to the sink and run cold water over it until the pressure is released completely.

Open the cooker and check the doneness of the beans. If the bean squashes easily between your fingers, it is cooked. If not, pressure cook for another 5 minutes, or until you achieve that softness. Transfer the cooked beans to a colander set over a pot and allow to drain. Reserve 1 cup (240 ml) of the soybean cooking liquid. Let the cooking liquid cool to 100°F (37°C). Put the beans back in the pot and mash until smooth, like hummus. Let the beans cool to 100°F (37°C).

Combine ½ cup of the reserved cooking water and the koji and mix well while still warm. Let stand for 5 to 10 minutes.

In a 4-quart (4 L) pot, combine 8 tablespoons of the sea salt and the koji mixture and mix well. Add the raw miso, if using, and the soybean mash. Knead the miso mash, turning it over until smooth, about 100 times. The mash should feel like cookie dough. If dry, add another ½ cup of the reserved cooking water and mix well.

Sterilize the 3-quart (3 L) wide-mouth container by wiping the interior with the *shochu* or vodka. Sprinkle 1½ teaspoons of the remaining salt over the bottom of the container, then spoon in the miso mash and pack it in firmly. Smooth the surface and sprinkle on 1½ teaspoons of the remaining salt. Cover the surface with cloth, butcher paper, or plastic wrap, and top with a drop lid (a flat plate or wooden disk) that will drop into the container, and then a 2-pound (910 g) weight. Cover the entire mouth of the container with butcher paper or cloth and tie closed to keep out dust. Or use a plastic bag, seal the mouth, and put a 2-pound (910 g) weight on top. Store in a cool place and allow to ferment for at least 4 to 6 months. Turn the miso over using a spoon after a month or two into the fermentation process. Remove the 2-pound (910 g) weight and replace it with a 1-pound (455 g) weight. When the miso is ready (taste and see), remove enough for several weeks and refrigerate. Cover the container and store in a cool place. The miso will keep for several years, continuing to ferment and getting saltier and darker. I try to use my miso within 1 to 2 years.

SHOYU (SOY SAUCE)

Soy sauce is an ancient seasoning of Chinese origin that dates back three thousand years. The precursor of soy sauce, *hishio*, was made by fermenting grains, fish, meat, or vegetables. The commonly used Japanese soy sauce is a descendant of *hishio* made with grains. It is fragrant with a complexity of flavors that encompass all the basic tastes: umami (savory), *amami* (sweet), *sanmi* (sour), *nigami* (bitter), and *shiomi* (salty).

I use naturally brewed Japanese soy sauce, primarily *koikuchi shoyu* (dark soy sauce) and *usukuchi shoyu* (light-colored soy sauce). If you can, choose soy sauce that is organic and made with *marudaizu* (whole soybeans), wheat, and koji (*Aspergillus* spores). Avoid nonbrewed soy sauce made from hexane (defatted soy meal) instead of whole soybeans, artificial food coloring, and other chemical preservatives.

You can also find artisan brands that use the traditional slow fermentation method of taking whole soybeans and aging them in wooden barrels for six to twenty-four months. Since most of the Japanese brewers produce small quantities and don't export overseas, look for them when you are traveling in Japan and bring them back! Japanese markets in the United States and various websites sell both major brands such Kikkoman, Yamasa, and Higashimaru, as well as a handful of artisan brands including Kinbue, Teraoka, Shimosa, and Shoda, to name just a few.

There are also a few microbrewers in the United States. One notable producer is Bluegrass Soy Sauce. Matt Jamie makes the soy sauce using non-GMO soybeans, soft red winter wheat, and limestone-filtered spring water—all sourced locally. He then ferments the soybean mash in repurposed bourbon oak barrels.

Japanese soy sauces can be divided into five categories based on their production methods and ingredients. Explore these five soy sauces to find what suits your palate and cooking needs.

How to Store Shoyu: Once a bottle of soy sauce is opened, store it in the refrigerator or in a cool place away from sunlight. For best fragrance and flavor, use it within 1 year (or sooner!).

KOIKUCHI SHOYU (DARK SOY SAUCE)

This dark and pungent soy sauce accounts for more than 80 percent of the market share and is the most popular all-purpose soy sauce. It is brewed with approximately equal amounts of soybeans and wheat. When I refer to "soy sauce" in this book, I mean *koikuchi shoyu*. It is rich in glutamic acids, which add deep umami flavors, aromas, and a sweetness that you won't find, for instance, in tamari. This is my all-purpose soy sauce.

USUKUCHI SHOYU (LIGHT-COLORED SOY SAUCE)

Usukuchi shoyu is thinner and lighter in color than regular soy sauce. It is made with equal amounts of wheat and soybeans, to which wheat gluten, rice, or *amazake* (a fermented rice drink) may be added to yield a distinctly light color. This soy sauce has a higher salt content than regular soy sauce, and it should not be mistaken for low-sodium soy sauce. Light-colored soy sauce doesn't darken the color of the food too much, the way regular soy sauce does. I use it for seasoning soups and braised dishes.

TAMARI SHOYU (TAMARI SOY SAUCE)

In ancient times, tamari was simply the liquid that pooled in miso. With time, the brewing methods of tamari have evolved, but the ingredients have remained basically the same: nearly 100 percent soybeans. This composition means that most tamari is gluten-free. Tamari is an excellent umami enhancer and is very stable as a basting sauce for grilled dishes such as *Yakibuta* Pork (Braised Pork Belly; page 258) and simmered dishes. More fragrant and thicker than regular soy sauce, tamari is appreciated for its nutritional value. It is higher in protein, and some brands are lower in salt than regular soy sauce. Tamari aids digestion and contains many antioxidants and minerals. If you are allergic or sensitive to wheat, tamari is a good alternative to regular soy sauce, but read the label to make sure that it is 100 percent wheat-free.

SAISHIKOMI SHOYU (TWICE-BREWED SOY SAUCE)

Saishikomi shoyu goes through two brewing processes, first with brine and then with soy sauce. This two-step process produces a darker and thicker soy sauce than regular soy sauce but with about the same level of saltiness. *Saishikomi* is used for seasoning sashimi and sushi.

SHIRO SHOYU (WHITE SOY SAUCE)

This is an amber-colored light soy sauce. It is a relatively modern soy sauce that came into being in the nineteenth century. It has a subtle sweetness and mellow flavor, but it is saltier than regular soy sauce. *Shiro shoyu* is suitable for seasoning simmered and steamed dishes; it is favored by chefs because it doesn't darken the color of foods. In that sense, its amber color helps retain the color of foods—something other soy sauces cannot do because they are dark to begin with, even *usukuchi shoyu*.

GYOSHO OR UO SHOYU (JAPANESE FISH SAUCE)

Fish sauce is another fermented seasoning like soy sauce that has been used in Asia since ancient times. There are three notable Japanese fish sauces that are made regionally in small batches that are starting to get broader appeal in Japan for their good flavor and versatile uses in cooking: *shottsuru* of Akita Prefecture, *ikanago* of Kagawa Prefecture, and *ishiri* of Noto Peninsula in Ishikawa Prefecture. Local fish is the primary ingredient. I had the pleasure of trying *ishiri* when I visited Noto Peninsula. *Ishiri* is made with the intestines of squid, which are pickled and fermented for two to three years. It is salty with a subtle sweetness. A few drops of *ishiri* in soups, pickles, and dressings enhance the umami in these dishes and is not fishy at all. Other regions use their local fish to make their sauces.

shoyu tare
(soy sauce–based seasoning)

Shoyu tare is an incredibly versatile base for dipping sauces, stews, and noodle soups. Make dashi and season it with *shoyu tare*, following these ratios for various uses. You can adjust the ratios according to your palate.

- Noodle dipping sauce: 1 part *shoyu tare* to 3 parts dashi
- Noodle soup: 1 part *shoyu tare* to 9 parts dashi
- Oil-free salad dressing: 1 part *shoyu tare* to 4 parts dashi

To make the soup or dipping sauce, combine the *shoyu tare* and dashi in a saucepan and bring to a boil over medium-high heat. Remove from heat. Keep in the refrigerator for 1 week.

In addition to its use as a base for dipping sauces, noodle soups, and salad dressings, *shoyu tare* can be used to baste chicken, marinate ramen eggs (see *Nitamago* [Marinated Soft-Boiled Eggs], page 83), and season braised dishes. For basting chicken (see Grilled Ginger Chicken with *Shoyu Tare*, page 139), fish, or other meats, use *shoyu tare* straight or add a couple of tablespoons of olive oil or sesame oil for deeper umami. For a sweeter *tare*, add more mirin, sake, sugar, or honey. You can spice up your *shoyu tare* with grated ginger, grated garlic, *shichimi togarashi*, and/or chopped scallions. I use regular soy sauce for making dipping sauces and *usukuchi shoyu* (light-colored soy sauce) for making soups and braised dishes.

MAKES ABOUT 2 CUPS (480 ML)

- ⅓ cup plus 1 tablespoon (80 ml) mirin (*hon mirin*, not mirin-type)
- 3 tablespoons cane sugar
- 2 cups (480 ml) soy sauce or *usukuchi shoyu* (light-colored soy sauce)

Combine the mirin and sugar in a small saucepan, place over medium heat, and stir to dissolve the sugar completely. Lower the heat, add the soy sauce, and heat until it starts to simmer, about 3 minutes. Remove from heat and set aside to cool to room temperature. Store in a nonreactive container in a cool, dry place or in the refrigerator, where it will keep for up to 3 months.

ponzu sauce

This is an all-purpose sauce that has a pleasant citrusy flavor. Ponzu sauce can be used as an oilless dressing on salads and to season hot pot dishes, grilled seafood, and meat. You can also make it richer by adding a few tablespoons of olive oil or sesame oil (light or toasted).

MAKES ABOUT ¾ CUP (180 ML)

- 3 tablespoons mirin
- 1 tablespoon sake
- ½ cup (120 ml) yuzu juice (or other citrus juice)
- 1 tablespoon rice vinegar
- ¼ cup (60 ml) plus 2 tablespoons soy sauce
- 1 piece kombu, 2 x 2 inches (5 x 5 cm)
- ½ cup (4 g) bonito flakes

Combine the mirin and sake in a small saucepan and bring to a boil over medium-high heat. Remove from heat and add the yuzu juice, rice vinegar, soy sauce, kombu, and bonito flakes. Pour into a glass container, cover, and refrigerate for 3 days. Strain out the kombu and bonito flakes. The sauce will keep, tightly covered, in the refrigerator for up to 2 weeks.

NUTS AND SEEDS

Nuts and seeds add texture and flavor as well as nourishment to dishes. Whole, roasted, chopped, sprinkled, or ground into paste—I use nuts and seeds in my cooking every day. I stock sesame seeds, pecans, pine nuts, almonds, pistachios, and walnuts throughout the year, and then chestnuts and ginkgo nuts when they are in season. Of all of these, ginkgo nuts are perhaps the least familiar to Western home cooks. These nuts are considered medicinal in Asia and have a rich cultural history. There was a ginkgo tree at our local shrine in Kamakura that was believed to be more than one thousand years old. People visited the tree to celebrate its beauty and longevity. My grandmother and I would go there to pick the nuts that had fallen from this old tree and then take them home to roast them and add them to rice. They looked like jewels on a bed of white.

At our ranch in Tehachapi, we have almond and pecan trees as well as an English walnut tree—all planted by a previous generation of farmers and ranchers who lived there before us. We monitor these old trees throughout their growing season, starting from when the first leaves sprout in early spring to the blooming of their flowers and the appearance of the nuts. It is not just my husband, Sakai, and I who do this, but also the wildlife around us: birds, gophers, deer, and squirrels. They want the nuts and seeds as much as we do. Sakai has built barricades to keep the creatures away, but they often get the best of the harvest. Nothing beats being at one with nature.

GRINDING SESAME SEEDS

There are two ways to grind sesame seeds: coarse or fine and creamy like tahini. You can grind them with a Japanese mortar and pestle, a spice grinder, or a food processor. The ground sesame seeds are used as seasoning sprinkles (*furikake*) on foods or blended with soy sauce, dashi, and mirin or sugar to make a salad dressing. The important thing is to toast the sesame seeds before grinding them.

surigoma (coarsely ground sesame seeds)

Surigoma is a *furikake* made with roasted sesame seeds that have been coarsely ground. It is a multi-purpose *furikake* that can be sprinkled on almost any food. You can add a couple of teaspoons of sea salt and turn *surigoma* into *gomashio furikake*. You can also blend it with soy sauce and a little sugar to make a versatile sesame dressing for vegetables.

MAKES 1 CUP (230 G)

1 cup (130 g) hulled white or black sesame seeds

Heat a medium dry skillet over medium-low heat. Add the sesame seeds, stirring constantly until the seeds become fragrant and lightly colored (but not browned), about 5 minutes. Black sesame seeds will not turn color but will become fragrant. When a few seeds pop, that is the sign to monitor carefully and start taking them off the heat. Transfer the hot toasted seeds into a mortar and crush the seeds with the pestle until your desired coarseness or smoothness is achieved (or grind them in a food processor). Leave some seeds whole for good texture.

Cool completely and store in an airtight container in a cool, dark place or in the refrigerator, where the seeds will keep for up to 1 month.

nerigoma (japanese-style tahini)

Nerigoma is the Japanese version of tahini. It is creamy and fragrant, and usually not salted. It can be made with black or white sesame seeds. I use *nerigoma* in salad dressings and in sweets. You can buy *nerigoma* at Japanese markets, but making it at home is easy and tastes so much better.

MAKES ¾ CUP (135 G)

1 cup (130 g) hulled white or black sesame seeds
¼ cup untoasted sesame oil

Heat a medium dry skillet over medium-low heat. Add the sesame seeds, stirring constantly until the seeds become fragrant and lightly colored (but not browned), about 5 minutes. Black sesame seeds will not turn color but will become fragrant. Be careful not to burn the seeds because that will make the paste taste bitter. Remove from heat and transfer to a baking sheet to cool.

Put the sesame seeds in a food processor and process until a crumbly paste forms, about 1 minute. Add ¼ cup of the oil and process for 1 minute more, stopping to scrape the sides of the machine.

Store in a covered container in the refrigerator for up to 2 weeks. It will separate over time, but you can revive it by giving it a good stir with a spoon before using it.

shichimi togarashi (seven-spice blend)

The classic *shichimi togarashi* combination is red chiles, *sansho* pepper, black sesame seeds, poppy seeds, hemp seeds, nori, and tangerine peel. This seasoning can be used in soups, noodles, grilled foods, rice, and salads. Japanese vendors of *shichimi togarashi* set up shop at temples and shrines in Japan during the festivals. They will make you a custom-made powder and put it in a small gourd-shaped wooden container that is quite charming. In the old days, real dried gourds were used as containers to store spices, because gourds absorb moisture and keep the spices dry.

MAKES ½ CUP (30 G)

EQUIPMENT
Dehydrator

One 1-inch piece (57 g) ginger, peeled and
  sliced ⅛ inch (3 mm) thick
2 teaspoons mandarin zest (or lemon or
  orange zest)
12 dried red chiles (Thai, Korean, Italian, or
  Mexican), seeded

1 teaspoon *sansho* peppercorns (or Sichuan
peppercorns to make it very spicy)

½ sheet nori, torn into small pieces

1 tablespoon hemp seeds or white sesame seeds

1 tablespoon poppy seeds

2 tablespoons toasted black sesame seeds

1 tablespoon sea salt (optional)

Spread the ginger and mandarin zest in a dehydrator and dehydrate at 135°F (57°C) for 3 to 4 hours,
until the ginger becomes completely dried and
snaps when bent. (You can also dehydrate them in
the lowest setting of your oven.) Process the ginger
and mandarin zest into a spice grinder until finely
ground. You should have about 2 teaspoons ginger
powder and 1 teaspoon mandarin peel powder. (If

you have more of either, save it to spice your tea.)
Sift the powders through a fine-mesh strainer to
remove any fibers. Transfer both to the same small
bowl and set aside. Next, process the chiles and
sansho peppercorns separately. Put the ingredient in the spice grinder and grind into a powder.
Sift the powder through a fine-mesh strainer. You
should have 1 tablespoon of chile powder and ½
teaspoon of *sansho* pepper powder. (If you have
more of either, save it to spice your noodle soup.)
Add both to the bowl. Last, put the torn pieces of
nori in the spice grinder and grind for 3 to 4 seconds, being careful not to overprocess it (you want
flakes not powder); add it to the bowl. Add the
hemp seeds, poppy seeds, toasted sesame seeds,
and salt, if using. Store in a glass container with a
tight-fitting lid in the pantry. Use within a couple
of months for best flavor.

OILS

I use oil—primarily nut and seed oils—with restraint,
not wanting to mask any natural flavors or fats in
foods. Unlike Western foods that are seasoned by
frying some garlic or onions in a pan with olive
oil, Japanese foods are seasoned in dashi, and oil
is used with more restraint. There are exceptions
for deep-fried dishes, of course, including tempura
(deep-fried seafood and vegetables introduced to
Japan by the Portuguese in the sixteenth century),
Tonkatsu (Pork Cutlet; page 155) and Crab Cream
Croquettes (page 214). All these deep-fried dishes
need to cook in plenty of fresh oil; skimping on oil
will produce a soggy, heavy dish. When deep-frying,
it is also important to get the oil temperature just
right. Oil that is too hot will burn food—and possibly you!—and oil that is not hot enough will just
soak into the food, resulting in a greasy taste and
texture. See more instructions about cooking with
oil in the recipe for Shrimp and Carrot *Kakiage*
Tempura (page 157).

I use rice bran oil and light sesame oil for deep-
frying because they have a high smoking point.

I use grapeseed oil for stir-frying. I also stock a bottle of good extra-virgin olive oil and some nut oils (such as walnut and almond) for seasoning salads. The only seasoned oil I make is *La-Yu* (Spicy Chile Oil; below), which is an essential companion to *Gyoza* (Fried Dumplings; page 145). And I must not forget butter. It was my mother's wish to always have butter in the fridge (she grew up during the war dreaming of having a big GE refrigerator stocked with cream and butter), so I carry on that wish and stock good unsalted butter and ghee (clarified butter) and use it for cooking and baking.

la-yu (spicy chile oil)

This is a spicy fragrant oil to season *gyoza* (fried dumplings) and *shumai* (steamed dumplings). It can also be used to season grilled meats—it is spicy, so a few drops go a long way.

MAKES ½ CUP (120 ML)

- ½ ounce dried red Japanese, Korean or Italian (Calabrian) chiles, seeded and sliced thinly, ¼ inch (6 mm) thick
- 1 teaspoon Sichuan peppercorns
- ⅓ cup (80 ml) untoasted sesame oil
- ⅓ cup (80 ml) toasted sesame oil
- 2 cloves garlic, chopped (optional)

In a small dry skillet, toast the chiles and Sichuan peppercorns over medium heat for 2 minutes, or until fragrant (but not browned). Transfer to a spice grinder and coarsely grind them, about 5 seconds. Put the ground spices in a small stainless steel bowl.

Heat the sesame oils in the skillet over medium-high heat. Add the garlic, if using, and cook for 1 minute. Pour half of the hot oil over the spice mixture and stir for about 30 seconds to combine well. Add the remaining half and mix well. Let cool to room temperature. Pour the oil through a fine-mesh strainer. Discard the garlic (if used) and ground spices. Transfer the strained oil into a glass or metal container with a tight-fitting lid. It will keep for up to 3 months in the refrigerator.

SWEETENERS

Used sparingly, sweeteners enhance flavors, add moisture, tenderize and preserve foods, and thicken sauces. For my everyday cooking, I use *hon mirin* (not mirin-type), cane sugar, *Amazake* (Fermented Rice Drink; page 289), and maple syrup. I also stock *kokuto*, a minerally rich and strong brown sugar rock obtained from the sugar canes of Okinawa. It is similar to muscovado in flavor and is used as a food medicine in Okinawa. I make *kokuto* syrup by adding 1 cup (136 g) of *kokuto* sugar and 1 cup (240 ml) of water to a saucepan and cooking them over low heat for 20 minutes or until it thickens into a syrup. This will make about ⅔ cup. I keep it in a jar and use it as an all-purpose simple syrup to sweeten foods.

herbs and aromatics

A *shirai* (garnishes) in Japanese cooking have their own language; they have various names, roles, and symbolism that initially can appear complex to home cooks in the West, where garnishes are often considered mere decorations. But understanding garnishes—aromatic leaves, roots, edible flowers, citrus fruits—is very important to Japanese cooking.

While there are specific plants used as garnishes (see below), there are also specific types of garnishes used with sashimi (thinly sliced fresh raw fish). Sashimi can also apply to sliced meat, *yuba* (tofu skin), *konnyaku* (yam cake), vegetables such as cooked fresh bamboo shoots, and other dishes. Three of the main types of garnishes used for sashimi are called *ken*, *tsuma*, and *karami*. *Ken* in Japanese cooking translates into "needle-fine cuts," most often used with daikon radishes or carrots served with fresh sashimi. *Ken* is also the Japanese word for "sword," so it is not hard to see the association with the sharp, fine cuts of the radish or carrot. *Ken* clears the palate and adds flavor, dimension, and color to a plate. It also absorbs fishiness and keeps sashimi fresh longer.

Tsuma (embellishment) is another type of garnish, also placed on the side as an accent to sashimi. Some *tsuma* express the season of a dish: a twig with a cherry blossom is a breath of spring, while cucumber flowers suggest summer. *Tsuma* in Japanese also means "wife," so on the plate the wife (*tsuma*) and the husband (sashimi) support each other.

Karami (spicy flavor), also called *yakumi*, is a category of spicy garnish that includes wasabi, ginger, and mustard, which act as antiseptics and good flavor. There are also garnishes such as grated daikon radish or *umeboshi* (pickled *ume* plum) that aid digestion.

Home cooks can use garnishes to create contrast in flavors and colors in a dish, bring seasonality, and improve digestibility. A simple grater and a vegetable slicer can help you in the kitchen. The threads of daikon radish may not come out as fine as those of a skilled sushi chef, but they fulfill their roles as garnishes. No matter what herbs and aromatics you are using, what is important is to always use the freshest ingredients and to never add so much that you overwhelm the flavor of your dish. A garnish should enhance your dish, not become the dish itself.

TYPES OF GARNISHES

ALLIUM: CHIVES, SCALLIONS, RAMPS, AND ONIONS

I use chives straight from my garden, chopped, to add to salads and soups. I soak sliced or chopped scallions and onions in ice water for about 5 minutes to crisp them up and remove any gooeyness before using.

BUDS AND EDIBLE BLOSSOMS: CHERRY BLOSSOMS, BORAGE, CUCUMBER BLOSSOMS, SQUASH BLOSSOMS, AND *MYOGA*

I love to use edible buds and blossoms to add accents of color and flavor to dishes. It is best to avoid big flowers and keep it small.

Myoga, which you can find at Japanese markets, is herbaceous and tastes like a cross between ginger and mild onion. The lovely pale pink bud of the plant—not the root—is eaten. I slice up *myoga* to garnish soups, salads, tofu, rice, noodles, and pickles. *Myoga* will grow easily in a pot, so it is something you might like to have in your kitchen window or garden. I used to go digging for *myoga* in my grandmother's garden.

CITRUS FRUIT AND CHILES: LEMON, LIME, YUZU, *SUDACHI*, CHILE PEPPER

The peel and zest of fruits, mostly citrus, but also *togarashi* (chiles), add colorful accents and tantalizing fragrances to dishes. I make a fragrant and spicy *yakumi* paste, *Yuzu Kosho* (Spicy Yuzu Paste; recipe follows), made with yuzu peels. and Thai chilies. I also grow a variety of other chiles—including jalapeno, serrano, Calabrian, and ahi amarillo (Peruvian chile pepper)—and use them in my cooking.

yuzu kosho (spicy yuzu paste)

Yuzu kosho is a fragrant spicy seasoning made of chiles, yuzu peel, and sea salt and allowed to ferment. It can be used in sashimi; *somen*, udon, soba, and ramen noodles; hot pots; *tonkatsu* (pork cutlet); *shumai* (steamed dumplings); *gyoza* (fried dumplings); and grilled meats and vegetables. Another type of citrus, such as Meyer lemon, lime, *sudachi*, or Buddha's hand citron, can be substituted for the yuzu. Be careful when handling chiles. Wear rubber gloves.

MAKES ABOUT ⅔ CUP (157 ML)

> About ¾ cup (2½ oz/70 g) zested yuzu, from about 3 dozen yuzu
>
> About ¾ cup (2½ oz/70 g) fresh green chiles, such as Thai chiles, stems and seeds removed and chopped
>
> 1½ tablespoons sea salt
>
> Juice of 1 yuzu

In a medium bowl, combine the grated yuzu, chiles, and salt. Let stand for 30 minutes. Transfer to a food processor or high-speed blender, add the yuzu juice, and process until pureed with some texture left. Transfer to a sterilized small jar, cover, and refrigerate for 3 days. It will keep, refrigerated, for up to 1 month or in the freezer for up to 3 months.

LEAVES, HERBS, AND MICROGREENS: *KINOME*, *MITSUBA*, *SHISO* LEAVES

Kinome are the highly aromatic and slightly minty young leaves of the prickly ash (*sansho*) tree. The fresh young leaves and the little green pods are packed with citrus flavor and a (pleasant) tongue-numbing sting; they are used to accent soups, tofu, rice, grilled seafood, and meats. You can find *kinome* in Japanese markets, but, of course, growing your own tree is even better. Store *kinome* in a damp paper towel in the refrigerator, where it will keep for 3 to 5 days.

Mitsuba is a three-leaf herb that resembles Italian parsley—in fact, it belongs to that family—though it is tenderer and tastes subtly like celery leaf. It is used mostly as a garnish to accent soups, *chawanmushi* (steamed custard), salads, and tempura.

Shiso is an aromatic and minty herb, also known as perilla or beefsteak plant, that comes in two types: green and red. The green leaves, which can be used like basil, are well suited to both Japanese and American cooking, but the red leaves are more specific to Japanese dishes. They are used primarily as a natural coloring and good flavor agent for *umeboshi* (pickled *ume* plums); the spent leaves

can also be dried and made into *yukari* (red shiso *furikake*; see page 92), which is delicious on rice. *Shiso* will grow well in your herb garden. Be sure to cut off the stems of the leaves before you use them. And the flower buds of *shiso* can be eaten.

Other microgreens include the young versions of arugula, onion, buckwheat, and kale, as well as daikon radish and broccoli. You can find many varieties of sprouts in the market; all can be used in Japanese dishes such as sashimi and salads, where they accent the flavors and clear the palate.

There are also leaves that are used merely as garnishes such as camellia, bamboo, fern, persimmon, and maple. The leaf is placed underneath or beside a dish for color contrast, or to send a seasonal message. Some of these leaves are also used to wrap foods; the leaf infuses its fragrance on the food. Every fall my mother would make *kaki no ha zushi* (persimmon leaf sushi) stuffed with cured salmon, amazu ginger, and seasoned sushi rice and wrapped in persimmon leaves. It was the most stunningly beautiful sushi.

ROOTS AND RHIZOMES: DAIKON RADISH, GINGER, WASABI

Daikon is a mild, peppery, large white radish that originated in the Mediterranean but is popular throughout Asia. The radish can grow up to twenty inches (fifty centimeters) long, so it might feel like a commitment to buy a whole one, but you will find that daikon is very easy to consume. The upper part of the daikon—near the leaves—is milder and sweeter in flavor than the root end. I use sliced daikon in soups, salads, stir-fries, and braised dishes. I use fresh grated daikon (*daikon*

oroshi) as a sauce to brighten the flavor of grilled fish, meats, tofu, and vegetables as well as tempura.

Ginger can be used in so many ways. I add slices of the root to my braised dishes to remove the odor of fish or meat. Grated ginger can jazz up a piece of tofu. *Amazu Shoga* (Pickled Ginger; page 87) is a staple accompaniment to sushi (though in the sushi world, it is called *gari*) and grilled foods; no matter what it is called, it aids digestion. Ginger acquires a pink or red color when pickled in rice vinegar or plum vinegar (*umezu*) or added to red vegetables such as red carrot or beet. When *amazu shoga* is dyed red, it is called *beni shoga*. It is commonly used as a garnish for *Yakisoba* (Stir-Fried Noodles; page 257) and *okonomiyaki* (see *Okonomiyaki* Pancakes with Bonito Flakes, page 261). Choose ginger that has smooth skin, is firm to the touch, and seems heavy for its size. Young ginger is especially pleasant to work with. It is easier to peel and cut, less fibrous, and fragrant. An easy way to peel ginger is to scrape it with the edge of a spoon. And an easy way to cut ginger is to first soak it in water for 15 minutes, which will soften its fiber.

Wasabi is a member of the Brassicaceae family, like horseradish and mustard, that is grown in clean streambeds or river valleys. When it is fresh, wasabi is an invigorating green rhizome. It is less harsh in flavor and more aromatic than horseradish. Grated wasabi is used as a condiment for sushi, sashimi, and soba noodles. You can buy fresh wasabi, which is sold as a stem, at Japanese markets and online; it is expensive, which is why I save it for special occasions. Use it from the leaf end (not the root end) and only partially peel it to expose the light green flesh just before grating. When you are ready to grate, do it at the table so the wasabi stays fresh and fragrant, and use the traditional fine-toothed Japanese grater called *oroshi-ki*, which can be easily found online (see Resources, page 291).

Serve wasabi immediately after grating to make the most of its full aroma and flavor potential. To store, wrap fresh wasabi in a damp paper towel (not plastic wrap) and refrigerate for up to 1 week.

Wasabi paste and wasabi powder are not substitutes for fresh, but they are reasonable alternatives if they are made with real wasabi. Look for the tubes that say *hon wasabi*, or "real wasabi"—most wasabi pastes are actually made with horseradish as a base, which is then mixed with mustard, food coloring, vegetable oil, salt, and other additives. Store wasabi paste in the refrigerator and use within a year. If you can't find fresh wasabi or wasabi paste, use grated ginger, grated daikon radish, or lemon juice for a comparable effect.

daikon oroshi (fresh daikon radish sauce)

This is one of the most popular and refreshing fresh sauces, made from pure daikon radish. It contains natural enzymes that aid digestion and is served on the side as a garnish with fresh, grilled, and deep-fried dishes. When grated or cut and left standing, daikon emits a slightly sulfurous smell common to cabbage and mustard families. To minimize this unpleasant effect, grate the daikon just before serving and use it right away.

If you can't find daikon radish specifically, American farmers grow a variety of heirloom radishes that are colorful and just as tasty. I use purple radishes that are milder in flavor than daikon radish; the grated sauce looks pretty in purple.

To grate the daikon, you might want to invest in *oroshi-ki*; these graters can be found in Japanese markets and are designed not only to grate radishes and roots such as daikon and ginger but also to collect their juices, so that absolutely nothing is wasted. Drink the spicy juice or pour it over your noodles. It is an invigorating and versatile tonic.

MAKES ABOUT ½ CUP (113 G) GRATED DAIKON RADISH

8 ounces (230 g) daikon radish, peeled

Grate the daikon by moving the daikon against the grater in a circular motion. Be patient and continue grating even though you will notice that you are producing mostly juice. Lightly press the grated daikon to get rid of excess juice, but don't discard the juice. Drink it straight or blend it with orange or apple juice. It is a restorative beverage that aids digestion. Serve the sauce with grilled and deep-fried dishes.

VARIATIONS

Daikon Oroshi can be combined with many other herbs, spices, and vegetables to create fresh aromas, colors, and seasonings.

Citrus: Add the zest of ½ lemon or yuzu to the grated daikon to enhance grilled meat and seafood dishes.

Ginger: Grate ginger to equal 1 tablespoon on top of the grated daikon for tempura, noodles, and tofu dishes.

Togarashi: Cut the daikon radish crosswise. Make two holes, about 2 inches (5 cm) deep with chopsticks and stick seeded dried *togarashi* (chiles) in each hole. Grate the daikon to produce *momiji oroshi*, a spicy and speckled red grated daikon that is named after the autumnal maple leaf. It is an all-purpose sauce.

Wasabi: Grate fresh wasabi and add to the top of the grated daikon, which will add a pop to grilled dishes and *nabemono* (hot pot dishes).

Cucumber: Grate cucumber (with the skin on) and top off the grated daikon, which works well with grilled seafood.

everyday *okazu*
(pantry recipes)

The recipes in this chapter are devoted to simple *okazu* (dishes) that I like to cook and eat. Japanese home cooks love to use the word *teiban* (regular) when they talk about their favorite *okazu*, and I'm no different. These *teiban okazu* are my staple family dishes and the recipes that I teach in my Japanese pantry workshops.

The pantry recipes might look complicated with a lot of ingredients. I want you to understand that Japanese food is a medley of components that are assembled into one—so everywhere there is dashi (stock; pages 23–31) or *Shoyu Tare* (Soy Sauce–Based Seasoning; page 105). These are staple pantry recipes that you can always make ahead and have on hand, which will make the recipes simpler. Some of the recipes can be made in less than 20 minutes and some have components that need to be rested or marinated overnight. Always read the full recipe before starting so you know how much time you will need to complete the dish.

These recipes represent essential Japanese dishes—from miso soup to dumplings and tempura. They use key ingredients and cooking techniques that, when taken as a whole, will teach you the basics of Japanese cooking and will set you up well for the recipes in part two.

two basic soups

Suimono (Clear Soup) and *Misoshiru* (Miso Soup)

Soup is an essential part of the traditional Japanese meal. You can have some soup at the start of a meal to whet your appetite, and that first sip will bring you the taste of the season. Soup also can be served at the finish of the meal to clear your palate. And soup can be served during the middle of a meal. At home, there are no strict rules.

Two basic Japanese soups to know are *suimono* (clear soup) and *misoshiru* (miso soup). *Suimono* is unadulterated dashi, while *misoshiru* is dashi with miso. You can choose from a variety of dashi. For the soup ingredients, here I have suggested simple combinations using mainly vegetables, seaweed, and tofu; in part two you will find more elaborate soups and hot pot recipes made with other proteins.

Japanese Soup Etiquette: Japanese soup bowls are smaller than their Western counterparts; they are meant to be held with your hands and brought up to your mouth for a sip. Small (¾ to 1 cup/ 180 to 240 ml) wooden and lacquerware bowls are most commonly used, but you can use any similar bowl of your choice. You want to use round bowls with some depth so you can pick up morsels of food with chopsticks (shallow soup bowls do not work well for Japanese soups). Japanese soups usually are not eaten with a spoon, but you can use one if you'd like.

suimono (clear soup)

This soup is usually served at the start of a meal to whet your appetite. It is composed of dashi and three or four soup ingredients: a bite-size morsel of tofu, meat, fish, seafood, or vegetable is the first and main ingredient; the second ingredient is a vegetable, which supports the first and expresses the season; the third ingredient is the garnish, which brightens the soup with flavor, texture, and aroma and can be as simple as a peel of yuzu or lemon. In a Japanese restaurant, the *suimono* can be a signal of the skill of a chef because it is the very first sip of dashi that the diner tastes. But in the home kitchen or at a restaurant, a good-tasting soup raises the anticipation of the dishes to come. Here I will show you simple and nonfussy methods for making soups that put primary emphasis on the freshness of the ingredients. To enjoy the full fragrance of *suimono*, do not serve it too hot.

MAKES 4 SERVINGS

> 3½ cups (830 ml) Dashi (choose one, pages 23–31)
> Soup Combinations (choose one, page 121)
> ½ teaspoon sea salt, or more to taste
> 1 teaspoon sake
> 2 teaspoons *usukuchi shoyu* (light-colored soy sauce), or more to taste

In a medium saucepan, bring the dashi to a boil over medium-high heat. Turn the heat down to low to maintain a low simmer. Add the soup combinations according to the instructions below except for the garnish and continue simmering over low heat until your vegetables reach the desired tenderness. If using root vegetables such as potato, or brassicas such as cauliflower or cabbage, they will need to cook longer than leafy vegetables or tofu.

Add the salt, sake, and soy sauce. Taste the soup and adjust the seasonings as needed. Divide the soup among bowls, making sure that the soup combinations are distributed evenly and attractively. Add the garnish and serve.

misoshiru (miso soup)

Miso soup is also a traditional breakfast soup. A good ratio of miso to liquid is 1 tablespoon of miso per 1 cup (240 ml) of dashi. But the saltiness of miso varies, so you should always taste and make adjustments.

You can use a variety of miso paste to make soup, or even make your own. To bring out the full fragrance and umami of miso soup, it should be served around 140°F (60°C); at this temperature, the probiotic cultures in unpasteurized miso can remain vital. However, most store-bought misos are pasteurized. Add the miso mixture just before serving.

MAKES 4 SERVINGS

> 3½ cups (830 ml) Dashi (choose one, pages 23–31)
> Soup Combinations (choose one, page 121)
> 3 tablespoons miso, homemade (see Miso, page 101) or store-bought; white, red, or any combination you prefer, or more to taste

In a medium saucepan, bring the dashi to a boil over medium-high heat. Turn the heat down to low to maintain a low simmer. Add the soup combinations according to the instructions below except for the garnish and continue simmering over low heat until your vegetables reach the desired tenderness. If the dashi evaporates below 3 cups (710 ml), replenish with filtered water or dashi to bring it back up to 3½ cups (840 ml).

Dilute the miso in a small bowl using ¼ cup (60 ml) of the dashi from the pot. Add the miso mixture to the pot and mix well. Taste the soup and adjust the seasonings as needed. Divide the soup among bowls, making sure that the soup combinations are distributed evenly and attractively. Add the garnish and serve.

SUGGESTED SOUP COMBINATIONS

Mushrooms, Tofu, and Yuzu Peel: 2 ounces (57 g) mushrooms of your choice, stems removed and sliced ¼ inch (6 mm) thick; 4 ounces (113 g) soft or medium-firm tofu, cut into ¼-inch (6 mm) dice; 1 teaspoon yuzu (or lemon) peel, pith removed. First, add the mushrooms to the heated dashi over medium heat and simmer for 2 to 3 minutes, until the mushrooms reach your desired tenderness. Then add the tofu and continue simmering just until heated, about 1 minute. To serve, garnish with the citrus peel.

Corn, Tomatoes, and Zucchini: ½ cup (77 g) fresh corn kernels; 8 cherry tomatoes, halved; ½ medium zucchini, sliced ¼ inch (6 mm) thick; 2 scallions, thinly sliced. Add the corn, zucchini, and tomatoes to the heated dashi and cook for 3 to 4 minutes over low heat, until the vegetables reach your desired tenderness. Garnish with the scallions.

Note: You can serve this miso soup chilled with *Surigoma* (Coarsely Ground Sesame Seeds; page 107). When serving chilled, I add the cherry tomatoes raw as a garnish.

Kabocha Squash and Onions: 1 teaspoon vegetable oil (or duck fat for more umami!); ½ yellow onion, peeled and sliced ¼ inch (6 mm) thick; 6 ounces (170 g) kabocha or butternut squash, peeled and sliced ¼ inch (6 mm) thick; 2 scallions, thinly sliced. In a medium pot, heat the oil or duck fat and saute the onion over medium heat. Add the dashi and the squash and continue cooking for 5 to 7 minutes over medium heat, until cooked to desired tenderness. Garnish with the scallions.

Cherry Tomatoes, Wakame, and Tofu: ½ cup (60 g) cherry tomatoes, halved; 2 tablespoons dry wakame, hydrated in 2 cups (480 ml) water for 15 minutes (it should more than double in size), drained, and cut into 10-inch (25 cm) pieces, if the pieces are large; 4 ounces (113 g) medium-firm or silken tofu, cut into ⅜-inch (1 cm) square; 2 scallions, thinly sliced. Add the tomatoes and wakame to the heated dashi and cook over low heat for 2 to 3 minutes. Add the tofu and cook until just heated. Garnish with the scallions.

Broccolini and Cauliflower: 4 ounces (113 g) broccolini, sliced ¼ inch (6 mm) thick; 4 ounces (113 g) cauliflower, sliced ¼ inch (6 mm) thick; 2 tablespoons chopped chives. Cook the broccolini and cauliflower in the heated dashi for 4 to 5 minutes over medium heat, until cooked to your desired tenderness. Garnish with the chives.

Medley of Roots, Tofu, and *Konnyaku*: 2 ounces (57 g) Satsuma potato (Japanese sweet potato), cut into ½-inch (12 mm) cubes; 2 ounces (57 g) burdock, sliced ¼ inch (6 mm) thick crosswise; 2 ounces (57 g) daikon radish, sliced ¼ inch (6 mm) thick crosswise and then cut each disk into quarters; 2 ounces (57 g) *konnyaku*, cut into ½-inch (12 mm) cubes; 2 ounces (57 g) carrot, sliced ¼ inch (6 mm) thick crosswise; 2 ounces (57 g) medium-firm tofu, cut into ½-inch (12 mm) cubes; 4 snow peas, strings removed; 1 scallion, sliced thinly, crosswise; pinch of *shichimi togarashi*. Cook all the ingredients except the tofu, snow peas, scallion, and *shichimi togarashi* in the heated dashi for 6 to 8 minutes, until cooked to desired tenderness. Add the snow peas and tofu and cook for another minute. Garnish with scallions and *shichimi togarashi*. Serve this as miso soup. For a heartier soup, add 4 ounces (113 g) pork belly, thinly sliced *sukiyaki*-style, or 4 ounces (113 g) chicken, diced ½ inch (12 mm), until cooked thoroughly, about 1 minute.

chawanmushi with manila clams and shiitake mushrooms

Chawanmushi is a savory, soupy warm custard. It makes a wonderful first course served either hot or cold. The clams and shiitake mushroom dashi impart a rich and subtly salty flavor to this custard, and the herb is a very important garnish to brighten this dish. Be sure to start by hydrating the dried mushrooms the night before you plan to serve the custard.

MAKES 6 SERVINGS

EQUIPMENT

Fine-mesh strainer

Cheesecloth or paper towels

Six 6-ounce (180 ml) ramekins or small cups

Stackable steamer with a flat, perforated base to accommodate the ramekins

3 dried shiitake mushrooms soaked in 1 cup (240 ml) water overnight

2 tablespoons dried wakame or ½ cup (20 g) fresh wakame

8 medium Manila clams or 16 littleneck clams

2 cups (480 ml) filtered water

2 tablespoons sake

3 large eggs

1½ teaspoons mirin

1½ tablespoons *usukuchi shoyu* (light-colored soy sauce)

¼ teaspoon sea salt (optional)

6 *mitsuba* (Japanese parsley, leaves only), chervil, or Italian parsley (leaves only)

6 Nasturtium leaves (optional)

Drain the shiitake mushrooms and slice to ⅛ inch (3 mm) thick. If using dried wakame, soak it in 2 cups (480 ml) of water for 15 minutes, then drain. If using fresh wakame, rinse it well and drain. Cut the wakame into ½-inch (12 mm) pieces.

In a medium pot, combine the clams, water, and sake and cook over medium-high heat until the clams open, about 4 minutes. Remove the clams and reserve the cooking liquid. Strain the cooking liquid through a fine-mesh strainer lined with cheesecloth or paper towels. Reserve 1¾ cups (420 ml) of the dashi (stock). Let cool to room temperature. Remove the clams from the shells and discard the shells. Place the clam meat in a small bowl.

Bring a stackable steamer to a boil over high heat and then keep it at a simmer.

In a medium bowl, combine the eggs, mirin, and soy sauce. Taste and add the salt if needed. Be careful not to beat the egg mixture too much; doing so will cause air bubbles to form on the surface of the custard. Add the reserved liquid and then run the egg mixture through the strainer. Divide the egg mixture, clams, shiitakes, and wakame into the ramekins.

Cover each ramekin with foil. Place the ramekins on the steamer rack and set the rack back on the pot. Steam the custards for 2 minutes over high heat, then reduce the heat to low and continue to steam for 6 minutes, or until the custard sets. Remove and discard the foil. Garnish with the herbs of your choice. Serve the custard warm or cold with a spoon.

chilled *ohitashi* (dashi-infused) heirloom tomatoes

Ohitashi is a vegetable salad that is briefly blanched and infused in light savory dashi, which enhances the natural flavors of the vegetables. The tomatoes are blanched just to remove the skin and allow the dashi to penetrate into the meat of the tomatoes. This is an incredibly versatile dish; instead of tomatoes, you can use blanched asparagus, green beans, cabbage, spinach, sprouts, okra, mushrooms, mizuna, bitter melon, chrysanthemum leaves, cabbage, corn—you name it. You can add bonito flakes for another layer of umami and smokiness to the dish, but that is optional. And for the garnish, you can stay with the plant theme and use julienned *shiso* or other herbs of your choice.

MAKES 4 SERVINGS

FOR THE *OHITASHI* DRESSING
  2 cups (480 ml) dashi, preferably Bonito and Kombu Dashi (page 27) or *Shojin* (vegan) Dashi (page 30)
  2 tablespoons *usukuchi shoyu* (light-colored soy sauce)
  1 tablespoon mirin
  Sea salt

FOR THE SALAD
  1 pound (455 g) heirloom tomatoes (about 2 large tomatoes)
  6 *shiso* or basil leaves, julienned
  Freshly ground black pepper
  ¼ cup (2 g) bonito flakes (optional)
  ½ teaspoon toasted sesame seeds

To make the dressing, in a small pot, combine the dashi, soy sauce, and mirin and season with salt. Bring to a boil over medium heat. Remove from heat and let cool. Taste and adjust the seasonings as needed. It should be drinkable like *suimono* soup.

To blanch the tomatoes, bring a medium pot of water to a boil over high heat. Score a cross about ¹⁄₁₆ inch (1.5 mm) deep across the top of each tomato, then drop the tomatoes into the water. When you see the skin of the tomatoes start to crack and peel, 30 to 40 seconds, remove them from the water with a slotted spoon and immediately move them into a bowl of ice water. When they are cool enough to handle, peel the skin with a paring knife, trying not to scar the surface of the tomato.

Cut the tomatoes into 8 wedges and place them in a medium serving bowl. Pour the seasoned dashi over the tomatoes, cover, and let them marinate for 30 minutes to 1 hour in the refrigerator. To serve, garnish with *shiso*, black pepper, the bonito, if using, and sesame seeds.

the japanese pantry

sunomono (cucumber, wakame, and harusame salad)

Sunomono is a classic Japanese salad, similar in lightness to *ohitashi* (dashi-infused) salads but with rice vinegar to brighten the dressing. This recipe uses a classic dressing called *sanbaizu*, which means "three cups," representing the formula for the dressing that is traditionally equal parts vinegar, mirin, and soy sauce. Today, the ratio varies. People use less soy sauce and some people use cane sugar instead of mirin for a sweeter taste. I use a little less soy sauce. I use *sanbaizu* when I want a light oil-free dressing. I briefly cook the dressing in a small saucepan to get rid of the alcohol in the mirin and the sharpness of the vinegar to yield a mellower dressing. You can also add a teaspoon or two of toasted sesame oil and turn this recipe into a Chinese-style *salada*.

For the salad, you can use a variety of vegetables (such as blanched cabbage), and seafood (such as cooked shrimp, crab, or sashimi-grade scallops), or meat (such as shredded, steamed chicken) to make *sunomono*. I also like to add *harusame* (glass noodles) to the salad; made from potato and bean starches, these dried noodles will take on the flavors of the seasonings they are cooked with, and they add a nice chew to the dish.

MAKES 4 SERVINGS

FOR THE *SANBAIZU* DRESSING
- ¼ cup (60 ml) mirin
- ¼ cup (60 ml) rice vinegar
- 2 tablespoons *usukuchi shoyu* (light-colored soy sauce)

FOR THE SALAD
- 1 ounce (28 g) dried *harusame* noodles
- 2 Persian cucumbers or 1 Japanese cucumber, sliced crosswise ⅛ inch (3 mm) thick
- ½ teaspoon sea salt
- ¼ cup (5 g) dried wakame, hydrated for 10 minutes then cut into bite-size pieces
- ½ teaspoon toasted white sesame seeds
- 1 teaspoon grated ginger

To make the dressing, combine the mirin and vinegar in a small saucepan over low heat and bring to a boil. Remove from heat. Add the soy sauce and let cool. Taste and adjust the seasonings as needed. You can make the dressing in advance; it will keep in the refrigerator for 3 to 4 days.

To cook the noodles, bring a medium pot of water to a boil over medium-high heat. Add the *harusame* noodles and cook until tender, about 2 minutes. Drain and rinse, then cut into 3-inch (7.5 cm) pieces. Set aside.

Remove excess water from the cucumbers by gently massaging the slices with salt for about 1 minute, then let stand for 5 minutes. Squeeze out excess water. Place the cucumber slices in a medium bowl. Do not rinse.

To serve, pour ¼ cup (60 ml) of the dressing over the salted cucumber. Gently squeeze out excess dressing with your hand and discard the dressing. Add the wakame and *harusame* noodles and the remaining dressing and toss gently. Divide among small serving dishes and garnish with the sesame seeds and grated ginger.

kombu-cured thai snapper sashimi

This recipe uses *kobujime*, a method of curing fish and vegetables using seasoned kombu. Allow 4 hours to prepare this dish. Make sure to ask your fishmonger if the fish is sashimi-grade quality.

I serve this dish in a salad of greens and micro herbs dressed with Ponzu Sauce (page 105) or pair it with *yuzu kosho* (spicy yuzu paste) and quick-pickled cucumbers, which make a nice accompaniment. This cured snapper can also be used to make *Mari Zushi* (page 205).

MAKES 4 SERVINGS

FOR THE KOMBU MARINADE

> 1 cup (240 ml) filtered water
>
> 1 cup (240 ml) rice vinegar
>
> ¼ cup (50 g) cane sugar
>
> 2 teaspoons sea salt
>
> 2 pieces kombu (preferably *hidaka* kombu) about 3 x 10 inches (7.5 x 25 cm)

FOR THE SASHIMI

> 1 pound (455 g) sashimi-grade Thai snapper (about 2 fillets)
>
> 1½ teaspoons sea salt
>
> 1 unpeeled Persian cucumber, sliced crosswise ⅛ inch (3 mm) thick

TO SERVE

> 1 tablespoon *Yuzu Kosho* (page 112) or Ponzu sauce (page 105)

To make the kombu marinade, combine the water, vinegar, sugar, and salt in a small bowl. Whisk to dissolve the sugar and salt. Add the kombu and leave to marinate in the dressing until tender, about 1 hour. Lightly wipe off the dressing with a clean kitchen towel or paper towel and reserve the dressing to make the quick-pickled cucumbers.

Slice the fish against the grain at about a 30-degree angle ¼ inch (6 mm) thick. Sprinkle ¾ teaspoon of the salt on a cutting board, then spread the slices on the salted surface so that the strips do not overlap with one another. Sprinkle the remaining ¾ teaspoon salt on top of the strips and let stand for 15 minutes. The amount of salt to use for salting fish is about 1½ percent of the total weight of the fish (1½ percent of 1 pound/455 grams is about 1½ teaspoon/7 grams of salt). Gently wipe off the moisture that is released from the fish with a paper towel to remove any lingering fishiness.

Place the moist kombu on a baking sheet and place the snapper sashimi on top so it covers only half of the kombu, again without overlapping. Cover with the remaining kombu by folding it over on top. If your kombu is too short, use several pieces to make two sheets to cover the fish completely. Wrap tightly with plastic wrap and let stand in the refrigerator for 3 to 4 hours.

When the fish is almost ready, make the quick-pickled cucumbers by marinating the cucumber slices in ¼ cup (60 ml) of the reserved kombu dressing for 20 minutes. Remove the cucumbers from the marinade and gently squeeze out the excess dressing.

To serve, remove the fish from the refrigerator and arrange it on a plate. Add the cucumber pickles and serve with *yuzu kosho*.

arame with carrots and ginger

This recipe is a riff on *kimpira*, a stir-fried sweet and savory root vegetable dish traditionally made with burdock and carrots seasoned with *shoyu tare*. In this recipe, I use arame in place of the burdock. Arame is high in iodine, iron, vitamin A, magnesium, and calcium. The onion is not traditional, but it adds a subtle sweetness to the dish. If you want a little more sweetness and umami, you can also add a small splash of *kokuto* syrup. Serve as a nibble dish, about ¼ cup (60 g) per person, or as a topping for a grain bowl.

MAKES 4 SERVINGS

½ cup (10 g) dried arame

3 tablespoons toasted sesame oil

2 tablespoons peeled and minced ginger

¼ cup (40 g) finely chopped yellow onion

4 medium carrots, peeled and julienned

1 tablespoon *Shoyu Tare* (page 105)

1 tablespoon sake

1 tablespoon *kokuto* syrup (page 109) (optional)

FOR THE GARNISHES

½ teaspoon toasted white or black sesame seeds

Pinch of *Shichimi Togarashi* (page 107)

Rinse the arame in water, then place in a small bowl, add fresh water to cover, and soak for 5 minutes. Drain.

Heat the oil in a large skillet over medium heat. Add the ginger and onion and cook for 2 minutes. Add the carrots and arame and cook for another 2 minutes, until the carrots are evenly coated with the oil. Add the *shoyu tare*, sake, and *kokuto* syrup, if using, reduce the heat to low, and continue cooking until most of the liquid is absorbed, about 4 to 5 minutes. Taste and make adjustments with the *shoyu tare*, if you like it saltier, or add a pinch of sea salt. Remove from heat and let cool. Garnish with sesame seeds and *shichimi togarashi*. Serve hot or at room temperature. This dish is meant to be served as a nibble. It will keep in the refrigerator for 3 to 4 days.

nishime (dashi-infused root vegetables)

Nishime is a dish of vegetables simmered in dashi and *shoyu tare*; it is like a stew but much lighter because the soup is not thickened with a roux. *Nishime* literally means "to simmer." I use bonito and kombu dashi, but you can also use a lighter kombu dashi if you like. You can make *nishime* with a variety of vegetables, but root vegetables—carrots, burdock, bamboo shoots, lotus root, and taro root—are the main attraction. Root vegetables symbolize groundedness in Japanese culture, so *nishime* is featured during New Year's as a good luck dish.

To preserve the shape and integrity of the vegetables, some of the vegetables are blanched and precooked so they cook at about the same rate as other vegetables. Green beans and carrots are left out of the pot until the end so they don't overcook and lose their color.

This dish features a few unique ingredients. The first is *konnyaku*, a gelatinous, flavorless gray or white block made from the corm (a part of the stem) of the konjac plant, which belongs to the yam family. Its nickname is "broom of the stomach," and it is considered a health food because it aids digestion. Like plain gelatin, *konnyaku* doesn't have much flavor, but in this recipe it takes on the flavor of the seasoned dashi. The other distinctive ingredient in this dish is *koya* tofu (freeze-dried tofu). When hydrated, it has a spongy texture. Like tofu, it is bland, but, like *konnyaku*, it takes on the flavor of the seasoned dashi.

If you want a meatier and easier-to-make *nishime*, try *Chikuzen-ni* (Braised Chicken and Vegetable Stew; page 231). *Nishime* tastes even better a day or two after you make it, as the vegetables have time to soak up even more of the seasoned dashi, making it a great addition to a bento box.

MAKES 4 SERVINGS

FOR THE DASHI

6 cups (1.4 L) Bonito and Kombu Dashi (page 27)

FOR THE STEW

12 ounces (340 g) taro root, about 4 large

1¼ teaspoons sea salt

8 green beans or snow peas, strings removed and ends trimmed

One 9-ounce (255 g) block gray or white *konnyaku* (yam cake)

1 medium lotus root, about 8 ounces (230 g), peeled, cut in half crosswise, then sliced ¼ inch (6 mm) thick

One 8 oz (255 g) vacuum-pack or can whole bamboo shoots, drained and quartered lengthwise and cut into 2-inch-long (5 cm) pieces

2 blocks (35 g) *koya* tofu (freeze-dried tofu), hydrated in 2 cups (480 ml) water for 30 minutes, drained, and quartered (optional)

2 medium carrots, cut into flower shapes using a cookie cutter

4 dried shiitake mushrooms, hydrated in 2 cups (480 ml) of filtered water overnight, liquid reserved

SEASONING

¾ cup (180 ml) *Shoyu Tare* (page 105)

1 tablespoon *kokuto* syrup (page 109)

1 tablespoon sake, or to taste

½ teaspoon sea salt, or to taste

To make the stew, peel the taro roots and rub them with 1 teaspoon salt to remove the sticky surface film. Rinse and drain the taro roots, then cut them in half. Set aside.

Bring a 2-quart (2 L) pot of water to a boil over medium-high heat and add the remaining ¼ teaspoon salt. Add the green beans and blanch for 1 minute. Remove them from the pot using a slotted spoon or spider and place in a small bowl.

Blanch the block of *konnyaku* in the same water for 1 minute, then remove from the pot and rinse under cold water. Blanch the taro roots in the same water for 2 minutes. Remove from the pot and place in a separate bowl. Drain the water from the pot.

Slice the block of *konnyaku* crosswise into ¼-inch-thick (6 mm) rectangles. To make ribbons, make a 1-inch (2.5 cm) slit in the center of each rectangle. Take one end of the rectangle and loop it through the hole to make a twisted ribbon. *Konnyaku* is slippery by nature, so don't get discouraged; you may have to practice a few times.

Heat oil in a 4-quart (4 L) saucepan over medium-high heat. Lower heat to medium and add the *konnyaku* ribbons, the taro roots, lotus roots, bamboo shoot, carrots, and tofu and gently stir-fry for a couple of minutes. Then add the dashi, kombu, mushrooms, and *shoyu tare* and bring to a boil over medium heat. Turn the heat

to low and simmer for 10 minutes. Using a slotted spoon, transfer the taro roots and carrots to a bowl so they don't overcook.

Cover the vegetables with a lid that fits inside the pot to prevent them from bouncing around and simmer for another 20 minutes, or until the liquid is reduced by half. Taste the vegetables and make adjustments with salt or soy sauce as needed. To make it sweeter, add a teaspoon or two of mirin, sake, or sugar.

Return the carrots and taro roots to the pan and cook for another 10 minutes. At this point you can either serve the *nishime* or cool, cover, and leave the vegetables soaking in the dashi overnight in the refrigerator. Serve at room temperature or reheat before serving with or without the seasoned broth. It will keep in the refrigerator for 3 to 4 days. Garnish with the blanched green beans just before serving.

inari zushi (seasoned fried tofu stuffed with sushi rice)

Inari is a kind of sushi wrapped in fried tofu. Its name derives from that of the Japanese god known for protecting rice, agriculture, and fertility. *Inari* is sometimes manifested as a foxlike creature said to have a soft spot for *abura-age* (deep-fried tofu pouches). So if you visit a Japanese shrine, you will sometimes find these pouches set out as offerings. These "footballs," as some Japanese Americans call them, are stuffed with sushi rice, chopped herbs, and toasted sesame seeds. You can garnish them with herbs such as *kinome* (*sansho* leaves) or with a sprinkle of toasted sesame seeds.

MAKES 10

FOR THE SEASONED TOFU POUCHES

Ten 4½-ounce (125 g) *abura-age* (deep-fried tofu pouches), 2¾ x 2¾ inches (7 x 7 cm)

1½ cups (360 ml) Bonito and Kombu Dashi (page 27) or filtered water

2 tablespoons mirin

2 tablespoons soy sauce

1 tablespoon cane sugar

1 tablespoon *kokuto* syrup (page 000) [[ms 162]] or dark brown sugar

FOR THE FILLING

1½ cups (300 g) short-grain or medium-grain white rice

1½ cups (360 ml) filtered water

1 tablespoon sake

1 piece kombu, 2 x 4 inches (5 x 10 cm)

2 ounces (57 g) ginger, peeled and minced (about 2 tablespoons)

20 *shiso* leaves, stems removed and minced

½ cup (64 g) toasted white sesame seeds

FOR THE SUSHI VINEGAR

¼ cup rice vinegar

2 tablespoons cane sugar

1 teaspoon sea salt

FOR THE GARNISHES

1 tablespoon toasted sesame seeds or 10 *kinome* (*sansho* leaves)

Amazu Shoga (page 87)

Bring a medium pot of water to a boil. Blanch the *abura-age* for 1 minute to remove excess oil. Drain.

To make the seasoned fried tofu pouches, combine the *abura-age*, dashi, mirin, soy sauce, and sugars in a large saucepan and bring to a boil over medium-high heat. Lower the heat to low and simmer for 7 to 8 minutes. Turn the pouches over and continue cooking until most of the liquid is absorbed by the tofu pouches, another 7 to 8 minutes. Remove from heat and let cool. Cut a slit at one end of each of the *abura-age*, to form an opening for the pouch. You can make the *abura-age* 4 or 5 days in advance and store them in the refrigerator.

In a medium bowl, rinse the rice under cool running water for about 20 seconds. Then drain the water completely. Gently stir the rice with your hand about 30 times, drain, and rinse again under cool running water. Drain the starchy water. Combine the measured filtered water and rice in a heavy-bottomed 2-quart (2 L) pot with a tight-fitting lid. Let the rice soak in the water for at least 30 minutes and up to overnight.

To cook the rice on the stovetop, add the sake and kombu to the pot of rice and bring to a boil, uncovered, over medium-high heat. This should take about 6 to 7 minutes and the water should be bubbling around the edges of the pot. Then place the lid on the pot, turn the heat down to very low, and cook without peeking for 15 to 18 minutes. Remove from heat and, without opening the lid, let the rice rest for 10 minutes. Then remove the lid, discard (or eat!) the kombu, and gently fluff the rice with a rice paddle or wooden spoon. Replace the lid and allow the rice to rest for another 5 minutes.

Make the sushi vinegar by mixing the vinegar, sugar, and salt in a small bowl.

Transfer the cooked rice into a large bowl or *handai* (wooden sushi rice container), add the vinegar to the rice and toss, using a rice paddle at a diagonal to avoid squashing or slicing the grains. Add the ginger, *shiso*, and toasted sesame seeds to the rice and toss gently.

Prepare a small bowl of water and a cutting board or clean counter. Moisten your hands with water to keep the rice from sticking to them.

Divide the rice into 10 equal portions of about ⅓ cup (50 g). Gently open a tofu pouch, without tearing it, and stuff it with one portion of the seasoned sushi rice. Do not overstuff, or the pouches will rip. Place them slit-side up or down on a plate.

Either decorate with *kinome* (*sansho* leaves) or sprinkle sesame seeds on top of each stuffed pouch.

Serve with *amazu shoga* on the side.

grilled *onigiri* (rice balls)

When it comes to grilling, the Japanese have a long tradition. They even grill rice—shaped into balls and brushed with some soy sauce until they are brown and crispy. You don't need anything else to make grilled *onigiri* taste good. The preparation is easy, and you can even use day-old rice. Old rice has a way of perking up with heat. Besides the straight soy sauce, you can add miso to the soy sauce to make your *onigiri* taste savorier; add mirin if you want to add a little sweetness. The thing you want to remember is to serve *onigiri* right off the grill while they are still hot. That way they are crispy and really delicious. You can also turn this into *Ochazuke* (Rice Tea Soup; page 162) by pouring some hot tea or *Suimono* soup (page 118) over the *onigiri*.

MAKES 6

> 1 batch Basic White Rice (page 46)
>
> 1 cup (240 ml) filtered water
>
> ¼ cup (60 ml) *Shoyu Tare* (page 105) or plain soy sauce
>
> 2 tablespoons untoasted sesame oil or chile oil

Set up a cutting board to serve as a staging station for making the *onigiri*. Pour the water into a small bowl to wet your hands so the grains don't stick to them. Place it near the cutting board.

While the rice is still warm, divide it into six equal parts. Lightly moisten your hands with the water. Place one portion of rice in your moistened palm. For a triangular shape, use one hand to hold the rice ball and the other to create the top corner of the triangle, shaping it with your thumb and index finger. Rotate the ball and repeat until you have three corners; it should be about 1 inch (2.5 cm) thick and firm on the outside but soft and pillowy on the inside. Brush each triangle with a little oil to prevent it from sticking to the grill.

Heat a grill pan or grill over medium-high heat until hot. Or set a rack about 6 inches (15 cm) from the heat source, preheat the broiler, and line a baking sheet with foil.

Grill or broil the *onigiri* until crisp and slightly toasted, about 5 to 8 minutes on each side depending on the strength of the heat, basting with the *shoyu tare* on each side a few times until it is absorbed and becomes crisp; the *onigiri* should not be moist when finished. Keep an eye on them to make sure they don't burn. Serve immediately.

an impromptu *onigiri* lunch party

Onigiri (rice balls) were the heart of one of my favorite recent memories: a visit to Colleen Hennessey's pottery studio in Mendocino, California. The visit turned into an impromptu lunch gathering with friends—we served freshly cooked rice, *umeboshi* (pickled *ume* plums), and herbs and aromatics from the garden of Colleen and her wife, Adele Horne.

Colleen studied sculpture in college but her interest in food took her on a culinary path working for some major restaurants in Los Angeles for fifteen years. However, there was always a potter in her, and one day she decided to get back into pottery, eventually making the switch from being a chef to a full-time potter and leaving Los Angeles to live in Mendocino—a quieter, rural setting.

Colleen's pottery is simple and functional, with clean lines and light warm glazes, some with specks of ash. I can see how her background as a chef is reflected in the utilitarian quality of her pottery.

For our *onigiri* lunch, Adele dry-roasted some wild nori she had harvested from a local tide pool, which we crumbled into *furikake* (seasoning sprinkles). We filled the *onigiri* with *umeboshi*, pickled shiitake, and cured olives. As we all molded the rice into round and triangular shapes, the grains stuck to our fingers and some of the *onigiri* fell apart. But we managed to glue them back together (thanks to the sticky rice) and create a plate of whimsical *onigiri*, dressed with nori, flower petals, and herbs from the garden, including basil and dill (garnishes I had never used before in Japanese cooking). To accompany the *onigiri*, I made *Misoshiru* (Miso Soup; page 118) and *tamagoyaki* (a Japanese omelet; see *Dashi-maki Tamago* [Dashi-Flavored Omelet], page 82) filled with wakame. It was a beautiful gathering of new friends and good food. Later, Colleen made me some nice noodle bowls, which I use every day, as they are meant to be. They serve as a lovely reminder of our day together.

takikomi–gohan (vegetables and chicken rice)

Every rice-loving country has its own version of a rice dish cooked with meat and vegetables. The Japanese version is called *takikomi-gohan*, a colorful dish with a variety of vegetables and seaweeds. I make it here with arame. You can simplify this dish by using only one vegetable; just increase the volume of that vegetable to make up for whatever you are not using. So if you omit burdock, for example, double up on the carrots. The dashi is the hidden seasoning that makes this rice dish absolutely delicious; here I use dried shiitake mushroom dashi. The chicken thigh in this dish also imparts good umami.

**MAKES 4 SERVINGS, ABOUT 7½ CUPS (1 KG)
COOKED RICE**

2¼ cups (450 g) short-grain white rice

4 dried shiitake mushrooms

1 tablespoon arame

2 pieces *abura-age* (deep-fried tofu pouches)
  2¾ x 2¾ inches (7 x 7 cm)

2 tablespoons toasted sesame oil or
  grapeseed oil

2 large boneless skin-on chicken thighs, cut
  into ½-inch (12 mm) cubes

2 ounces (57 g) burdock, scrubbed lightly,
  julienned, and cut into 1-inch (2.5 cm) lengths

2 ounces (57 g) carrot, peeled and julienned

4 tablespoons *Shoyu Tare* (page 105)

2 tablespoons sake

2 tablespoon mirin

½ teaspoon sea salt

GARNISHES FOR THE TABLE

2 tablespoons thinly sliced *shiso* (about 4 leaves),
  mitsuba (Japanese parsley), or chervil leaves

1 teaspoon yuzu, *sudachi* (Japanese lime), or
  lemon zest

Shichimi Togarashi (page 107)

½ sheet nori, crumbled

Rinse the rice in water for 20 seconds, then drain. Stir the rice gently with your hands about 30 times. Rinse again and drain the starchy water. Set aside for 30 minutes.

Soak the shiitake mushrooms in 4½ cups (1 L) of water for 1 hour or up to overnight. Drain, reserving the mushroom dashi (soaking liquid). Coarsely mince the mushrooms. Place the arame in a small bowl and cover it with water. Hydrate for 10 minutes, then drain and set aside. Blanch the *abura-age* in a pot of boiling water, drain, and cut into ¼-inch (6 mm) pieces. (The blanching will freshen the tofu and remove any odors it has picked up.)

In a medium saucepan, heat the oil over medium heat. Add the chicken and cook until the pieces turn white, about 5 minutes. Then combine the mushrooms, burdock, carrot, *abura-age*, and arame and cook for 3 minutes, until the vegetables are evenly coated with oil. Add 3 cups of the mushroom dashi and bring to a boil. Reduce the heat to maintain a simmer. Add the *shoyu tare* and sake and simmer for 5 minutes. Remove from heat and drain, reserving the liquid. Measure 2½ cups (600 ml) of the liquid in a measuring cup. If short, add mushroom dashi.

Transfer the reserved liquid into a 3-quart (3 L) heavy-bottomed pot with a tight-fitting lid. Add the rice and mix it into the liquid. Put the chicken and vegetables on top. Do not stir. Bring to a boil on the stovetop, 7 to 8 minutes, until the liquid is bubbling around the edges. Place the lid on the pot, turn the heat down to the lowest possible level, and cook, without peeking, for 18 minutes. Turn off the heat and let stand, without peeking, for 15 minutes. Open the lid and gently fluff the rice, meat, and vegetables with a rice paddle or wooden spoon. Replace the lid and allow the rice to rest for another 5 minutes. (If you are using an electric rice cooker or *donabe*, follow the manufacturer's instructions.)

Serve with the *shiso* leaves, yuzu zest, *shichimi togarashi*, and crumbled nori.

grilled ginger chicken with *shoyu tare*

This is a nice chicken dish I make using *shoyu tare* (soy sauce–based seasoning). The skin here comes out super crispy and the meat is very tender—a beautiful contrast. I like to make a large batch of *shoyu tare* and use it for dipping sauces and for seasoning noodle soups and braised dishes. Serve the chicken as a topping for your grain bowl or as part of your bento box with some *Amazuzuke* (Quick Vinegar Pickles; page 86) or First Garden Soba Salad with Lemon–White Miso Vinaigrette (page 247).

MAKES 2 TO 4 SERVINGS

4 boneless skin-on chicken thighs
½ teaspoon sea salt
1 tablespoon ginger juice
1 tablespoon untoasted or toasted sesame oil
¼ cup (60 ml) *Shoyu Tare* (page 105)

Position the top rack of your oven about 7 inches (17 cm) from the broiler and preheat the broiler. Line a rimmed baking sheet with aluminum foil.

Make ½-inch (12 mm) slits on the meaty side of each chicken thigh, about 2 inches (5 cm) apart. Sprinkle the salt over the meat and rub it all over with the ginger juice and oil. Spread the thighs on the baking sheet, skin-side down.

Broil the thighs until they start to brown lightly, about 3 minutes, then start basting with the *shoyu tare*. Let the chicken brown some more and then baste again, repeating a few more times at 2-minute intervals. Allow 8 to 9 minutes cooking time on the meat side before you flip the chicken.

Turn the chicken over so it is skin-side up. Baste again with *shoyu tare* and broil until the skin is browned and crispy and the chicken is cooked and no longer pink inside, about 2 minutes. Do not flip, or the skin will lose its crispiness. Remove from the oven and let the chicken rest for 3 to 5 minutes, then slice it crosswise 1 inch (2.5 cm) thick and serve.

grilled eggplant with herbs

This dish celebrates the deliciousness of eggplant. You may be used to slicing the eggplant, salting it, and cooking it in oil, but this dish leaves the eggplant alone. I grill or broil the whole unpeeled eggplant until it is scorched and steamed inside. It is easy to peel once it is cooked.

> 2 pounds (900 g) Japanese eggplants, about 6 to 8 eggplants
>
> 3 scallions, sliced about ⅛ inch (3 mm) thick
>
> 2 tablespoons ginger juice, from 5 ounces (142 g) of peeled and grated ginger
>
> 4 to 6 *shiso* leaves, chopped
>
> 2 to 3 *myoga* buds, thinly sliced crosswise (optional)
>
> 3 tablespoons bonito flakes (optional)
>
> 1 tablespoon *Surigoma* (page 107)
>
> Soy sauce for serving

Position the top rack of your oven about 7 inches (17 cm) from the broiler and preheat the broiler. Line a rimmed baking sheet with aluminum foil.

Use the tip of a sharp knife to pierce the eggplant in one place to allow steam to escape while it cooks. Put the eggplant on the prepared baking sheet and broil, turning every 3 to 4 minutes, until the skin is browned and a little burnt and the eggplant feels tender inside, about 12 to 15 minutes.

Rinse the eggplants under cold running water as soon as you remove them from the broiler (this makes them easier to peel). Use a paring knife to peel the eggplant, starting from the stem end of the eggplant and working your way down. Be careful not to peel away the flesh.

You can serve the eggplant whole and let people tear it apart with chopsticks or forks or slice each eggplant crosswise into disks about 2 inches (5 cm) thick. Garnish the eggplant with scallions, ginger juice, *shiso* leaves, *myoga*, and bonito flakes, if using. Serve piping hot or chilled with soy sauce on the side for your guests to add as they like.

koji-marinated salmon

This is my "no-recipe" salmon dish. Simply smear the *shio koji* (fermented koji salt) all over the salmon fillets and let marinate overnight or up to 2 days in the refrigerator. You can find *shio koji* online or in Japanese markets, but it is easy to make at home. I use *shio koji* to marinate meat, seafood, and vegetables. The amount of *shio koji* to use is about 5 to 7 percent of the weight of the fish. So, for example, if you have 6 ounces (170 g) of fish, use about 1½ teaspoons (8.5 g) to 2½ teaspoons (12.5 g) *shio koji*.

This recipe also works well as a marinade for other fish such as mahi-mahi, yellowtail, opah, ocean whitefish, snapper, halibut, cod, scallops, squid, or shrimp, as well as for meat including pork, chicken, and beef. This makes a perfect entry for your bento box.

MAKES 4 SERVINGS

3 tablespoons *Shio Koji* (page 95)
4 salmon fillets, about 1½ pounds (680 g)
  total with skin
Vegetable oil for basting

FOR THE GARNISH

6 ounces (170 g) daikon radish, peeled
  and grated
1 tablespoon grated ginger

Evenly spread the *shio koji* all over the salmon fillets, including the skin, and let them marinate in the refrigerator overnight or for up to 3 days. The longer the fish marinates, the saltier it will become. When you are ready to cook the salmon, wipe off the *shio koji* with a paper towel or give the fish a quick rinse and then wipe down with a paper towel.

Position the top rack of your oven about 7 inches (17 cm) from the broiler and preheat the broiler. Line a rimmed baking sheet with aluminum foil.

Brush the fillets with oil and place them skin-side down on the prepared baking sheet. Broil for 5 to 6 minutes, until the fish is lightly browned and you can flake it easily with a fork.

Serve with the daikon radish and grated ginger.

soba salad with kabocha squash and toasted pepitas

This is the salad that I served at one of my first soba pop-ups in Los Angeles, working with my chef friends Roxana Jullapat and Daniel Mattern of Friends & Family. Roxana and Dan came up with the idea to add a little pumpkin seed oil to the dressing and garnish with toasted pepitas, which opened my mind about the possibilities of soba.

MAKES 4 SERVINGS

FOR THE *AMAKARA* (SWEET AND SAVORY) *SHOYU TARE*

2 tablespoons *kokuto* syrup (page 109)

2 teaspoons *Shoyu Tare* (page 105) or soy sauce

FOR THE SALAD

1½ pounds (680 g) kabocha squash (about half of a medium squash), peeled and diced into ½-inch (12 mm) cubes

2 tablespoons plus 1 teaspoon untoasted sesame oil or olive oil

1 teaspoon sea salt

Freshly ground black pepper

½ cup (70 g) pepitas (pumpkin seeds)

8 ounces (230 g) dried or fresh Soba Noodles (page 58)

10 ounces (284 g) mixed baby greens, such as arugula, spinach, and kale

FOR THE PUMPKIN SEED VINAIGRETTE

¼ cup (60 ml) orange juice

1½ tablespoons rice vinegar

2 teaspoons ginger juice

2½ tablespoons lemon juice

2 tablespoons soy sauce

1 tablespoon pumpkin seed oil or other nut oil (such as almond, walnut, or pecan)

¼ cup (60 ml) extra-virgin olive oil or untoasted sesame oil

Shichimi Togarashi (page 107), to taste

Sea salt and freshly ground black pepper, to taste

Preheat the oven to 400°F (200°C). Line a large baking sheet with parchment paper.

Combine the *kokuto* syrup and *shoyu tare* in a small saucepan.

To roast the squash for the salad, toss the squash with 1 tablespoon of the oil and season with salt and pepper. Place the squash on the prepared baking sheet and roast for about 15 minutes, basting with the *shoyu tare* after the squash has had a chance to roast for 7 minutes. Brush again after 5 minutes. Roast until the squash can be pierced with a fork but is still slightly firm and the bottom is slightly browned. There is no need to turn the squash. Remove from the oven and let cool.

Lower the oven temperature to 325°F (163°C).

In a small bowl, toss the pepitas in the remaining 1 teaspoon oil and place them on a baking sheet in a single layer. Place in the oven and toast until lightly browned, 8 to 10 minutes, stirring once or twice so they don't burn. Remove from the oven and let cool.

To make the vinaigrette, whisk together all the ingredients in a medium bowl. Taste and adjust the seasonings as needed.

Cook the soba noodles in a pot of boiling water until al dente. If you are using store-bought noodles, follow the instructions on the package. If you are using homemade noodles, the cooking time will depend on the thickness of your noodles; it will be anywhere from 1½ minutes for thin noodles to 3 to 4 minutes for thicker noodles. Vigorously rinse the cooked noodles under cold running water to remove the starch, then shock the noodles in a bowl of ice water for 3 seconds. Drain the noodles very well.

Arrange the greens and soba in a serving bowl and toss with the dressing. Top with pieces of the roasted squash and garnish with the pepitas. Add sea salt, *shichimi togarashi*, and freshly ground pepper to taste. Serve immediately.

how to clean and cut a squash for cooking

I overcame my fear of cutting squash after I learned this method. In this demo I use a kabocha squash.

Using a heavy kitchen knife, cut a square hole around the stem of the kabocha, about 2 x 2 inches (5 x 5 cm). Turn the kabocha over and cut the same size square on the bottom. (You can use a pumpkin saw to do this part if you feel safer.)

Hold the kabocha down firmly with one hand. Cut down the length of the squash from the top hole to the bottom. Turn the squash and repeat on the other side. Split the kabocha open with your hands. Scrape out the seeds and fibers using your hands and a spoon.

Cut the squash into wedges. Peel each piece; the Japanese like to leave a little skin on the kabocha for color. Then cut each wedge into smaller pieces. Use your knife to bevel the edges of each wedge for a cleaner finish.

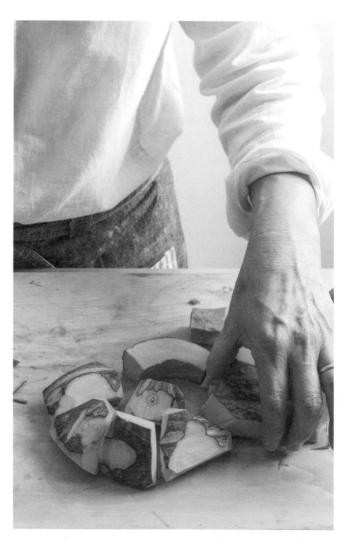

gyoza (fried dumplings)

Dumplings are always a crowd pleaser. I make a classic ground pork, shrimp, and cabbage filling. You can prepare the filling a day in advance. Fill the wrappers while you are entertaining your guests in the kitchen before the meal—I can assure you that people will love to watch you wrap and fry the dumplings. Some might even offer to help you wrap, and it is totally okay to accept their help and wind up with some crooked-looking or otherwise oddly shaped dumplings.

I cook my dumplings in a 10-inch (25 cm) nonstick skillet or well-seasoned cast-iron pan, which fits about 25 to 30 dumplings. I make one batch and let people stand in the kitchen and enjoy them right out of the pan, then I do a second batch. I serve them with a simple side dish of *namuru*—blanched bean sprouts shocked in ice water and seasoned with a dash of toasted sesame oil, a pinch of salt, and *shichimi togarashi* (seven-spice blend). It is very refreshing and makes a nice foil to the rich, hot *gyoza*.

MAKES ABOUT 60

FOR THE PORK FILLING

About 4 cups (12 oz/340 g) Napa cabbage, finely chopped

2 teaspoons sea salt

1 pound (455 g) ground pork (preferably pork shoulder)

2 cloves garlic, grated

1 cup (3 oz/90 g) garlic chives, finely minced, or scallions, finely minced

2 tablespoons finely grated ginger

½ cup (120 ml) chicken broth or Kombu Dashi (page 27)

1 tablespoon soy sauce

1 tablespoon sake

2 teaspoons toasted sesame oil

Freshly ground black pepper

FOR THE WRAPPERS

One 10-ounce (284 g) package *gyoza* skins (about 60 wrappers) or 1 recipe Dumpling Wrappers (page 65)

2 tablespoons toasted sesame oil, plus an additional 1 teaspoon for extra-crispy *gyoza*

FOR THE TABLE

La-Yu (page 109)

Kurozu (amber rice vinegar) or lemon wedges

Soy sauce

Rice vinegar or *kurozu* (black rice vinegar)

To make the pork filling, combine the cabbage and 2 teaspoons salt in a medium bowl and massage the cabbage for 2 minutes. Let stand for 15 minutes, then squeeze out excess moisture and discard the liquid. You should have about 1 cup of wilted minced cabbage.

Combine the pork, cabbage, garlic, garlic chives, ginger, chicken broth, soy sauce, sake, and sesame oil and season with pepper. Knead the mixture for 4 to 5 minutes, until it is well combined and smooth. Cover and refrigerate for at least 1 hour or up to overnight.

Fill a small bowl with water and put it next to a cutting board, where you will form the *gyoza*. The water will be used to dampen and seal the *gyoza* wrappers. Line a baking sheet with parchment paper and set it next to the cutting board for your wrapped *gyoza*.

Place the wrappers next to one another on the cutting board without overlapping. Spoon approximately 1 scant tablespoon of the filling into the middle of each wrapper. The amount of filling will depend on the size of the wrapper; you don't want to be skimpy, but you also don't want too much filling on your wrapper, as the contents might spill out as they cook.

To wrap a *gyoza*, dip your fingertip into the water and use it to dampen the whole edge of the

wrapper. Lift the front and back edges and pinch them together in the center; the dampness will form a seal between the two edges. Begin pleating along the front edge and folding the pleats so that the folds point toward the center. Fold two or three pleats on the right. Do the same with the left, with the pleats pointing toward the center. Press firmly on each pleat to completely seal the wrapper. Place the sealed uncooked *gyoza* on the baking sheet, flattening the bottom so it stands upright with the pleated edge at the top. Repeat with the remaining wrappers.

To cook the *gyoza*, heat 1 tablespoon sesame oil in a 10-inch (25 cm) nonstick skillet over medium-high heat. You will get the best results when the pan is heated evenly.

Place half of the *gyoza* into the pan, forming three rows with all the dumplings facing in the same direction and standing in the pan, not lying down. Fry the *gyoza* for 3 to 4 minutes, until the bottoms are evenly browned. Pour about ¾ cup (180 ml) water, enough to cover the bottom third of the *gyoza*, into the pan. Be ready to cover the pan immediately with a lid because the water will sizzle and splash. Lower the heat and simmer with the lid on until almost all the liquid is gone, 5 to 6 minutes.

Remove the lid and increase the heat to medium-high. Cook until the bottom of the *gyoza* become dry and crispy, 3 to 4 minutes. For an even crispier finish, add ½ teaspoon sesame oil to the pan and swirl it around, lifting the *gyoza* up with a spatula so the oil can spread evenly beneath. Continue to cook for about 1 minute, until the bottoms of the *gyoza* are crisp. Remove from heat and loosen the *gyoza* with a spatula. Transfer to a serving plate, bottom-side up. While your diners are eating the first batch, cook the remaining batch in the same way.

Serve immediately with *la-yu*, soy sauce, and *kurozu* (amber rice vinegar)—pick one or any combination—for dipping.

noodle soup with egg and shiitake mushrooms

This is a versatile noodle soup that uses fresh or dried soba, *somen*, or udon noodles.

To make the soup, you will prepare four components: a dashi-based seasoned broth, an egg omelet, the noodles, and the garnishes. The seasoned broth and the egg omelet can be made a day in advance. You can substitute *Nitamago* (Marinated Soft-Boiled Eggs; page 83), another protein (such as grilled chicken or shrimp), or vegetables for the omelet, if you prefer. The *shoyu tare* used to season this soup is made in a larger batch; it can be stored in the pantry for up to six months. *Shoyu tare* is my all-purpose sauce that I use for seasoning soups and basting grilled meats and grilled rice balls. If you have these ingredients prepped, this noodle soup will be very easy to put together.

MAKES 4 SERVINGS

> 8 cups (2 L) Bonito and Kombu Dashi (page 27) or other dashi of your choice (pages 23–31)
>
> Scant 1 cup (200 ml) *Shoyu Tare* (page 105)
>
> 1 tablespoon sake
>
> 1 recipe *Dashimaki Tamago* (page 82)
>
> 1 tablespoon untoasted or toasted sesame oil or grapeseed oil
>
> 8 fresh shiitake mushrooms, sliced ¼ inch (6 mm) thick or left whole if they are small
>
> 1 baby spring onion, sliced ⅛ inch (3 mm) thick
>
> 1 pound (455 g) dried or fresh soba, *somen*, or udon noodles

FOR THE GARNISHES

> 4 scallions, white and light green parts thinly sliced crosswise about ⅛ inch (3 mm) thick
>
> 2 tablespoons grated ginger
>
> 1 tablespoon citrus peel (yuzu, lemon, lime) in 1-inch-long (2.5 cm) julienned strips
>
> *Shichimi Togarashi* (page 107)

Bring the dashi to a boil in a large saucepan over medium-high heat and add the *shoyu tare* and sake. Reduce the heat to medium and cook for 3 to 4 minutes. Remove from heat. Taste and adjust the seasonings as needed. You can make the soup 2 to 3 days in advance and keep it in the refrigerator; reheating when you are ready to make the soup.

Cut the omelet, if using, crosswise into ½-inch-thick (8 mm) pieces.

In a medium skillet, heat the oil over medium-high heat. Add the mushrooms and spring onion and cook until softened, about 2 minutes. Set aside.

Bring the dashi to a boil over high heat, then lower the heat to maintain a simmer while you cook the noodles.

Bring a large pot of water to a rolling boil over high heat. Add the noodles. They will take between 2 and 10 minutes to cook, depending on the type of noodles you are using; cook them to your desired tenderness, letting your teeth be your guide. Rinse the noodles vigorously under running water to remove the surface starch, then drain. Divide the noodles into individual soup bowls.

Arrange the sliced omelet, mushrooms, and onions on top of the noodles in the bowls. Pour the piping hot soup into the bowls and garnish with scallions, ginger, and citrus slivers. Serve immediately with *shichimi togarashi* on the side.

nikujaga (beef, *shirataki*, and potato stew)

This is a Japanese-style beef stew. It is lighter than a traditional stew because it uses no roux to thicken the sauce. The dish is made with *shirataki* (yam noodles), which add volume and texture without any added calories. The noodles absorb the rich umami flavor of the meat; when I make this dish, the noodles are the first thing to disappear out of the pot. Here we will use thinly sliced *sukiyaki*-style or *shabu shabu*–style beef or pork. The thin cut, available in Asian markets, enables the meat to cook very quickly.

MAKES 4 SERVINGS

12 snow peas, strings removed

7 ounces (200 g) *shirataki* (yam) noodles (1 package)

2 tablespoons vegetable oil

1 large yellow onion, cut in half lengthwise, then cut into ¼-inch-thick (6 mm) slices

8 ounces (230 g) *sukiyaki*-style or *shabu shabu*-style beef or pork tenderloin, sliced thin and cut into 4-inch (10 cm) pieces

1½ pounds (680 g) Yukon Gold potatoes (about 4), peeled and quartered

1 medium carrot, cut into 1-inch (2.5 cm) coins (optional)

½ cup (120 ml) *Shoyu Tare* (page 105)

¼ cup (60 ml) sake

1 tablespoon *kokuto* syrup (page 109) or dark brown sugar (optional)

4 cups (960 ml) Bonito and Kombu Dashi (page 27) or Kombu Dashi (page 27)

Bring a small pot of water to a boil over medium-high heat. Add the snow peas and blanch for about 1 minute, until tender. Remove the snow peas from the boiling water and set aside to use as a garnish. Using the same water, blanch the *shirataki* for 1 minute. Drain the noodles and cut them into 4-inch (10 cm) pieces. Set aside in another bowl.

Heat the oil in a 4-quart (4 L) pot over a medium heat. Add the onion and cook for 4 to 5 minutes, until it is tender. Add the meat and cook for another 2 to 3 minutes, until the meat is cooked through. Add the blanched *shirataki* noodles, potatoes, and carrots and cook for another 4 to 5 minutes, until the potatoes are cooked.

Add all the ingredients for the *shoyu tare*, sake, and *kokuto* syrup to the pot along with the dashi and bring to a boil. Lower the heat, cover the pot, and simmer for 15 to 20 minutes, or until half of the liquid is absorbed into the noodles, meat, and vegetables and the potatoes are cooked. Taste and adjust the seasonings. Serve warm in a medium bowl with the broth and garnish with the blanched snow peas.

japanese chicken curry with relish of the seven lucky gods

My mother always made curry with S&B or House Foods curry bricks, just as convenient as bouillon cubes. I like the convenient part, but I don't care for all the additives that go into most of these store-bought brands. So I started making my own by blending a variety of spices including turmeric, which gives my curry a bright mustardy yellow color and pungent flavor. First you will need to make your own Japanese Curry Brick which you can keep in the fridge for 1 week or in the freezer for 3 months. The base stock is a cold-brew kombu and shiitake mushroom dashi, which can, like the curry brick, be made ahead of time. The curry is traditionally served with rice or noodles and *fukujinzuke*, a classic pickle made with seven vegetables, a perfect crunchy counterpart to the soft, mild curry.

MAKES 4 SERVINGS

2 tablespoons vegetable oil

1½ pounds (680 g) boneless, skinless chicken thighs, cut into 1-inch (2.5 cm) chunks

2 onions, halved and thinly sliced

2 cloves garlic, minced

2 tablespoons minced ginger

2 carrots, cut into bite-size pieces

1 celery stalk, cut into bite-size pieces

1 pound (455 g) Yukon Gold, russet, or other potatoes, peeled and cut into bite-size pieces

8 cups (1.9 L) Bonito and Kombu Dashi (page 27) or chicken stock

1 tablespoon honey

2 tablespoons soy sauce, or to taste

2 tablespoons sake

⅓ recipe Japanese Curry Brick (recipe follows)

Salt and freshly ground black pepper

1 recipe *Fukujinzuke* (page 89)

Heat the oil in a large saucepan over medium heat. Add the chicken and cook until lightly browned, 6 to 8 minutes.

Reduce the heat to low and add the onions, garlic, and ginger. Cook until softened, about 5 minutes. Add the carrots, celery, potatoes, dashi, honey, soy sauce, and sake, increase the heat to medium-high, and bring to a boil. Lower the heat and simmer for 20 minutes, or until the liquid is reduced by a third. Add the curry brick, stir to break it down, and continue simmering until the sauce is thickened but still pourable and reduced by about two-thirds, about 30 minutes. Season with salt and pepper as needed. Remove from heat and serve with rice and *fukujinzuke*.

japanese curry brick

Most Japanese cooks rely on prepared curry bricks to make curry. These are basically blocks of seasoned roux—the shape of a chocolate bar—made of spices (including turmeric, coriander, cumin, and fennel), salt, flour, and butter that can be dissolved in water to make an instant curry sauce. My brick is on the mild side, so if you like it spicier, add the cayenne pepper. To make your curry block gluten-free, chickpea flour is a good alternative that is used in Indian curries. If using chickpea flour, it will be soupy in consistency. You can add a tablespoon of *mochiko* (glutinous rice flour) diluted with equal amounts of water to thicken the curry.

One curry brick in this recipe makes about three batches of Japanese-style curry. You can break up the brick into three pieces and store it in the refrigerator. This recipe makes more curry powder than you will need for the brick. You can use the remaining powder to sprinkle on vegetables and salads or save it for the next batch of brick.

FOR THE CURRY POWDER

    1 tablespoon brown or black mustard seeds

    One 2-inch (5 cm) piece of cinnamon stick, broken into small pieces

    1 bay leaf

    2 to 3 cardamom pods

    1 tablespoon coriander seeds

    1 tablespoon fennel seeds

    1 tablespoon cumin seeds

    1 teaspoon fenugreek seeds

    ½ teaspoon whole cloves

    1½ teaspoons black peppercorns

    1 teaspoon sweet paprika

    1 tablespoon ground ginger

    1 tablespoon ground turmeric

    1 tablespoon sea salt

    1 teaspoon cayenne pepper (or more to taste)

FOR THE ROUX

    ½ cup (1 stick/115 g) unsalted butter

    ⅔ cup (70 g) all-purpose flour or chickpea flour

the japanese pantry

In a medium skillet, toast mustard seeds, cinnamon, bay leaf, cardamom pods, coriander seeds, fennel seeds, cumin seeds, fenugreek seeds, and cloves over medium heat, stirring until fragrant, about 2 minutes. Remove from heat.

Transfer the toasted spices to a spice grinder, add the peppercorns, and grind at the highest speed for 30 seconds. Shake the grinder a couple of times to make sure the cinnamon stick is pulverized. Sift the ground spices through a fine-mesh strainer set over a bowl. Add the paprika, ginger, turmeric, salt, and cayenne, if using. You will have ⅔ cup (50 g) of the ground spice mix.

To make the curry brick, put the butter in a medium nonstick skillet and place over medium-high heat. When the butter is nearly melted, turn the heat to low. Add the flour and cook, stirring constantly, until the roux turns light brown, 15 to 20 minutes, being careful not to let it burn. Add ⅓ cup (36 g) of the curry powder and mix well. Transfer the seasoned roux to a small container or a mini aluminum loaf pan measuring 5¼ x 3½ x 2 inches (14.5 x 8.5 x 5 cm). Let stand at room temperature until the roux is set, about 3 hours. But you can start using the curry brick in liquid form if you wish to make curry right away.

To store, take the curry brick out of the container and wrap in parchment paper or plastic wrap and store in the refrigerator for up to 1 month or in the freezer for up to 3 months.

tonkatsu (pork cutlet) with *ume shiso* paste

Tonkatsu is a breaded and deep-fried pork cutlet. The secret to getting the brittle crispy skin is using *panko*–Japanese bread crumbs, which are much larger and coarser than Western-style bread crumbs. You can make a plain *tonkatsu*, which is a good place to start, or add a layer of tanginess with *ume shiso* paste made from *umeboshi* (pickled *ume* plums) and *maesil chung*, a Korean green plum syrup. Most Japanese season *tonkatsu* with store-bought *tonkatsu* sauce, which to me tastes too sweet. Instead I prefer to make my own or simply use soy sauce and a squirt of lemon on my cutlet. You can also make a delicious *katsu sando* (deep-fried pork cutlet sandwich) using leftovers. Brush Japanese Milk Bread (page 67) with *Tonkatsu* sauce (recipe follows) and place sliced *tonkatsu* on top with shredded cabbage for a good crunch.

MAKES 4 SERVINGS

EQUIPMENT

    3-quart (3 L) cast-iron Dutch oven or
       heavy-bottomed pot

    Deep-fry thermometer

    1¼ pounds (560 g) boneless pork chops,
       about four ¾-inch-thick (2 cm) cutlets

    1 teaspoon sea salt

    Freshly ground black pepper

    1 cup (130 g) all-purpose flour

    2 large eggs, beaten

    2 cups (120 g) *panko*

    3½ cups (830 ml) rice bran oil, light sesame oil,
       or grapeseed oil

    8 ounces (230 g) cabbage, shredded

FOR THE *UME SHISO* PASTE (OPTIONAL)

    3 to 4 *Umeboshi* (page 90), seeded and minced

    8 *shiso* leaves, minced

    2 teaspoons *maesil chung*, homemade (see *Ume* Syrup, page 288) or store-bought

FOR THE TABLE

    1 lemon, cut into 8 wedges

    Tonkatsu Sauce (recipe follows) or soy sauce

Trim the fat around the edges of the pork chops. Pound them with a meat mallet to slightly flatten them and rub them with the salt and pepper.

If you are making the *ume shiso* paste, mix the *ume* paste with the *shiso* leaves and *maesil chung*. Make a lengthwise incision 3 inches (7.5 cm) long on both sides of each pork chop. Using a fork or your clean hand, smear 1 teaspoon of the paste in each incision.

You are now ready to start frying. Line up three small shallow bowls: one with the flour, one with the beaten eggs, and one with the *panko*. Take one pork chop and lightly flour it on both sides, patting to remove excess flour. Dip the chop into the egg and then coat it generously with *panko*. Repeat with the remaining chops.

Pour the oil into a 3-quart (3 L) cast-iron Dutch oven or heavy-bottomed pot and heat over medium heat until it reaches 350°F (175°C). Test the temperature by dropping a few bread crumbs into the oil. If the crumbs sizzle up instantly but do not burn, the temperature is right for frying. Add two chops to the oil and cook for 3 to 4 minutes, until they are lightly browned on one side. Flip and fry for another 3 to 4 minutes, until lightly browned on the second side. The timing will depend on the thickness of the meat and the temperature of the oil. Test for doneness by taking one chop out of the oil when it is lightly browned on both sides and slice it; it should not be pink inside. Be careful not to overcook the pork–you want your cutlets to be tender and juicy. Drain the chops on a paper towel–lined plate to remove excess oil. Fry the remaining two chops.

Slice the pork crosswise about ¾ inch (2 cm) thick and serve over the shredded cabbage with the lemon wedges and your choice of sauce.

tonkatsu sauce

I was teaching a *tonkatsu* class in Lima, Peru, when my students Mei and Miki and I realized we didn't have any *tonkatsu* sauce for the *tonkatsu* (pork cutlet). So it was an opportunity to make our own. After a little tweaking, we came out with something as good, and not as sweet as the store-bought varieties.

MAKES ABOUT ⅔ CUP (156 ML)

½ cup (240 ml) Bonito and Kombu Dashi
(page 27)

2 teaspoons *kokuto* syrup (page 109)
or dark brown sugar

¼ cup (60 ml) ketchup

3 tablespoons soy sauce

3 tablespoons Worcestershire sauce

½ teaspoon ground pepper

1 teaspoon kudzu or potato starch, dissolved in
1 teaspoon water

Bring the dashi to a boil in a small pot over medium-high heat. Add the remaining ingredients and cook until the liquid thickens and reduces by one-third, stirring frequently so it doesn't burn, about 10 minutes. Taste and make adjustments. If you like the sauce sweeter, add more ketchup, sugar, or mirin. If you want the savory flavors to come out, add more soy sauce and Worcestershire sauce. Keep in the fridge for up to 1 month.

shrimp and carrot *kakiage* tempura

This is a light and crispy fritter that combines a variety of chopped seafood and vegetables. I often serve this tempura with noodles or as *tendon* (tempura grain bowl). You can use other seafood here, such as clams, scallops, and different types of fish; and you can substitute other vegetables, such as asparagus, burdock, lotus, kabocha squash, and green beans in season. Be sure to read the Tempura Guidelines (page 159) before you start frying.

MAKES 3 TO 4 SERVINGS

EQUIPMENT

3-quart (3 L) Dutch oven or heavy-bottomed cast-iron pot or deep fryer

Deep-fry thermometer

1 pound (455 g) medium shrimp, peeled and deveined

2 large carrots

½ cup (12 g) *mitsuba* (Japanese parsley), parsley, chervil, cilantro, or dill leaves, roughly chopped

½ teaspoon sea salt

4 to 5 cups (960 ml to 1.2 L) vegetable oil

FOR THE DIPPING SAUCE

2 cups (480 ml) Bonito and Kombu Dashi (page 27)

1½ tablespoons mirin

½ cup (120 ml) *Shoyu Tare* (page 105)

FOR THE TEMPURA BATTER

1 large egg yolk, beaten

¾ cup (180 ml) ice-cold water

1 scant cup (120 g) cake flour, plus 2 tablespoons for dusting the shrimp mixture

1 tablespoon potato starch or cornstarch

2 cups (480 ml) ice cubes

FOR THE GARNISHES

8 ounces (230 g) daikon radish, peeled and grated

1 tablespoon grated ginger

Cut the shrimp into 4 pieces crosswise. Blot any excess moisture with a paper towel and place in a medium bowl. Cut the carrots into 2½-inch (6.5 cm) matchsticks and add them to the shrimp. Refrigerate until you are ready to fry.

To make the dipping sauce, bring the dashi to a boil in a medium pot over medium-high heat. Lower the heat and add the mirin and the *shoyu tare* and simmer for 2 minutes. Turn off the heat. Reheat the dipping sauce before serving or serve at room temperature. You can also make it ahead; it will keep in the refrigerator for 4 to 5 days.

To make the tempura batter, whisk the egg with the ice-cold water in a medium bowl. Sift 1 cup of the flour and the potato starch into a separate medium bowl. Add the dry mixture to the egg mixture and combine using a whisk or chopsticks. Do not overmix. Set the bowl in a larger bowl filled with the ice. Keep the batter away from the heat; it is important that the tempura batter remain chilled.

Remove the shrimp and carrots from the refrigerator and add the *mitsuba*. Season with the salt. Transfer the vegetables to a plastic bag and add the remaining 2 tablespoons flour and shake to coat the ingredients. Divide the mixture into 8 portions.

Pour the oil into a 3-quart (3 L) cast-iron pot and heat over medium-high heat to 325°F (163°C). It is crucial to maintain an even temperature.

In a small bowl, add one batch of the flour-coated shrimp and vegetable mixture to 1½ to 2 tablespoons of the chilled tempura batter, lightly coating the vegetable mixture with the batter. Slide (don't drop!) the mixture into the hot oil from the side of the pan, using another spoon to gently guide the batter into the oil. Quickly spread the batter with a pair of chopsticks to make an oblong or round fritter. When the fritter crisps, poke a couple of holes in the middle of it with chopsticks, then flip it. Fry until lightly golden on both sides, about 2 minutes.

the japanese pantry

Remove the fritter from the pot and place on a wire rack or paper towels set over a baking sheet. Check the oil to make sure the temperature remains at 325°F (163°C) and remove any flecks of batter or vegetables from the oil with a skimmer. Repeat with the remaining batter, adding batter for two fritters at a time.

As the fritters are finished, reheat the dipping sauce if you like and serve immediately with the dipping sauce and garnished with the grated radish and ginger.

tempura guidelines

Portuguese missionaries and traders residing in Nagasaki introduced this fritter dish to Japan in the sixteenth century; the name relates to its Portuguese origin. Like anything else, making tempura gets easier the more you do it. You can fry one ingredient at a time (shrimp, green beans, *shiso* leaf, etc.) or combine several ingredients together to make a fritter (see Shrimp and Carrot *Kakiage* Tempura, page 157). Here are a few guidelines to keep in mind:

The Ingredients

Use the freshest seasonal ingredients possible. Almost any vegetable will work for tempura, even *shiso* leaves, carrot leaves, and parsley. But leafy greens with a high moisture content, such as lettuce, will wilt. Serve tempura right out of the pot, as hot as possible.

I make tempura on a little butane stove on my patio. This keeps my kitchen clean and my house from smelling like fryer oil.

The Pot

Use a heavy-bottomed pot or cast-iron skillet. I use a 2- or 3-quart (2 or 3 L) pot depending on the amount of frying I want to do. It should have wide sides and plenty of depth; you will want oil 3 to 4 inches (7.5 to 10 cm) deep in the pot. A shallow or thin skillet will result in an initial high temperature that will suddenly drop when you add food to the pan. Don't overcrowd your pot; it should never be more than half full, so the food has space to move.

The Oil

Don't skimp on the oil; use plenty of it. Use an oil with a high smoke point. I use a variety of oils including rice bran, peanut, and light sesame oil. Some oils handle heat well; others start to smoke at relatively low temperatures. You'll want to avoid smoke, of course!

You can repurpose the spent oil and make another batch of tempura. I supplement with half fresh oil.

If you deep-fry ingredients that contain a lot of water, such as tofu, the oil will lose its vitality quickly, so you will not be able to reuse it. Press out the water from the tofu using a paper towel or dish towel. Dusting watery ingredients such as tofu, shrimp, and scallops with flour or starch helps contain some of the moisture and produce a crispy tempura.

The Temperature

Keep the temperature even and hot, starting with a relatively slow preheat while you are preparing the ingredients. I use a digital deep-fry/candy thermometer to check the temperature and always stay in the range of 325°F to 350°F (163°C–175°C). If the temperature is too low, you will get greasy tempura; if it is too high, the tempura will burn. Monitor the temperature throughout the frying process and adjust as needed.

The Batter

Use ice-cold water and fresh eggs, starch, and flour. The ice-cold water keeps the batter light and less doughy and the tempura crisp. Keep the batter ingredients, including the water and flour, in the refrigerator until just before you are ready to fry. There are different ratios of flour, water, egg, and starch. The standard recipe is 1 beaten egg yolk mixed with 1 cup (240 ml) ice-cold water to achieve a 1:1 ratio of liquid (egg and water) to cake flour. In a separate bowl, sift together the dry ingredients, which consist of 1 cup (150 g) cake flour and 1 tablespoon potato starch or rice starch. Sift this dry mixture into the egg mixture and combine using a whisk or chopsticks. Be careful not to overmix; it is okay to have a few lumps of flour in the batter. Keep the batter as chilled as possible by keeping the batter bowl afloat in a bowl of iced water, and never let it sit next to the heat. Finally, don't make too much batter at once. It is better to make a second batch later if you run low. If you prefer a lighter, gluten-free batter, try substituting rice flour for cake flour. Use a 1:1 ratio of liquid (egg and water) to rice flour. You can use beer instead of water and a pinch of salt for a crispy batter.

The Dipping Sauce

To make a good dipping sauce, make the dashi from scratch; I use Bonito and Kombu Dashi (page 27). The dashi is then seasoned with *Shoyu Tare* (page 105), which is a combination of soy sauce, mirin, and a little sugar (you can skip the sugar if you like). I use about 1 part *shoyu tare* to 3 parts dashi. You can make the tempura dipping sauce ahead and store it in the refrigerator for 3 to 4 days.

flower-viewing bento box

A bento box (*bento* meaning "lunch" or "lunch box") is far more than a food container. While it has become quite familiar in places outside of Japan, it retains a special place in Japanese culture. Since ancient times, bento boxes have been used to carry food to school, to work, and on trips so people can taste something that feels close to home. Thus a bento box is a portable, physical expression of a cook's love for his or her family and friends.

I remember when I used to take my mother's bento box to school in Japan; all the students would compare boxes. Some mothers devoted a great deal of time to them; I remember one that was an artful replication of a garden, complete with vegetables cut to look like flowers. On the other hand, there were simple bento boxes that spoke to less fortunate family circumstances. There was one boy in our class who had lost his mother; he brought *onigiri* (rice balls) made by his father to school every day. His box contained two plain rice balls wrapped in nori—they looked like tennis balls—and three dried sardines. He never complained.

Here is a loose recipe for some bento boxes I made for a group of friends one day when we were heading out to celebrate the springtime in Tehachapi, California. I prepared a big bento box with three *okazu* (dishes) and two rice dishes—made a few days before our outing—and then assembled them in separate bento boxes by category—rice, seafood, braised vegetables, and so forth. This family-style bento lends itself to a picnic where you are sharing food with everyone. You can also make individual bento boxes that contain a variety of *okazu*. (See Composing a Bento Box on page 161).

One of the goals of the bento box is to present a variety of food. In these boxes I included braised, grilled, and deep-fried dishes, as well as fresh vegetables and fruit to nibble on. The trick is to do some advance prep work and finish the dish on the morning of the picnic or serve the dish for dinner the night before and use the leftovers for the bento box. The rice should be fresh, so cook that on the day of your picnic. In addition to the dishes listed below, you can go through the book and find many other candidates for your bento box *okazu*. The goal is not to stress yourself out but to enjoy the creative process. People will appreciate your labor of love.

MAKES 6 TO 8 SERVINGS

OKAZU (DISHES)

    Nishime (Dashi-Infused Root Vegetables; page 129)

    Kasuzuke (Miso-Sake Lees Marinade) Mahi-Mahi; page 213)

    Crab Cream Croquettes (page 214)

THE RICE

    Grilled *Onigiri* (page 133) with Pickled Cherry Blossoms (page 271)

    Inari Zushi (Seasoned Fried Tofu Stuffed with Sushi Rice; page 131)

Preparation of the *okazu* can start 1 to 3 days ahead of time with the dishes kept on standby in the refrigerator. Here is the order in which I prepared the entries for the flower-viewing bento.

THREE DAYS BEFORE THE PICNIC

- Make the marinade for *Kasuzuke* and put the fish in the marinade.
- Make the *Nishime*.

TWO DAYS BEFORE THE PICNIC

- Season the tofu pouches for the *Inari Zushi*.
- Prepare the filling for the *Inari Zushi*.
- Prepare the base for the Crab Cream Croquettes.

ONE DAY BEFORE THE PICNIC

- Take the *Kasuzuke* fish out of the marinade and broil the fish.
- Rinse the rice for the *Inari Zushi* and *onigiri* and let it soak overnight.

ON THE DAY OF THE PICNIC

- Cook the rice for the *Inari Zushi* and *onigiri*.
- Make the *onigiri*.
- Stuff the *Inari Zushi* with the rice.
- Deep-fry the Crab Cream Croquettes.
- Reheat the *Nishime* and bring it down to room temperature.
- Cut the *okazu* (dishes) into bite-size pieces. Arrange the *okazu* and rice in bento boxes.
- Garnish with fresh vegetables, fruit, herbs, leaves, and flowers.

Enjoy the picnic!

composing a bento box

The everyday bento maker has to be simple, quick, and practical. Here are some general guidelines:

- Include something seasonal and fresh
- Welcome leftovers from last night's dinner
- Keep food at the same temperature to prevent spoilage
- Cut food in bite-size pieces so you can eat it with chopsticks or a fork
- Avoid watery foods to prevent leakage
- Make compartments in your bento box and group your food by category: rice, grilled foods, braised food, fruit, pickles
- Aim to achieve a balance among flavors and nutritional values
- Express creativity

ochazuke (rice tea soup)

Ochazuke (Rice Tea Soup) was always the last part of the meals we ate with our grandmother; my *obachama* didn't like seeing any grains go to waste. Tea soup is made with fresh or leftover rice in your rice bowl and green tea, but you can substitute chicken broth, *Misoshiru* (Miso Soup; page 118), or dashi (see pages 23–31) for the green tea. You can also make *ochazuke* a meal in itself by making it with more rice and toppings, which is what this recipe calls for. For the rice, use basic white rice. Enjoy this soup plain or with a variety of toppings, such as grilled fish, sashimi, pickled cod roe, *umeboshi* (pickled *ume* plums), and nori.

MAKES 2 SERVINGS

6 ounces (170 g) salmon or smoked salmon fillet

Sea salt

Freshly ground black pepper

1 teaspoon vegetable oil

2 cups (350 g) cooked Basic White Rice (page 46)

3 cups (710 ml) hot freshly brewed green tea

2 tablespoons *Surigoma* (page 107) or a combination of nori and toasted sesame seeds

2 tablespoons thinly sliced scallions, white and light green parts

1 tablespoon grated fresh wasabi or wasabi paste (optional)

Preheat the broiler. Line a baking sheet with aluminum foil and brush it with the oil.

Season the salmon with salt and pepper. Place the salmon on the baking sheet and broil for about 6 to 10 minutes, to desired doneness. If using smoked salmon, it will cook in half the time. Let cool and flake the meat.

Divide the rice among individual rice bowls and spoon the flaked salmon on top. At the table, pour about 1 cup (240 ml) of the hot tea over each and garnish with the *surigoma* or nori and sesame seeds, and scallions. Serve topped with the wasabi, if desired.

okazu, sweets, and beverages

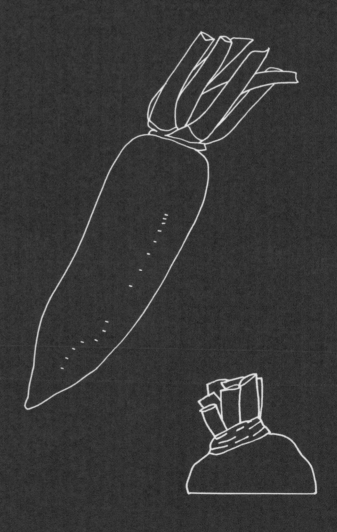

The recipes here build off the pantry recipes in part one into a full expression of Japanese home cooking. My emphasis is on adapting traditional recipes so that they work with the wide range of ingredients available to me locally in California and elsewhere in the United States. The result is a collection of recipes that make Japanese cooking more accessible to the Western cook. Some recipes call for preparing several elements in advance and assembling them later. Once you get used to this idea, you can organize your time and space to make the recipes easily and seamlessly.

In addition to the *okazu* (dishes) here, you will also find recipes for sweets and beverages. I will share some simple traditional Japanese *wagashi* (confections) as well as some sweet dishes inspired by Japanese flavors. The good news is that almost any ingredient needed for making Japanese sweets is available at Japanese markets or online.

breakfast

japanese american breakfast

I consider breakfast to be the most important meal of the day, and I was raised in a Japanese family that enjoyed a Western breakfast at home. My *obachama* (maternal grandmother) baked bread every week just so she could have toast for breakfast—decidedly non-Japanese fare. My parents also loved a big American breakfast, even after they moved back to Japan; my father liked his eggs sunny-side up with bacon.

My husband, Sakai, on the other hand, was raised in Japan on Japanese breakfasts, which follow the traditional meal composition of *ichiju sansai*: one soup and three *okazu* (dishes), with pickles and rice. He says that his engine won't start unless he has miso soup and rice in the morning. He doesn't even like bread that much! As a result, I adopted the practice of making a Japanese American breakfast for my family.

It sounds like a lot of food and a lot of work for the cook, but it really isn't. It takes me only a few minutes to assemble miso soup because I always have dashi on standby in the fridge. I heat up the dashi, add some chopped vegetables and tofu, and season it with miso. The rice cooker makes the rice; all I do is fill it with rice and water and press start. The toaster oven toasts the bread. Eggs or some grilled salmon are always part of our breakfast. I often serve natto (fermented soybeans) with the rice or toast.

The meal doesn't stop there, though. We have a glass of freshly squeezed juice, made with fruit from our grapefruit tree, and homemade yogurt with granola and sweetened *tamba* (black soybeans) or seasonal fruit. That is my *ichiju sansai* with a few additions depending on the day or season. After thirty-plus years of making a Japanese American breakfast every morning for my family, I have come to conclude that there is nothing quite as splendid and nourishing. While this section includes some wonderful breakfast recipes, don't overlook recipes from other parts of the book that can be great additions to the breakfast table such as:

- *Misoshiru* (Miso Soup; page 118)
- *Dashimaki Tamago* (Dashi-Flavored Omelet; page 82) or fried eggs
- Koji-Marinated Salmon (page 141)
- Steamed rice (preferably brown rice; see Basic Brown Rice, page 46) or Japanese Milk Bread (page 67) toast
- Nori (seaweed), cut into four pieces
- *Umeboshi* (Pickled *Ume* Plums; page 90)
- Natto (Fermented Soybeans; page 73)

homemade granola with lucky beans

Setsubun, which means "divide the season," is a Japanese festival that celebrates the arrival of spring. One of the rituals associated with the festival, said to bring luck into your house, is to throw roasted soybeans out the front door or at a member of the family wearing a demon mask while everyone shouts, "Demons out, luck in!" It is one of my favorite seasonal practices, so I like to add these lucky beans to my granola.

MAKES 6 CUPS (ABOUT 500 G)

½ cup (120 ml) maple syrup

½ cup (100 g) *kokuto* syrup (page 109) or dark brown sugar

¼ cup (60 ml) whole milk

¾ teaspoon sea salt

½ cup (120 ml) extra-virgin olive oil

2 tablespoons walnut oil

1 teaspoon vanilla extract

3 cups (240 g) rolled oats

½ cup (40 g) slivered almonds

½ cup (50 g) pepitas (hulled pumpkin seeds)

½ cup (45 g) walnut halves, coarsely chopped

3 tablespoons black sesame seeds

½ cup (100 g) Roasted Soybeans (recipe follows)

1 cup (125 g) raisins

Preheat the oven to 350°F (175°C). Line a baking sheet with parchment paper.

Combine the maple syrup, *kokuto* syrup, milk, and salt in a large saucepan. Bring to a simmer over medium heat and cook, stirring, until the sugar is completely dissolved. Add the olive oil, walnut oil, and the vanilla. Remove from heat.

In a large bowl, combine the rolled oats, almonds, pepitas, walnuts, and sesame seeds and mix well. Add to the maple syrup mixture and mix to coat the ingredients. Let stand for 15 minutes.

Turn the mixture onto the prepared baking sheet and spread it in an even layer. Bake for about 45 minutes, stirring every 10 minutes, until it is lightly browned around the edges. Remove from the oven and let stand on the sheet until cooled. The granola will continue to crisp.

Transfer the granola to a bowl. Add the roasted soybeans and raisins and mix well. Store in an airtight container at room temperature for 2 to 3 weeks or in the freezer for up to 1 month.

roasted soybeans

Roasted soybeans make a simple and delicious snack, and they also add a nice crunch and protein to granola. I use small non-GMO soybeans grown by Laura Soybeans, available online (see Resources, page 291).

MAKES ABOUT 1¼ CUPS (375 G)

½ cup (100 g) dried soybeans or *tamba* black soybeans soaked in 3 cups (710 ml) water overnight

Preheat the oven to 350°F (175°C) and line a baking sheet with parchment paper.

Drain the soybeans and spread them on the prepared baking sheet. Roast for about 45 minutes, stirring every 10 minutes, until the beans are toasted and crunchy but not browned. Remove the pan from the oven and cool to room temperature. Store the roasted soybeans in a glass jar with a tight-fitting lid in a cool place. They will keep for 1 month.

okara (soy lees) pancakes with blueberry syrup

The pancakes here are in the Japanese style (*oyaki*), which is a cross between a Western pancake and the Chinese pancakes that are stuffed with meat and vegetables. My mother's version was a pancake made with leftover brown rice, milk, egg, and flour. The addition of grains makes the pancakes dense and flavorful. I like to make *oyaki* with *okara*, the soy lees that remain when you make fresh Soy Milk (page 74). It has a similar effect as adding grains. *Okara* adds moisture with a subtle nutty flavor. *Okara* in *oyaki* is a great way to repurpose this part of the soybean. It is high in protein as well as iron, phosphorous, vitamin A, and fiber; as a bonus, it is also fat-free. You can buy *okara* at some Japanese markets that sell artisan tofu, but if you can't find it, you can use an equal amount of cooked grains such as rice, millet, rye, quinoa, farro, or oats, or a combination.

MAKES 4 SERVINGS

¾ cup (90 g) whole wheat flour

½ cup (60 g) all-purpose flour

1 teaspoon baking powder

1 teaspoon baking soda

1 tablespoon cane sugar

½ teaspoon sea salt

1 cup (100 g) *okara* (soy lees)

1 cup (150 g) cooked grains

1 large egg

1½ cups (360 ml) whole milk or soy milk

4 tablespoons (½ stick/60 g) unsalted butter

FOR THE BLUEBERRY SYRUP

2 cups (290 g) fresh blueberries

⅓ cup (65 g) cane sugar

1 tablespoon lemon juice

⅛ teaspoon sea salt

½ teaspoon vanilla extract

In a large bowl, whisk together the flours, baking powder, baking soda, sugar, and salt. In another bowl, whisk together the *okara*, cooked grains, egg, and milk. Whisk the dry ingredients into the *okara* mixture until just combined. Let the batter rest for 10 minutes.

While the batter is resting, make the blueberry syrup. Place 1 cup (145 g) blueberries in a small pot and mash them using a fork. Add the sugar, lemon juice, and salt. Bring to a boil over high heat, then lower the heat to maintain a simmer and cook for 1 minute, until it is thicker but still pourable. Add the vanilla and the remaining 1 cup (145 g) blueberries and stir to combine. Transfer the syrup to a glass container and let cool.

To make the pancakes, heat a large, well-seasoned cast-iron or nonstick skillet over medium-high heat. Add 1 tablespoon of the butter and allow it to melt. Add one quarter of the batter and spread it into an even circle. Cook until bubbles form on the top and the underside is golden brown, 4 to 5 minutes. Flip the pancake and continue to cook until browned on the second side, about 4 to 5 minutes. Transfer the pancake to a plate, then repeat with the remaining batter. Serve topped with the blueberry syrup.

mochi waffles with *tatsuta* (fried chicken) and maple *yuzu kosho*

I love mochi waffles. I use frozen mochi and put it directly onto the hot waffle maker. They come out crispy and light like crackers. I made this mochi waffle and served it with fried chicken to my son, Sakae, and his cousin, Miki, after Sakae gave Miki her first surfing lesson.

You will need to cut the mochi into thin slices so they fit evenly in the waffle maker. Allow about 2 ounces (57 g) mochi per serving. Mochi is filling, so that is probably enough for each person. The chicken is marinated in *shoyu tare* and deep-fried *tatsuta*-style. It is served with a maple *yuzu kosho* (spicy yuzu paste).

MAKES 2 TO 4 SERVINGS

EQUIPMENT
  2-quart (2 L) heavy-bottomed pot for frying
    or deep-fryer
  Waffle maker (preferably nonstick)

FOR THE CHICKEN
  ½ cup (120 ml) *Shoyu Tare* (page 105)
  1 tablespoon ginger juice (from grating ginger)
  ¼ teaspoon freshly ground black pepper,
    or to taste
  4 boneless skin-on chicken thighs
  3 cups (710 ml) grapeseed, rice bran,
    or peanut oil
  ½ cup (80 g) rice flour
  ½ cup (64 g) tapioca flour

FOR THE WAFFLES
  8 ounces (230 g) fresh or frozen mochi,
    sliced ¼ inch (6 mm) thick

FOR THE MAPLE *YUZU KOSHO*
  1 teaspoon *Yuzu Kosho* (page 112)
  ¼ cup (60 ml) maple syrup
  2 tablespoons soy sauce

To make the marinade for the chicken, whisk the *shoyu tare*, ginger juice, and ground black pepper in a large bowl. Add the chicken and marinate in the refrigerator for 30 minutes to 1 hour.

Heat the oil in a 2-quart (2 L) heavy-bottomed pot over medium-high heat to 330°F (165°C).

Take the chicken out of the marinade and dry lightly with paper towels. Slice each thigh at an angle into 1-inch (2.5 cm) pieces.

In a small bowl, whisk together the rice flour and tapioca flour. Lightly coat the chicken with the flour mixture and pat to remove excess flour.

Set a wire rack over a baking sheet or line the sheet with paper towels. Heat the oil in a 2- to 3-quart (2–3 L) heavy-bottomed Dutch oven over medium heat to 325°F (163°C). Add the chicken to the oil 4 or 5 pieces at a time and fry until lightly browned, 2 to 3 minutes. Remove the chicken from the oil and place it on the rack while you fry the other pieces. When all of the pieces are fried, raise the heat to medium-high and bring the oil to 350°F (175°C). Return the chicken to the hot oil 3 or 4 pieces at a time for a second quick frying, 1 to 2 minutes, until crispy and nicely browned. Remove the chicken from the oil and return it to the wire rack. Check that the meat is thoroughly cooked and no longer pink inside.

While you are frying the chicken, preheat the waffle maker to make the mochi waffles. Lay the mochi slices in the waffle maker. The amount of mochi will depend of the size of the waffle maker. The mochi will melt and spread, so try not to leave big gaps between the slices. Close the waffle maker. It may not want to close all the way, but it will as the mochi melts. Cook until the waffle is crispy and peels off easily, about 4 to 5 minutes. Repeat with the remaining mochi to make more waffles.

To make the sauce, combine the *yuzu kosho*, maple syrup, and soy sauce in a small bowl.

Arrange and serve immediately.

ojiya (porridge) with kabocha squash and ginger

Most Western steel-cut oat recipes are cooked with milk and sweetened with fruit and syrup, but my porridge is savory. One Japanese word for porridge is *ojiya*. It is usually made with rice or mixed grains; I like to make mine with steel-cut oats. Steel-cut oats have a coarse texture that resembles rice. The creaminess of this *ojiya* is similar to risotto but without the cheese. I add a little butter and chicken to the mix, but you can omit them to make a lighter, more traditional style of *ojiya*. Dashi is the base flavor, which is seasoned with a little salt, soy sauce, and ginger. It works very well as a savory dish for brunch or anytime you want something comforting and filling.

MAKES 4 SERVINGS

- 1 cup (115 g) steel-cut oats
- 1 teaspoon butter
- 4 cups Bonito and Kombu Dashi (page 27) or other dashi of your choice (see pages 23–31)
- 8 ounces (230 g) skinless chicken breast, cut into ½-inch (12 mm) pieces (optional)
- ¼ teaspoon freshly ground black pepper
- 6 ounces (170 g) kabocha or butternut squash, peeled and cut into 1-inch (2.5 cm) pieces
- 1 tablespoon ginger juice
- ½ teaspoon sea salt
- 2 teaspoons soy sauce
- 2 teaspoons grated ginger
- 2 scallions, white and light green parts thinly sliced

Melt the butter in a medium frying pan over medium-high heat. Add the steel-cut oats and stir frequently for 2 minutes, until slightly toasty. Turn off the heat. Set aside.

In a large sauce pan, bring the dashi to a boil over medium-high heat. Lower the heat and add the chicken, if using, and squash and cook until the chicken and squash are cooked through, 3 to 5 minutes. The squash should still have some firmness. Remove any surface scum with a slotted spoon or skimmer, then transfer the chicken and squash to a small bowl. Set aside.

Bring the dashi to a boil again over medium-high heat. Add the toasted steel-cut oats and turn the heat to low. Continue cooking for 25 minutes without stirring. Turn off the heat, return the chicken and squash to the pot, and cover. Let stand for 5 minutes for the porridge to thicken a bit more. Remove the lid and add the ginger juice, salt, and soy sauce. Stir, taste, and make adjustments as needed. Spoon into bowls, garnish with the grated ginger and the scallions, and serve immediately.

yogurt with *kuromame-no-amani* (sweetened black soybeans)

Yogurt is easy to make—it is just heated milk with dried starter added and kept in a warm place to ferment. There are a variety of yogurt starters and yogurt-making machines you can buy online. Follow the manufacturer's directions to make your yogurt. My son, Sakae, gave me a dehydrator, which I use regularly to make yogurt and dehydrate foods.

I like to serve yogurt with *kuromame-no-amani* (sweetened black soybeans). I prefer to use *tamba* (black soybeans) because they are plump and meaty. Black soybeans are eaten mainly during New Year's for good luck; the *tamba* variety only makes its appearance in the market in the late fall but the regular black soybeans are available all year round.

I serve these beans with yogurt, granola, tofu custard, or even ice cream. They also can be a component of a savory meal—served as a palate cleanser.

MAKES 1 QUART (960 ML) YOGURT

EQUIPMENT

Candy thermometer
1-quart (1 L) mason jar with lid
Dehydrator or yogurt maker

4 cups (960 ml) whole milk
1 teaspoon powdered yogurt starter
1 recipe *Kuromame-no-Amani* (page 78)

Heat the milk in a medium heavy-bottomed pot over low heat until the temperature reaches 180°F (82°C), 12 to 15 minutes. Remove from heat and allow the milk to cool to 73°F to 77°F (23°C–25°C).

Remove ¼ cup (60 ml) of the cooled milk and whisk the powdered starter into it until it dissolves. Pour the milk mixture into a 1-quart (1 L) mason jar and screw on the lid. Put the jar into a dehydrator at 100°F (37°C) or a yogurt maker set to the yogurt temperature setting. Leave for 8 to 12 hours, then check it. When the yogurt is firm but still moves a bit, take it out of the dehydrator or yogurt maker and store it in the refrigerator for at least 2 hours, where it will continue to firm up.

Serve the yogurt with some *kuromame-no-amani* stirred into it.

natto for breakfast

Natto is a very nourishing fermented food made from soybeans. I love it and eat it all the time, but I'm the first to admit that it is an acquired taste (and smell) for most non-Japanese. Natto can be enjoyed in many different ways, such as with a little soy sauce and mustard, garnished with chopped green onions, or with a beaten raw egg (be cautious about consuming raw egg). I enjoy natto with buttered toast lined with a piece of nori.

MAKES 2 SERVINGS

> ½ cup (3 ounces/85 g) Natto (page 73)
> ½ teaspoon mild prepared mustard
> 1 teaspoon soy sauce
> 2 slices bread of your choice or 2 cups (250 g) freshly cooked Basic White Rice (page 46)
> 2 teaspoons butter
> ½ sheet nori, cut into 4 pieces

In a small bowl, combine the natto, mustard, and soy sauce. Mix well until it becomes really stringy, about 1 minute.

Toast the bread then spread it with the butter. Line the toast with a piece of nori and top it with the natto mixture. If you are eating your natto with rice, spoon the rice into bowls and top with the natto mixture. You can serve the natto rice bowl with nori on top.

Serve immediately. The seasoned natto will keep in the refrigerator for up to 1 day.

vegetables and grains

kenchin-jiru (hearty vegetable soup with *sobagaki*)

When I don't have time to make soba noodles, I make these *sobagaki* (buckwheat dumplings) instead. I like to eat the hot dumplings straight, with a little soy sauce and wasabi, like soba noodles, but they also make a wonderful addition in soup. These buckwheat dumplings are light and easily digested, because they contain no gluten. I make the seasoned dashi and parboil the vegetables ahead of time and keep them on standby in the refrigerator, then I make the dumplings at the last minute. This is a hearty soup that works well for breakfast, lunch, or dinner.

MAKES 4 SERVINGS

FOR THE DASHI

> 5 cups (1.2 L) Bonito and Kombu Dashi (page 27)
>
> ⅓ cup (80 ml) *Shoyu Tare* (page 105)
>
> 1 tablespoon mirin
>
> 1 tablespoon sake
>
> Sea salt to taste

FOR THE VEGETABLES

> 4 fresh shiitake mushrooms, stems removed
>
> 8 ounces (230 g) medium-firm tofu, cut into ½-inch (12 mm) cubes
>
> About 4 (4 oz/120 g) small taro roots, peeled and sliced crosswise ¼ inch (6 mm) thick
>
> 1 medium carrot, sliced crosswise ¼ inch (6 mm) thick
>
> One 8-inch (20 cm) piece unpeeled burdock, sliced at an angle crosswise ¼ inch (6 mm) thick

FOR THE DUMPLINGS (MAKES 12 DUMPLINGS)

> ⅔ cup (156 ml) filtered water
>
> 1 cup (120 g) buckwheat flour

FOR THE GARNISHES

> 2 scallions, white and light green parts thinly sliced
>
> 1 tablespoon slivered lemon peel
>
> *Shichimi Togarashi* (page 107)

Bring the dashi to a boil in a large saucepan over medium-high heat. Add the soy sauce, mirin, and sake. Lower the heat to maintain a simmer.

To parboil the ingredients for the soup, bring a medium saucepan of water to a boil over medium heat. Lower the heat to maintain a simmer, add the mushrooms, and cook for 1 minute. Remove from the water using a slotted spoon and transfer to the pot of dashi.

Return the water to a boil over medium heat, add the taro roots and carrot, and cook for 3 minutes. Remove from the water using a slotted spoon and transfer to the pot of dashi. Return the water to a boil again, add the burdock, and cook for 5 minutes. Remove from the water using a slotted spoon and transfer to the pot of dashi. Add the tofu to the pot of dashi, bring the dashi to a low simmer, and leave it over low heat while you make the dumplings.

To make the dumplings, combine the filtered water and flour in a small saucepan and mix vigorously over medium heat until it turns into a paste, about 2 minutes. There should be no lumps. Remove from heat and continue stirring vigorously until the paste turns into a medium-soft dough. Prepare a small bowl with water to wet your hands. While the batter is still warm and moldable, use a spoon to scoop 1 scant tablespoon of batter and shape the batter with your wet hands into balls about ¾ inch (2 cm) in diameter, similar to melon balls. Set the dumplings on a baking sheet as you make them.

Add the dumplings to the soup and continue simmering over low heat for 2 minutes, until warm. The dumplings will cook in 1 minute. Turn the heat off, taste, and adjust the seasonings as you like. Add a pinch of salt if you like. Serve immediately, garnished with the scallions, lemon peel, and *shichimi togarashi*.

hiryozu (tofu fritters)

The best way to eat *hiryozu* is straight out of the hot oil, when the tofu fritters are crispy outside and soft inside. They can also be served as an appetizer with soy sauce and grated daikon or added to stews such as *Oden* (Vegetable, Seafood, and Meat Hot Pot; page 217) and *Nishime* (Dashi-Infused Root Vegetables; page 129), or even grilled like a hamburger patty (some people make tofu burgers out of them and melt cheese on top). In this recipe, the starchy root *yamaimo* (Japanese mountain yam) is used as a binder. You can buy *yamaimo* at Japanese markets. If you can't find it, substitute an egg white.

MAKES 12 SMALL FRITTERS

EQUIPMENT

 2-quart (2 L) Dutch oven or deep fryer
 Deep-fry thermometer

FOR THE FRITTERS

 One 14-ounce (396 g) block medium-firm tofu
 4 fresh shiitake or other mushrooms, minced
 1 small carrot, minced
 4 *shiso* leaves, minced
 4 ounces (113 g) *yamaimo* (Japanese mountain yam), peeled and grated, or 1 large egg white
 1 large egg yolk
 1 tablespoon kudzu, or potato starch or cornstarch
 ½ teaspoon cane sugar
 1 tablespoon sake
 1 tablespoon soy sauce, preferably *usukuchi shoyu* (light-colored soy sauce)
 ½ teaspoon sea salt
 1 tablespoon arame (optional), hydrated in ½ cup of water for 10 minutes and drained

FOR FRYING

 3 cups (710 ml) grapeseed or rice bran oil

TO SERVE

 1 cup (230 g) grated daikon radish
 2 tablespoons grated ginger
 ½ cup (120 ml) soy sauce

To remove the moisture from the tofu, wrap the block in a paper towel or clean kitchen towel, set it on a rimmed baking sheet, and place a cutting board on top of it. Let stand until the tofu is pressed down to about half of its original size, about 30 minutes. Transfer the pressed tofu to a bowl. Break it apart with your fingers and knead until smooth.

To make the fritters, combine all the ingredients in a food processor and process for 1 minute, or until smooth but not too finely pureed. Transfer the mixture to a medium bowl and form balls out of the tofu mixture using about 2 tablespoons of the mixture for each.

To fry the fritters, heat the oil to 350°F (175°C) in a 2-quart (2 L) heavy-bottomed Dutch oven or other saucepan. Slide—don't drop—the tofu balls into the oil and fry until they are browned and slightly crispy all around, 3 to 5 minutes. Only fry 3 or 4 balls at a time. Adjust the temperature so it stays at around 350°F (175°C). Remove the fritters from the oil using a slotted spoon and place on a wire rack; pat off excess oil with paper towels.

Serve with grated daikon radish, ginger, and soy sauce.

water kimchi with chilled *somen* noodles

This is a quick Korean pickle served with thin *somen* noodles. The noodles take no more than 3 minutes to cook. This is my staple summer dish and energy booster. You can drink the cold seasoned brine like soup. It is so easy to make and vegan friendly.

MAKES 4 TO 6 SERVINGS

1 large apple, peeled or unpeeled, sliced into ⅛-inch (3 mm) wedges

1 pound (455 g) daikon radish, peeled and cut into ⅛-inch (3 mm) disks then quartered

6 Persian cucumbers, sliced crosswise into ⅛-inch (3 mm) disks

1 carrot, peeled and sliced crosswise into ⅛-inch (3 mm) slices

4 Napa cabbage leaves, cut crosswise into 2-inch (5 cm) pieces

1 dried Japanese or Mexican or Italian chile, seeded and sliced thinly

2 quarts (2 L) filtered water

2 tablespoons sea salt

¼ cup (50 g) cane sugar

¼ cup (60 ml) rice vinegar

2 tablespoons minced ginger

2 cloves garlic, peeled and sliced in half

1 pound (455 g) dried *somen* noodles (preferably Moriwaki's Handa Somen)

3 cups (710 ml) filtered water

FOR THE TABLE

6 cups ice cubes

Juice of 1 lemon

4 tablespoons toasted pine nuts

1 tablespoon Korean dried chile threads or *Shichimi Togarashi* (page 107)

Combine the sliced apple, daikon, cucumbers, carrot, Napa cabbage, and sliced chile into a bowl.

Combine the water, salt, sugar, vinegar, ginger, and garlic in a large bowl and mix well. Pour over the sliced fruit and vegetables. Let stand for 30 minutes to overnight in the refrigerator.

Just before serving, cook the dried *somen* noodles in boiling water for 3 to 4 minutes, following the package instructions. Rinse under cool running water. Drain. Transfer to a bowl with the ice cubes and 3 cups (710 ml) filtered water. Bring to the table.

Add the lemon juice to the kimchi mixture and stir. Garnish with pine nuts and Korean dried chile threads or *shichimi togarashi* and serve in soup bowls with the chilled noodles.

potato *salada*

The Japanese flavors in this potato salad make it quite different from your standard American potato salad. Japanese call their version potato *salada*. I add *nerigoma* (Japanese-style tahini) to mayonnaise to give it a nutty flavor. You can also try adding miso, yuzu or lemon zest, and wasabi.

MAKES 4 SERVINGS

1 pound (455 g) Yukon Gold potatoes (about 3)

6 green beans, top ends trimmed and cut into 2-inch (5 cm) pieces

2 medium carrots, sliced ¼ inch (6 mm) thick

Pinch of sea salt

½ celery stalk, chopped

1 Persian cucumber, sliced ¼ inch (6 mm) thick

FOR THE *NERIGOMA* MAYO SAUCE

4 tablespoons *Nerigoma* (page 107)

¼ cup (60 ml) plus 2 tablespoons Japanese Mayonnaise (recipe follows)

1 tablespoon rice vinegar

1 tablespoon lemon or lime juice, or to taste

2 teaspoons soy sauce, or to taste

½ teaspoon cane sugar, or to taste

Salt and freshly ground black pepper

Fresh dill, for garnish

Place the potatoes in a medium pot and add water to cover by a few inches. Place over medium-high heat, bring to a boil, and reduce heat to low and cook until the potatoes are cooked through but still firm, 20 to 25 minutes. Drain and let cool.

Fill the pot with fresh water and bring to a boil over medium-high heat. Have a bowl filled with ice and water ready. Add a pinch of salt to the boiling water, then add the green beans and carrots and cook until they are al dente, about 3 minutes. Drain and transfer to the ice water to cool. Drain and set aside.

Peel the potatoes and cut them into ½ x 2½ x ¼-inch (12 mm x 6.5 cm x 6 mm) pieces.

In a small bowl, combine the *nerigoma*, mayonnaise, vinegar, lemon juice, soy sauce, and sugar. Taste and adjust the flavors as needed.

In a serving bowl, combine the potatoes, green beans, carrots, celery, and cucumber and toss with the dressing. Taste and season with salt and pepper. Garnish with dill and serve.

japanese mayonnaise

Japanese mayonnaise is made with a mild rice vinegar. If you want to add even more Japanese flavors, you can include 1 teaspoon miso, soy sauce, yuzu zest, pureed *umeboshi* (pickled *ume* plums), or wasabi.

MAKES 1 CUP (240 ML)

1 large egg yolk, at room temperature

½ teaspoon Dijon mustard

½ teaspoon sea salt, or to taste

1 teaspoon rice vinegar

1½ teaspoons lemon or yuzu juice

¾ cup (180 ml) olive oil

Freshly ground white pepper

In a medium bowl, whisk together the egg yolk, mustard, salt, vinegar, and lemon juice until blended. Add ¼ cup (60 ml) of the oil, drop by drop (about ¼ teaspoon at a time) and continue whisking until the mixture starts to thicken, about 4 minutes. (Adding the oil very slowly ensures that the mayonnaise emulsifies properly.) Add the remaining ½ cup (120 ml) a little faster (about 1 tablespoon at a time) and continue whisking until the mixture is fully emulsified and turns light yellow, about 8 minutes. Season with pepper. Taste and adjust the seasonings as needed. Transfer to a glass container, cover, and store in the refrigerator, where it will keep for up to 1 week.

caramelized satsuma potatoes with black sesame

This is a versatile candied vegetable side dish. Because the Satsuma potato is basically a sweet potato, you can serve it with grilled meats or even with your Thanksgiving turkey. It also makes a great snack. Substitute sweet potatoes if you can't find Satsuma potatoes.

MAKES 4 SERVINGS

- 1½ pounds (680 g) unpeeled Satsuma potatoes (1 large or 2 medium) or sweet potatoes (3 medium)
- 4 tablespoons cane sugar
- 1 tablespoon soy sauce
- 4 tablespoons mirin
- 1 tablespoon filtered water
- ¼ cup (60 ml) vegetable oil, or grapeseed or rice bran oil
- 1 teaspoon toasted black sesame seeds

Cut the potatoes into ½-inch-thick (12 mm) pieces. Soak them in a bowl of water for 20 minutes to remove the starch. Drain and dry the potatoes with a paper towel.

Combine the sugar, soy sauce, mirin, and water in a small saucepan and bring to a boil over medium-high heat and cook, stirring frequently, until it comes to a boil. Lower the heat and cook for another minute. Remove from heat.

Heat the oil in a large nonstick or well-seasoned cast-iron skillet over low heat. Pan-fry the potatoes, turning frequently, until toasted (but not burned) on both sides and a toothpick pierces a piece easily, about 3 minutes per side. Transfer the potatoes from the pan to a bowl.

Clean out the skillet, add the sauce, and cook over low heat until it begins to boil, about 1 minute. Return the potatoes to the pan and cook, stirring with a spatula for another minute, or until they are coated with the caramelized sauce.

Remove from heat and serve topped with the sesame seeds.

chirashi zushi with pomegranate seeds

Chirashi zushi is a cheerful rice salad that can be the centerpiece of a festive meal. You can prepare the fillings a day or two in advance, so all you have to do is make the sushi rice on the day you plan to serve the dish.

In this *chirashi zushi*, I have included the five basic colors: red (pomegranate seeds, carrot), green (snow peas), yellow (egg), white (rice), and black (nori). The pomegranate seeds were a last-minute addition–they are not a traditional ingredient in sushi, but they work! You can also use salmon eggs or flaked cooked salmon for the red accent; and for the green, you can use asparagus, fava beans, or green beans instead of snow peas. And you can use a variety of herbs–parsley, basil, or dill–to accent your rice. You can turn this into a seafood *chirashi* by adding sliced sashimi, cooked shrimp, or crab, or salmon eggs on top of *shiso* leaves. *Chirashi zushi* pairs well with miso soup and grilled meats and seafood.

FOR THE VEGETABLES

- 8 dried shiitake mushrooms, hydrated in 2 cups (480 ml) filtered water overnight and drained, reserving the soaking liquid
- 3 tablespoons *Shoyu Tare* (page 105)
- 1 tablespoon *kokuto* syrup (page 109) or dark brown sugar
- 2 medium carrots, quartered lengthwise
- ½ teaspoon salt
- 8 ounces (230 g) snow peas, strings removed

FOR THE EGG RIBBONS

- 4 large eggs, beaten
- 1 teaspoon cane sugar
- ½ teaspoon sea salt
- 2 tablespoons grapeseed or rice bran oil

FOR THE SUSHI RICE (MAKES ABOUT 10 CUPS/ 1.3 KG COOKED RICE)

- 2 batches freshly cooked Basic White Rice (page 46)
- ⅓ cup (80 ml) unseasoned rice vinegar
- 3 tablespoons cane sugar
- 2 teaspoons sea salt

FOR THE GARNISHES

- 3 tablespoons peeled and minced ginger, or to taste
- 20 *shiso* leaves, stems removed and minced
- ¼ cup (32 g) toasted sesame seeds
- ½ cup (87 g) pomegranate seeds
- 2 sheets nori, cut into ⅛ x 2-inch (3 mm x 5 cm) strips

To prepare the shiitake mushrooms, combine the hydrated mushrooms and their reserved soaking liquid in a small saucepan and bring to a boil over medium heat. Reduce the heat to maintain a simmer and add the *shoyu tare* and *kokuto* syrup. Simmer until most of the liquid is absorbed, about 20 minutes. Let cool, then drain. Mince the shiitake mushrooms.

To prepare the carrots and snow peas, bring a small pot of water to a boil over medium heat. Add the carrots and salt and cook until al dente, about 2 minutes. Remove from the water, cool, and mince the carrots. Bring the water back up to a boil and add the snow peas. Cook for 1 minute, then remove from the water, cool, and slice thinly crosswise.

To make the egg ribbons, whisk the eggs, sugar, and salt in a small bowl. In a well-seasoned 10-inch (25 cm) cast-iron or nonstick skillet, heat 1 tablespoon of the oil over medium-high heat. Spread the oil evenly over the pan with a paper towel. Add one quarter of the beaten egg mixture and spread it over the pan to make a thin crepe, about 1 minute. When one side is cooked, carefully flip the crepe over and cook the other side just until the egg sets, about 1 minute more. Flip or slide the cooked crepe onto a cutting board and let cool. Repeat with the remaining oil and eggs to make 4 crepes. When all the crepes have cooled, cut each in half and stack them. Slice the stack into ⅛ x 2-inch (3 mm x 5 cm) ribbons. Place in a bowl.

To make the vinegar dressing for the rice, whisk the vinegar, sugar, and salt in a small bowl until the salt and sugar are dissolved. Transfer the freshly cooked hot rice into a large bowl or *handai* (wooden sushi rice container) and add the vinegar dressing and toss to combine, moving the rice paddle at a diagonal to avoid squashing the grains. If using a *handai*, be sure to wet it first, give it a light wipe with a clean kitchen towel, and then add the rice to prevent the grains from sticking to the *handai*.

Add the minced mushrooms, carrots, ginger, *shiso*, and toasted sesame seeds. Mix gently to avoid squashing the grains.

Garnish with the egg ribbons, snow peas, pomegranate seeds, and nori strips. Serve immediately. If you make the components for this dish ahead, be sure to eat the finished dish within a day, as the sushi rice will harden quickly.

chimaki (wrapped steamed rice dumplings)

The tradition of wrapping sweet and savory glutinous rice in leaves (bamboo, banana, lotus, persimmon, and other types) is practiced throughout Asia. Wrapped Japanese rice or rice dumplings are called *chimaki*. The wrappers lend their herbaceous aromas to the food and keep the rice moist, but they are not eaten. Allow a full day to make this rice dish, including overnight soaking time for the rice.

Japanese eat *chimaki* on Children's Day, May 5, which falls on the fifth day in the fifth month of the Chinese lunar calendar. This festival originated in China to commemorate Qu Yuan (d. third century B.C.E.), the beloved poet who was banned by the king and drowned himself in the Miluo River. To protect Qu Yuan's spirit, the people scattered rice dumplings wrapped in chinaberry leaves, said to be disliked by the mythical soul-eating dragon, and tied the dumplings with strings in the five colors of red, yellow, blue, black, and white to ward off bad spirits. In addition to eating *chimaki*, Japanese fly carp-shaped wind streamers, also decorated with the five colors, on Children's Day.

Here I have used a number of fillings to make the *chimaki*. You can simplify the recipe by using just two or three. If you can't find dried bamboo leaves or other leaves to wrap the rice, use aluminum foil instead. Glutinous rice (also called sweet rice) is sold at Asian markets.

MAKES ABOUT 12 TO 16 DUMPLINGS

EQUIPMENT
  Stackable steamer

  3 cups (600 g) sticky (glutinous) rice
  12 large dried bamboo or dried lotus leaves, or aluminum foil cut into sixteen 8-inch (20 cm) squares

FOR THE PORK OR CHICKEN
  1 tablespoon sake
  1 tablespoon ginger juice
  1 tablespoon soy sauce
  ½ teaspoon ground black pepper
  ½ pound (225 g) boneless pork shoulder or skinless boneless chicken thigh, diced in ½-inch (12 mm) cubes
  1 tablespoon dried small shrimp, hydrated in ¼ cup (60 ml) water overnight
  5 dried shiitake mushrooms, hydrated in 2 cups (480 ml) filtered water overnight
  ¼ cup (60 ml) light sesame oil
  2 shallots, minced
  1 medium carrot, peeled and minced
  3½ ounces (100 g) burdock, unpeeled and minced
  8 ounces (230 g) canned cooked sliced bamboo shoots, coarsely minced
  12 roasted or canned cooked ginkgo nuts or chestnuts (optional)

FOR THE *CHIMAKI* SEASONING
  4 tablespoons *Shoyu Tare* (page 105)
  1 tablespoons sake
  2 teaspoons cane sugar
  1 tablespoon grated ginger
  ½ teaspoon sea salt
  ¼ teaspoon freshly ground black pepper

Rinse the sticky rice in a bowl and soak in 6 cups (1.4 L) of water for at least 5 hours. Drain in a mesh strainer. Let stand for 30 minutes.

To prepare the bamboo leaves, bring 5 quarts (5 L) of water to a boil in a large pot. Add the leaves and boil for 1 minute; remove from heat and soak in the water for 15 minutes. Cover lightly with a dish towel. Drain and then press the leaves with a heavy cutting board to keep them from curling. Wipe each leaf with a well-wrung wet towel before you wrap the dumplings. Japanese dried bamboo leaves are thick and long, so you will use just one leaf to wrap each dumpling. Chinese dried bamboo leaves may be smaller, so you may need to use more than one leaf to hold each dumpling in place.

In a medium bowl, combine the sake, ginger juice, soy sauce, and black pepper, then add the diced pork or chicken. Let stand for 15 minutes.

Remove the shrimp and mushrooms from their soaking water. Reserve the shrimp soaking liquid and the mushroom soaking liquid, which will serve as the dashi to season the rice. If the shrimp are large, cut them in half. Remove and discard the stems from the mushrooms and mince the mushroom caps. Set aside.

In a large wok or skillet, heat 2 tablespoons of the sesame oil over medium-high heat. Remove the pork or chicken from the marinade and saute until the color changes, about 2 minutes. Lower the heat to medium. Add the shallots and cook, stirring, until the shallots are tender, about 2 minutes. Add the shrimp, mushrooms, carrots, burdock, and bamboo and cook, stirring, for 2 minutes. Add the seasoning ingredients along with the shrimp and mushroom soaking liquids and continue to cook, stirring, for about 8 minutes, until 1 cup of the liquid remains in the wok. The ingredients will not be completely cooked at this point. They are being prepared for the steamer. Transfer the food to a bowl and add the ginkgo nuts, if using.

Clean the wok and heat the remaining 2 tablespoons of sesame oil over medium-high heat. Add the rice and cook, stir-frying the rice until it begins to turn transparent. Add the seasoned pork and vegetables and cook over medium-low heat until most of the liquid is absorbed into the rice, about 5 minutes. Remove from heat. Let the rice mixture cool down to room temperature. The rice is still not fully cooked at this stage.

To assemble the dumplings, hold one bamboo leaf vertically. Bring the bottom end of the leaf over to the other side to make an open-mouthed cone shape and tuck some of the top end of the

leaf to make an inner lining in the cone. The inner lining will help keep the grains from falling out through the gap. Holding the cone upright with one hand, put 4 tablespoons of the rice filling into the cone, making sure to include pieces of pork or chicken, shrimp, shiitake mushrooms, carrot, bamboo, and ginkgo nuts, if using. Seal the mouth of the cone by folding over the remaining part of the leaf around the cone to make a tight triangular shape. Use a long piece of kitchen twine or a thin strip of bamboo leaf to tie a knot around the triangle to hold the dumpling together. Repeat with the remaining leaves and fillings. If you are using aluminum foil, position the dumplings in the center of the foil and wrap the balls.

To cook the dumplings, heat a stackable steamer over high heat and steam the dumplings for 45 minutes to 1 hour. The dumplings can be made in advance, cooled, frozen, and resteamed (straight from the freezer) over medium-high heat for 15 to 20 minutes. Serve immediately.

koji-marinated mushrooms with rice

This fragrant rice dish combines *shimeji* and shiitake mushrooms and sliced *abura-age* (deep-fried tofu pouches) marinated in *shio koji*. *Shio koji*, or koji salt, is a probiotic seasoning made with fermented rice. I think *shio koji* is the next best thing to miso; in fact, it is a cousin of miso. It is available at Japanese markets and online, but you can easily make your own.

Marinating the mushrooms in *shio koji* deepens their umami flavor. If you would like, you can skip the deep-fried tofu and double the amount of *shimeji* mushrooms. This rice pairs well with grilled meats and seafood.

MAKES 3 TO 4 SERVINGS

> 1½ cups (300 g) short-grain white rice or *haiga* rice
>
> 1½ cups (360 ml) filtered water
>
> 1 tablespoon sake
>
> 2 teaspoons *Shio Koji* (page 95)
>
> 1 piece kombu, 2 x 2 inches (5 x 5 cm)

FOR THE KOJI-MARINATED MUSHROOMS

> 2 tablespoons untoasted sesame oil or butter
>
> 3.5 ounces (100 g) *shimeji* mushrooms, trimmed
>
> 2.5 ounces shiitake mushrooms (about 3 large), sliced about ⅛ inch (3 mm) thick
>
> 2 small (2¾ x 2¾ inch/7 x 7 cm) *abura-age* (deep-fried tofu pouches), minced
>
> 1½ tablespoons *Shio Koji* (page 95)

FOR THE GARNISHES

> 1½ tablespoons peeled and minced ginger
>
> Zest of ¼ lemon
>
> Handful of *mitsuba* (Japanese parsley), Italian parsley, or chervil leaves
>
> *Shichimi Togarashi* (page 107)

To clean the rice, place it in a bowl, add water to cover, and gently swirl the grains with your fingers until the water is nearly clear, about 20 seconds. Repeat. Drain, and let wet rice stand for 30 minutes.

Combine the rice, filtered water, sake, *shio koji*, and kombu in a 3-quart (3 L) heavy-bottomed saucepan, electric rice cooker, or *donabe* and leave to soak for 20 minutes. Follow the manufacturer's instructions for cooking with an electric rice cooker. If you are cooking on the stovetop, bring to a boil over medium-high heat. When the surface of the water begins to boil vigorously, cover the pan and decrease the heat to very low. Cook for 17 minutes without peeking. Remove from heat and let the rice rest, still covered, for 5 minutes.

While the rice is cooking, make the marinated mushrooms. Heat the oil in a medium skillet over medium heat. Add the mushrooms and cook, stirring, for 2 minutes, or until they are tender. Combine the mushrooms and the *abura-age* with 1 tablespoon of the *shio koji*. Let stand for 10 to 15 minutes. Set the marinated mushrooms and *abura-age* in a fine-mesh strainer to drain excess liquid.

Open the rice pot and discard (or eat) the kombu. Add the mushroom and *abura-age* mixture to the surface of the rice, spreading it evenly across the surface, then toss everything together with a moistened wooden paddle. Cover and let the rice rest for another 5 minutes.

Serve in bowls garnished with the ginger, lemon zest, *mitsuba* leaves, and, if you like a little kick, an accent of *shichimi togarashi*.

the life cycle of cooking

During the year I spent writing this cookbook, my cooking went beyond the kitchen and into the garden.

My garden in Los Angeles is urban; it is a small patch. I have a half dozen young and old fruit trees including a Meyer lemon, Sand Mexican lime, Santa Rosa plum, Fuyu persimmon, Hachiya persimmon, and three *sudachi* (Japanese lime) a student grafted and gave to me. I thought the last severe drought had done the garden in, but I hoped it would regenerate by giving it the attention it needed. My son, Sakae, gave me a composting book for Christmas, and I made a New Year's resolution to rejuvenate my garden.

okazu, sweets, and beverages

The first thing I did was to get rid of a plastic compost bin that was broken and leaking foul-smelling black ooze. I set up a clay compost pot, right under my kitchen window. Now I can easily come out and feed the pot with kitchen scraps, and it is pleasant to look at. I keep the brown waste, leaf clippings, and twigs in a clay pot. Every time I feed the pots with green waste, I layer it with brown waste. Part of my inspiration to try clay composting came from a YouTube posting by an Indian woman who used the balcony of her small apartment in Mumbai to make compost in multiple clay pots. Clay composting is a simple way to start composting on a small scale. My ultimate goal was to start a worm farm or vermiculture by putting some wiggler worms into the mix to help decompose the food waste into a nutrient-rich compost capable of restoring my soil.

In my garden I forecasted some mustard seeds as a cover crop and waited for spring to come. After I began regenerating my compacted soil, the next step was to build berms around the yuzu, lemon, persimmon, and plum trees to create a deep, wide moat to collect rainwater for their root system. I had some resourceful friends and students who volunteered to help in the garden; they

also brought trays full of garlic chives and red *shiso* from their gardens. I made them lunch as a way to thank them, but they always gave me more. The weeds were pulled by hand. The only tilling done to the soil was for the berms. Then the mustards were cut and set down, in lasagna-style layers, so the soil could gently rejuvenate.

After two months, the soil in the garden was loosened and ready for planting the summer crops in the vegetable patch. We planted Chioggia beets, squash, melons, San Marzano tomatoes, Lacinato kale, Japanese eggplant, Sun Gold cherry tomatoes, peppers, a medley of lettuces, lemon verbena, basil, chives, cilantro, garlic chives, and more. I learned how to properly water, pull weeds, and cut up kitchen scraps to speed up the composting process, and to collect coffee grounds from my local coffee shop. Now when I do my workshops at home, I invite my students to visit the small garden and pick the vegetables and fruit. I save the kitchen scraps to feed the always hungry worms in the compost bin. But turning kitchen scraps into soil can take a long time—six months to a year. The book project is finished, and the garden restoration project is ongoing. The full cycle of cooking begins and ends with the garden.

fish

temaki zushi (sushi hand rolls)

I make this sushi by hand, without using a bamboo mat. This is the way we made sushi at home when I was growing up. The fillings will depend on what is available at your local market. Talk to the fishmonger and select sashimi-grade raw fish. If you cannot find sashimi-grade fish, use smoked fish such as salmon or sardines. Use the freshest, preferably seasonal, vegetables–daikon radish, purple radishes, asparagus, cucumbers, *shiso* leaves–from the farmers' market. Slice up an assortment of sashimi, vegetables, and garnishes, pass the nori and sushi rice around, and have everyone wrap their own rolls. It is a great activity for children too. This sushi doesn't really require much in the way of technique! Some people may prefer to eat the sashimi straight, with garnishes, soy sauce, and wasabi.

I cook and make the sushi rice 30 minutes before serving the meal, so it stays fresh. I use short-grain and medium-grain white rice. These rice varietals are sometimes also sold as sushi rice. It is just another way to market the same varieties. See "A Fish Lesson by Niki Nakayama and Carole Iida of n/naka," page 206, for instructions on slicing and arranging sashimi and sushi. Serve *temaki zushi* and sashimi with *Misoshiru* (Miso Soup; page 118).

MAKES 6 TO 8 SERVINGS

FOR THE SUSHI RICE

2 batches Basic White Rice (page 46), freshly cooked and hot (makes about 8 cups/1.4 kg cooked rice)

⅓ cup (80 ml) unseasoned rice vinegar

3 tablespoons cane sugar

1 tablespoon sea salt

SUGGESTED SUSHI FILLINGS

1 pound (455 g) Santa Barbara spot prawns or other fresh shrimp, peeled and deveined

8 ounces (230 g) *uni* (sea urchin), removed from the shell

8 ounces (230 g) Thai snapper fillets, sliced about ⅛ inch (3 mm) thick

8 ounces (230 g) *kinki* (rock cod) fillets, sliced about ¼ inch (6 mm) thick

8 ounces (230 g) ocean whitefish fillets, sliced about ⅛ inch (3 mm) thick

4 Japanese or Persian cucumbers, seeded and julienned

1 ripe avocado, cut into 1-inch (2.5 cm) wedges

24 *shiso* leaves

½ cup (64 g) toasted sesame seeds

6 ounces (170 g) purple radish, julienned

6 *Umeboshi* (page 90), seeded and minced

3 scallions, white and light green parts thinly sliced

1 cup (50 g) daikon radish sprouts or other microgreens

1 head radicchio or Treviso, leaves separated

1 head butter lettuce, leaves separated

1 lemon, thinly sliced crosswise

1 recipe *Dashimaki Tamago* (page 82), cut into ½ x 5-inch (12 mm x 12 cm) strips

TO SERVE

Soy sauce or tamari

Grated fresh wasabi or wasabi paste

Amazu Shoga (page 87)

12 sheets nori, cut in half

To make the dressing, whisk together the vinegar, sugar, and salt in a small bowl.

While the rice is still hot, add the rest of the ingredients for the sushi rice, and gently toss, mixing the rice at an angle so you don't squash the grains. Taste and adjust the seasonings. Put a wet but well-wrung dish towel on top of the rice to keep it from drying out.

Remove the head and shells of the prawns. Firmly hold a prawn at the head with one hand. Using your other hand, firmly grip the abdomen. Try holding it as close to where the tail meets the head as possible and pull it apart. Repeat with the

remaining prawns. Devein the prawns and rinse the tails. Check with your fishmonger to make sure they are safe for eating raw. If not, cook them in boiling water until the flesh turns pink, about 1 minute, and shock in ice water. Drain. Arrange on plate with slices of lemon.

Arrange the fish fillets and other fillings on a platter, with the fish in one section and the vegetables and sliced *dashimaki tamago* in another. Put the soy sauce, wasabi, *amazu shoga*, and sheets of nori in separate bowls (but don't open the bag of nori until you are ready to wrap your sushi, or it will wilt with moisture).

Give a short stack of nori—4 to 6 pieces—and plates to each person, and you are now ready to wrap whatever combination of fillings you like. Take about 2 tablespoons of the rice and lay it on a piece of nori, spreading it with chopsticks. Next comes a dab of wasabi, followed by one, two, or more fillings on top of the bed of rice. Take the edges of the nori and wrap it around the rice and fillings. Dip it in soy sauce. Freshen your palate with a few bites of pickled ginger and then move on to your next hand roll.

mari zushi

Mari zushi is a charming ball-shaped sushi made with pressed rice and fish and vegetable toppings, served with the same toppings as sushi hand rolls. To prepare the fish, cut a fillet across the grain about ¼ inch (6 mm) thick, drawing the knife toward you in one even stroke. To assemble the *mari zushi*, drape a piece of plastic wrap in the palm of your hand. The plastic wrap will serve as a guide to shape the ball and will keep the rice from sticking to your hands. Place a bite-size piece of fish or sliced vegetable into the plastic wrap, then put a tablespoon or two of sushi rice to cover the fish or vegetable. Lift the plastic wrap, along with the rice ball, with your hands and twist the ends of the plastic wrap, gently molding the mixture into a ball. Don't twist too tightly; you want the ball to be firm on the outside but fluffy and a bit airy inside. Unwrap the plastic wrap and transfer the *mari zushi* to a platter. Continue making balls, reusing the plastic wrap as you go. Garnish the sushi with a pinch of lemon zest, grated ginger, minced chives, or sprig of dill and serve with wasabi and soy sauce.

a fish lesson
by niki nakayama
and carole nakayama
iida of n/naka

Niki Nakayama and her partner, Carole Nakayama Iida, have a renowned *kaiseki*-style Japanese restaurant in Los Angeles called n/naka. *Kaiseki* cuisine consists of a multicourse seasonal dinner rooted in Japanese tradition, and nowhere is a chef's culinary skill better demonstrated than in the elegantly and meticulously arranged dishes in a *kaiseki* meal. Niki's approach is fundamental: respect the integrity of the ingredient. Within this guiding principle, she explores modern ideas and showcases local ingredients, including sustainable seafood and vegetables. We have a lot in common.

I asked Niki and Carole if they would give me a fish lesson in exchange for a noodle lesson. Happily they agreed. Most of us home cooks seldom work with a whole fish; instead we buy fish already filleted. But I believe it is still good to know how to get from a whole fish to a fillet.

On the day of the fish lesson, Seiichi Yokota of Yokose Seafood, a Los Angeles–based fishmonger who imports and exports seafood, brought three fish caught in local coastal waters for us to practice on: a bright big red *kinki* (rock cod; also known as "idiot fish" due to its large head and small body), an ocean whitefish, and black cod.

Using a pre-scaled and gutted fish, Niki and Carole showed me how to do a *sanmai oroshi* (three-section fillet), which includes the bone section as the third piece. This method can be used for round-bodied fish such as cod and snapper. (There are other ways to fillet fish; for example, flat fish such as flounder get a five-section fillet.) But here I will focus on the three-section fillet.

THREE-SECTION FILLETING

For firm white fish: Cut off the head by sliding the knife under the bone close to the gills. This will require turning the fish over to cut through the spine. Discard the head or use it to make dashi (see below).

Holding the fish with one hand, separate the meat from the bones by sliding the knife along the belly. Start at the head, cut through the back of the rib cage, and finish at the tail. This will give you two fillets, one with bones and the other boneless. Set the boneless fillet aside.

To remove the bones from the first fillet, turn it bone-side down. With the knife nearly parallel to the cutting board, cut from the head end by sliding the knife as close as possible to the bones. This will give you two fillets, plus the skeleton with some meat on it. You now have your three-section fillet: the two you have just made and the original boneless fillet.

Now remove the skin. Place a fillet skin-side down. Hold the fillet in one hand and make an incision as close as

possible to the tail end. When the blade of the knife reaches the skin, pull the skin to the left with one hand while the other hand guides the blade to the right at a slight angle, drawing the knife back and forth and as close to the skin as possible until you reach the other end. Discard the skin.

TRIMMING A FILLET

Further filleting is necessary to make sashimi slices. Only the finest part of the fillet is used for sashimi.

First cut away the ribs by sliding the knife at an angle just underneath the bones. Then slice just above the lateral line containing the bones by drawing the knife toward you. Slice off the bone along the lateral line.

Trim the bones from the other fillet in the same way. Using tweezers, pull out any bones embedded in the fillet.

SLICING SASHIMI

There are various ways to prepare the fish:

Hirazukuri (the basic cut): This technique can be used on any type of fish. It is a rectangular cut, producing slices measuring from ⅜ inch (1 cm) to ½ inch (12 mm). Place the fillet lengthwise on a clean cutting board. The narrow end of the fillet should be facing toward you. Draw the knife from the end closest to you to the tip in one single motion, slicing through the fillet without much pressure other than the weight of the knife. Slice each piece about ⅜ inch (1 cm) thick. The firmer the fish, the thinner it can be cut. Soft-fleshed fish such as tuna should be cut rather thick, about ½ inch (12 mm). Occasionally wipe the knife with a well-wrung damp cloth to remove fresh oils.

Usuzukuri (the wafer-thin cut): This method is applied to firm fish such as Thai snapper, ocean whitefish, and flounder. Place the fillet lengthwise on a clean cutting board. The narrow end should be facing toward you. Tilt the knife toward the thick part of the fillet and slice as thinly as possible, drawing the knife from base to tip in one single motion, cutting across the grain.

Rosette sashimi: To shape the sashimi like a rosette, hold the knife inclined to the right and make wafer-thin angle cuts through the fillet in one single motion, cutting across the grain. Repeat. When you are finished, line up the pieces of the cut fish slightly overlapping one another. Carefully roll up the fish and gently open the "petals" of the rose to arrange on the plate.

SERVING SASHIMI

Serve sashimi in odd numbers—three or five pieces (avoid four pieces; four is a bad-luck number in Japan because it rhymes with *shi*, which means "death"). A dish of sashimi should have something from the sea *and* land, so you could combine sashimi with julienned daikon radish. A simple way to serve sashimi is to make a small bed of julienned daikon radish on the plate. Place a piece of *shiso* on top and then three pieces of tuna or salmon (red or pink meat). Then make another bed, using three pieces of *hamachi* (yellowtail) or snapper (white meat), alternating the type of fish to bring contrast in colors, textures, and flavors. A small chrysanthemum flower from your garden, sliced cucumbers, or citrus peel would make an excellent garnish to tuck between the sashimi or arrange on the side. See "Types of Garnishes,"

Hirazukuri (the basic cut)

Usuzukuri
(the wafer-thin cut)

Rosette sashimi (1)

Rosette sashimi (2)

Rosette sashimi (3)

page 111, for an explanation of the various herbs and aromatics you can use as garnishes. You can serve sashimi in individual small dishes or on one large dish and let everyone help themselves. Serve with wasabi and soy sauce.

ushio jiru (fish bone soup)

Every part of the fish is good, especially the bones. Fresh fish heads and bones make really good dashi to use as a base for clear soups and miso soup. My *obachama* (grandmother) was particularly fond of fish bone soup. One New Year's Eve, someone gifted her a whole Thai snapper. My mother and aunties sliced the fish into sashimi and we had a feast. But Obachama was thinking about the fish bone soup. She asked my mother about the head. It was missing. It turned out that someone had thrown it away. Obachama was furious. She sighed, "*Mottainai*" (what a waste!), for days about the lost head and the soup we never had for New Year's. The story is legendary in our family. *Ushio jiru* is served with the bones, but if you prefer not to deal with them, strain them out.

MAKES 4 TO 6 SERVINGS

- 2½ pounds (1.2 kg) fish heads and bones (such as Thai snapper, rock cod, or ocean whitefish)
- 2 teaspoons sea salt, plus more for seasoning the soup
- 1 piece of kombu, 3 x 3 inches (7.5 x 7.5 cm)
- 1 tablespoon sake
- 1 teaspoon *usukuchi shoyu* (light-colored soy sauce), or to taste
- 1 tablespoon very thinly sliced ginger (1-inch/ 2.5 cm slices)
- 3 scallions, white and light green parts thinly sliced, or *mitsuba* leaves or daikon radish sprouts

Split and cut the fish heads in half and cut the bones into smaller pieces. Rub the salt into the bones and let stand for 15 minutes. (Salting helps remove the odor of the fish.)

Bring a medium pot of water to a boil. Add the fish heads and blanch for 1 minute, then add the bones and blanch for 20 seconds. Remove from the pot and rinse in a bowl of ice water. Remove any visible fish clots with a toothpick and discard the blanching water.

Clean the pot. Add 1½ quarts (1.5 L) fresh water, the kombu, and the blanched fish heads and bones and turn the heat to high. Just before the water comes to a boil, lower the heat to maintain a simmer and remove any surface scum with a ladle. Simmer until no more visible scum rises to the surface of the soup, about 15 minutes. Add the sake and soy sauce. Taste and add more salt or soy sauce as needed. Remove the fish heads. Divide the soup and bones (or no bones) in soup bowls garnished with the ginger and scallions.

wakame soup with manila clams

This soup is inspired by *miyeok guk*, a Korean seaweed soup traditionally served on birthdays and after women give birth. I decided to make it during our trip to the Mendocino coast, where we harvested wild seaweed and did photography for this book (see "Harvesting Seaweed with Barbara Stephens and John Lewallen," page 40). It is a nurturing soup with great flavors. I used kombu as a dashi base and wakame in the soup to celebrate two of my favorite seaweeds, both of which were available fresh out of the pristine ocean of the Mendocino coast.

MAKES 4 SERVINGS

- 1 tablespoon toasted sesame oil
- 2 cloves garlic, minced
- 1 ounce (28 g) dried wakame, hydrated in 1 quart (960 ml) water, drained, and cut into 1-inch (2.5 cm) pieces
- ¼ cup (60 ml) sake
- 1½ tablespoons *usukuchi shoyu* (light-colored soy sauce)
- 6 cups (1.4 L) Kombu Dashi (page 27)
- 12 Manila clams in their shells, degritted (*see note*)
- 2 teaspoons sea salt, or to taste
- Freshly ground black pepper or *sansho* pepper
- 2 scallions, white and light green parts thinly sliced

In a large saucepan, heat the oil over medium heat, add the garlic and cook, stirring, for 2 minutes. Lower the heat and add the wakame, sake, and soy sauce and cook for an additional 3 to 4 minutes.

Add the kombu dashi, increase the heat to medium-high, and bring to a boil. Lower the heat to medium-low and add the clams. Cover and cook until the clams open, about 3 minutes. Discard any clams that don't open. Season with salt and pepper, spoon into bowls, and serve garnished with the scallions.

How to Select and Degrit Clams: Select clams that are unbroken and unopen. Unwrap them when you get home from the store so they can breathe, and store them in the refrigerator. To degrit the clams, soak them in fresh water for 20 minutes. The clams will do the work of pushing salt water and sand out of their shells. Remove the clams from the soaking liquid and discard it. Brush the clams with a firm brush and rinse to remove any remaining sand before cooking.

kasuzuke (miso-sake lees marinade) mahi-mahi

Sake lees are the leftover bits of lees from the production of sake. Here, the combination of the lees with miso makes a subtly sweet and delicious marinade and tenderizer. It works well with meaty fish such as mahi-mahi, cod, opah, halibut, or salmon. I grill or broil the marinated fish and serve it with grated daikon radish or *amazu shoga* (pickled ginger) on the side. The marinade keeps for up to 3 weeks in the refrigerator.

Chicken, pork, and beef will also marinate well in a *kasuzuke* base, and *kasuzuke* can be used for pickling vegetables such as radishes, cucumbers, and carrots as well, but you will need to pickle the vegetables in separate marinades.

MAKES 4 SERVINGS

> 1½ pounds (680 g) or 4 skin-on mahi-mahi fillets about 1 inch (2.5 cm) thick
>
> 2½ teaspoons sea salt
>
> 1 teaspoon untoasted sesame oil or grapeseed oil

FOR THE MISO-SAKE LEES MARINADE

> 4 ounces (113 g) sake lees, quartered
>
> 4 ounces (113 g) white or red miso
>
> 1 tablespoon mirin or 2 teaspoons cane sugar
>
> 1 tablespoon sake

FOR THE GARNISHES

> *Amazu Shoga* (page 000) [[ms 123]]

Sprinkle the salt on both sides of the fillets. (The salting is not for seasoning but to extract the fishy water from the flesh.) Give the thick parts of the fillets extra salting. Arrange the fillets on a wire rack set inside a baking dish so they do not touch the fishy liquid. Let stand for 20 minutes, then rinse the fillets and wipe dry with a paper towel.

To make the marinade, combine the sake lees, miso, mirin or sugar, and sake in a food processor and process until smooth.

Spread half of the sake lees mixture over the bottom of a rectangular glass container large enough to hold the fillets in a single layer (about 8 x 5 x 2 inches; 20 x 13 x 5 cm). Cut a double layer of cheesecloth to 14 x 8 inch (35 x 20 cm). Lay the cheesecloth inside the container so that 4 inches (10 cm) of the fabric hangs over the longer edges. Lay the fillets on top without overlapping. Fold the cheesecloth over the fillets to cover and spread the remaining sake lees mixture on top of the cheesecloth.

Cover the container with plastic wrap and refrigerate for 1 to 2 days. The longer you keep the fish in the marinade, the stronger and saltier the flavor will be; you could even leave them for up to 3 days. Remove the fillets from the marinade, unwrap the cheesecloth, and wipe off the marinade with a paper towel.

Set an oven rack 7 inches (17 cm) from the heat source and preheat the broiler. Line a baking sheet with aluminum foil. Lightly brush the surface of the foil with the oil.

Place the fillets on the prepared baking sheet and broil until the top is browned, 5 to 6 minutes. The fish can burn easily, so keep a close eye on the fillets.

Serve hot with *amazu shoga*. Or cool the fish to room temperature and add it to your bento box.

crab cream croquettes

The base of this croquette is made with crab meat, onions, shiitake mushrooms, and béchamel sauce. The thickened sauce is shaped into little barrels, coated with *panko* (Japanese bread crumbs), and deep-fried into a crispy croquette. These croquettes are similar to the Italian rice croquettes called *arancini* in that both are hard to resist when they are piping hot right out of the oil.

MAKES ABOUT 12 CROQUETTES

EQUIPMENT

2-quart (2 L) cast-iron pot or deep fryer
Deep-fry thermometer

6 ounces (170 g) fresh cooked crabmeat (Dungeness or Alaskan king crab), shredded
1 tablespoon sake
1 tablespoon chopped tarragon or parsley
½ teaspoon sea salt
Freshly ground black or white pepper

FOR THE BÉCHAMEL

2 tablespoons unsalted butter
½ yellow onion, minced
4 fresh shiitake mushrooms, minced
¼ cup (30 g) all-purpose flour
1 cup (240 ml) whole milk

FOR FRYING

4 cups (960 ml) grapeseed, rice bran, or peanut oil
1 cup (120 g) all-purpose flour
2 large eggs, beaten
2 cups (112 g) *panko*

FOR THE TABLE

8 ounces (230 g) cabbage, shredded
1 lemon, cut into 8 wedges
2 tablespoons grated ginger
Soy sauce
Japanese mustard

Put the crab in a medium bowl, pour the sake over it, mix, and let stand for 10 minutes. Drain.

To make the béchamel sauce, melt the butter in a medium well-seasoned cast-iron or nonstick skillet over medium-low heat. Add the onion and cook, stirring, for 3 minutes, or until it is nearly translucent. Add the mushrooms and cook for 2 more minutes. Add the flour, reduce the heat to low, and cook, stirring, for about 3 minutes. Slowly pour in the milk, stirring constantly until it reaches a thick and creamy but still pourable consistency, 5 to 7 minutes.

In a medium bowl, combine the crab, tarragon, and salt and season with pepper. Taste and adjust the seasonings to your liking. Add the crab to the sauce and transfer to the prepared baking sheet and cool completely. Refrigerate for at least 3 hours or overnight, so it can harden enough to shape. Divide the mixture into 12 equal pieces and shape into round barrels or golf ball–size balls.

To fry the croquettes, heat the oil in a 2-quart (2 L) cast-iron pot until it reaches 350°F (175°C). Set up the kitchen counter with three bowls: the first bowl for the flour, the second for the eggs, and the third for the *panko*. Start by dipping one barrel into the flour and pat to remove any excess. Then dip the barrel into the beaten eggs and finally into the *panko*. Repeat with the rest of the barrels, then, to ensure a good coating of *panko*, go back and dip the barrels in the eggs and *panko* once more. Place the barrels back on the baking sheet as you finish.

When the oil gets to 350°F, fry the croquettes, up to 3 at a time, for about 1 to 2 minutes until they are lightly browned on all sides. Do not overcrowd the pot or the temperature of the oil will drop. Remove the barrels from the oil using a slotted spoon and put them on a baking sheet lined with paper towels to absorb excess oil.

Serve the croquettes with the shredded cabbage, lemon wedges, grated ginger, soy sauce, and mustard.

satsuma-age (fish fritters)

Satsuma-age is a fried fish cake made with fresh fish paste mixed with a variety of vegetables such as onions, mushrooms, and seaweed. Cod is used in this version, but you could also use mahi-mahi, haddock, scrod, halibut, or flounder. The mixture is shaped into round, rectangular, or oval shapes. They make a great hot appetizer right out of the oil and served with grated ginger and soy sauce or mustard; they are also the star of *oden* and other hot pots or can be served over noodles.

Most Japanese buy premade *satsuma-age*, but I find most store-bought versions contain undesirable preservatives, flavor enhancers, and food coloring.

MAKES 4 SERVINGS

EQUIPMENT

    2-quart (2 L) cast-iron pot or deep fryer
    Deep-fry thermometer

    1½ tablespoons potato starch or cornstarch
    1 tablespoon filtered water
    1 tablespoon sake
    One 8-ounce (230 g) skinless, boneless cod fillet
    6 ounces (170 g) shrimp, peeled and deveined
    2 teaspoons cane sugar
    1 large egg white
    2 tablespoons grated ginger
    ½ teaspoon sea salt
    Freshly ground black pepper
    2 scallions, white parts only, minced
    ½ cup (50 g) unpeeled burdock, minced
    ½ medium carrot, minced
    About 4 cups (960 ml) grapeseed, rice bran, or peanut oil
    2 tablespoons toasted sesame oil (optional)

FOR THE TABLE

    1 recipe *Daikon Oroshi* (page 115)
    Yuzu, *sudachi*, lime, or lemon wedges
    Soy sauce
    Japanese mustard

In a small bowl, whisk the potato starch in the water and sake to dissolve.

Cut the fish and shrimp into 1-inch (2.5 cm) pieces.

In a food processor, combine the cod and shrimp and process into a paste. Add the sugar, potato starch mixture, egg white, 1 tablespoon of the ginger, and the salt and season with pepper. Process until smooth, about 30 seconds. Transfer the paste to a medium bowl and stir in the scallions, burdock, and carrot. At this point the paste can be covered and refrigerated for up to 12 hours if you want to use it later.

When you are ready to fry, prepare a small bowl of water for lightly wetting your hands to prevent the paste from sticking. Using your hands, make little nuggets or balls using about 1 tablespoon of fish paste. You can also make other shapes, such as patties.

Fill a deep, heavy-bottomed saucepan with enough grapeseed oil to come at least 2 inches (5 cm) up the sides of the pan. Add the sesame oil for a more aromatic flavor, if you like. Heat the oil to 320°F (160°C). Make sure to maintain this temperature so the fritters don't brown too quickly while remaining raw in the center. The temperature will drop when the fritters are added to the oil, so you will need to make adjustments.

Drop 4 or 5 fish balls into the oil and fry until they are golden and puffy, 3 to 4 minutes. Remove them with a slotted spoon. Slice one in half to check that it is cooked in the middle. Continue frying until all the fritters are cooked. Drain on paper towels. The fritters will deflate slightly upon cooling. Serve hot or at room temperature garnished with the remaining 1 tablespoon grated ginger, *daikon oroshi*, and citrus wedges. The fritters are best eaten while piping hot. They also freeze well; they will keep for up to 1 month in the freezer. To reheat, simply warm them on the grill or add them to a warm dish, such as *Oden* (Vegetable, Seafood, and Meat Hot Pot; page 217) or noodles.

oden (vegetable, seafood, and meat hot pot)

Nabemono (hot pot) is a big hearty soup that the chef brings in its cooking pot right to the table. It is a very convivial way to dine, with everyone helping themselves while the host is in charge of replenishing the pot with ingredients and dashi. With a diligent host, everything in the pot is always hot and freshly cooked. See page 218 for my general guidelines for making hot pot.

Oden is one of the oldest and most popular Japanese hot pots. What goes into *oden* varies from home to home, shop to shop, and region to region. Most Japanese cooks make *oden* with store-bought *oden* ingredients, but I try to make as many of the entries from scratch as possible because I don't like all the preservatives that industrial manufacturers use—my constant refrain. So my *oden* is unique in that way. It takes a little more work than buying premade ingredients, but it is well worth the effort. My process is to choose two or three items to make a day or two ahead and then a few more to make the day I serve the *oden*. Despite the time it takes to make *oden*, it is my most popular hot pot workshop. Patricia Judice, a student and friend who tested this recipe, split the task of making the *oden* entries with several of her friends and turned it into a potluck party. It was a big success! *Oden* tastes better the day after it is made and the ingredients have had a chance to soak up a bit of the broth, but you can start eating it the day you make it.

MAKES 4 TO 6 SERVINGS

MAKE-AHEAD *ODEN* ENTRIES
The following entries can be kept in the refrigerator, and among them the fish fritters and tofu fritters can be stored in the freezer and kept for up to 1 month.

Kobumaki (Pork Kombu Roll; page 229)
Satsuma-Age (Fish Fritters; page 215)
Hiryozu (Tofu Fritters; page 189)

DAY OF, OR ONE DAY IN ADVANCE *ODEN* ENTRIES
These entries will go straight into the pot, without any advance preparation.

Mochi-Stuffed Fried Tofu Pouches
    (recipe follows)
Cabbage Rolls (recipe follows)
1½ pounds (680 g) daikon radish
One 9-ounce (255 g) block *konnyaku* (yam cake)
6 hard-boiled eggs, peeled
2 large carrots, sliced into ½-inch (12 mm) coins
1 pound (455 g) Yukon Gold potatoes (about 3),
    peeled and cut in half

FOR THE DASHI
4½ quarts (4.5 L) Bonito and Kombu Dashi
    (page 27)
¾ cup (180 ml) *usukuchi shoyu*
    (light-colored soy sauce)
¾ cup (180 ml) mirin
¼ (60 ml) cup sake
1 teaspoon sea salt, or to taste

FOR THE TABLE
Soy sauce
Japanese or Dijon mustard

Hot Pot Guidelines

- Use a 4- to 5-quart (4 to 5 L) *donabe* (clay pot) or other wide-mouthed heavy-bottomed pot.

- Make your dashi. You will need 3 to 4 quarts (3 to 4 L) stock. It can be as simple as cold-brewed Kombu Dashi (page 27) or Bonito and Kombu Dashi (page 27). You will need to replenish the hot pot with more dashi, as the dashi will reduce as the hot pot cooks. It is your job as the chef to always make sure there is enough dashi in the pot. Use the lid of the pot to control the temperature of the hot pot; it should always be simmering.

- Put together a variety of entries. Freshness and presentation are the keys to making an attractive and tasty hot pot.

- The components go into the pot and can be heated over your kitchen stove and then brought to the dining table or cooked on a portable cooking unit at the table (see page 19). Vegetables cook at different rates; you can parboil those that take longer, such as daikon radish, potatoes, and burdock. If you have leafy vegetables such as Napa cabbage or spinach, take care not to overcook them. You want the cabbage to still have a crunch and the spinach to look bright green. I add the leafy greens at the very end to wilt them, just before serving.

- Keep the pot on a simmer, never a boil.

- To serve, give each diner a bowl, a pair of chopsticks, and a spoon to scoop up the delicious broth. All should help themselves from the pot. Don't forget to put the condiments on the table.

- When all of the components have been eaten and only the rich broth is left in the pot, it is the cook's job to add more fresh ingredients. Make sure you have enough prepared ingredients to replenish the pot two or three times.

- You may finish the hot pot with porridge or noodles cooked in the rich dashi (see *Zosui* [*Nabe* Broth Rice Porridge], page 236).

Choose 4 or 5 entries from the lists above for your *oden*.

For the daikon radish, peel and slice it into disks approximately ¾ inch (2 cm) thick. Use a knife to score one side of each disk in a crisscross pattern so the dashi can penetrate the daikon in the hot pot.

For the *konnyaku*, bring a small pot of water to a boil over high heat. Add the *konnyaku* and blanch for 2 minutes to remove any odor. Drain. Slice the *konnyaku* crosswise into thirds, then cut each rectangle diagonally in half to make 6 triangles total. Score one side of each triangle in a crisscross pattern so the dashi can penetrate during cooking.

Season the dashi with the soy sauce, mirin, sake, and salt and mix well. You can store it in the refrigerator, where it will keep for up to 1 week.

Once all of your components are completed and assembled, you are ready to make your *oden*. Bring 8 cups (2 L) of the seasoned dashi to a boil over medium heat in a large saucepan or *donabe*. You will have a little more than 8 cups (2 L) in reserve. Use it to replenish the pot. Add the *kobu-maki*, *satsuma-age*, *hiryozu*, mochi-stuffed fried tofu pouches, cabbage rolls, daikon, *konnyaku*, eggs, carrots, and potatoes to the pot. Turn heat to low and simmer for 30 to 40 minutes.

Group the food by category to allow diners to choose easily rather than search through a hodgepodge of a soup. Bring the heated pot of *oden* to the table and set it on a hot plate so it can continue to simmer over low heat. Invite diners to help themselves directly out of the pot. Replenish the pot with ingredients, including dashi, as needed.

Serve with soy sauce and mustard.

mochi-stuffed fried tofu pouches

I love how *abura-age* (deep-fried tofu pouches) can be used as edible pillows to hold food. The hard mochi will melt inside while it cooks in the *oden* broth, so when you bite into it, the mochi will be soft, chewy, and delicious.

> 6 small (about 2¾ x 2¾ inch/7 x 7 cm) *abura-age* (deep-fried tofu pouches), blanched in boiling water for 20 seconds and drained
>
> Three 1½-ounce (50 g) pieces mochi

Slit one end of each pouch with a knife to make an opening. Cut each piece of mochi into 6 pieces and stuff each pouch with a piece. Use toothpicks to stitch or close the mouth of each pouch. Set aside to add to the *oden*.

cabbage rolls

I love a good cabbage roll. Whenever I see cabbage roll on a menu, I go for it. I have tasted Russian, Polish, Romanian, American, and Chinese cabbage rolls, and more. My cabbage roll recipe is pretty loose, so you can deviate and add cooked grains or other spices if you like. You can also substitute the ground chicken with ground pork or flaked salmon. This is one of my favorite entries for *oden*.

MAKES 8 CABBAGE ROLLS

> 8 large green or Savoy cabbage leaves (the large, outer leaves)
>
> 8 ounces (230 g) ground chicken
>
> 3 fresh shiitake mushrooms, minced
>
> ½ medium yellow onion, minced
>
> 1 tablespoon of ginger juice
>
> 1 tablespoon potato starch or cornstarch
>
> 1 tablespoon sake
>
> 2 teaspoons soy sauce
>
> ½ teaspoon sea salt

Bring a medium pot of water to a boil over medium-high heat and have a bowl filled with ice water ready. Add the cabbage leaves and blanch for 2 minutes. Remove from the pot and transfer to the ice water. Drain. Cut the white vein from the bottom of each leaf, making a V-shaped cut. Set aside.

Combine the ground chicken, mushrooms, onion, ginger juice, potato starch, sake, soy sauce, and salt and mix with your hands until very smooth. Make 8 balls of the mixture. Place one ball on a cabbage leaf and overlap the cut ends of the leaf. Fold in the sides toward the middle of the leaf, beginning from the cut end, then fold in the left and right sides. Hold the roll together at the end with a toothpick. Cook the cabbage rolls in the dashi as instructed in the *oden* recipe.

considering the ocean with seiichi yokota

I lived near the sea in Kamakura, thirty miles west of Tokyo, in the 1960s, back when the waters were pristine. I loved going to the beach with Obachama (my grandmother) at dawn. We would buy fish directly from the fishermen who were sorting out their morning's catch, mostly small fish such as mackerel and sardines. At home we seldom ate big fish from the deep sea such as tuna or yellowtail; they were precious and reserved for special occasions. But at school they sometimes fed us whale-meat fritters, because whale was an economical and nourishing protein. We all ate a lot of fish, but there seemed to be plenty of it in the ocean.

In the fifty years since my whale-meat school days, however, we have experienced an alarming decline in the health of the oceans due to overfishing, pollution, and climate change. There is less fish to eat in Kamakura, and most of the fishermen are gone. Marine biologists such as Sylvia Earle have given us the grim reality about the ocean: we have eaten more than 90 percent of the big fish in the sea, half of the coral reefs have disappeared, and there is a mysterious depletion of oxygen in large areas of the Pacific Ocean that is causing the sea life to die.

Seiichi Yokota of Yokose Seafood, a seventh-generation wholesale fish business, moved to Los Angeles from Toyama Prefecture in Japan to expand his family business. According to Yokota, part of the problem is that people have grown accustomed to eating the most popular fish, such as tuna and salmon. It echoes what is happening to the farmlands in the United States, where farmers are growing primarily corn and soybeans—monocropping for the sake of yield but at the expense of the health of our soils.

Since Yokota's arrival in California four years ago, he has been bringing fish from Japan, but also working with fishermen in Southern California and along the central coast to explore local fish. The good news is that a variety of coastal fish are thriving—albacore tuna, *kinki* (rock cod), halibut, ocean whitefish—and he is slowly experiencing an upward trend in his business by selling these local fish. Chefs are discovering that there are more than decent fish to be had in our coastal waters. Yokota is also making a difference by improving the way fish is processed in the United States. He says that proper handling of fish can preserve its freshness and improve its flavor. He uses *ikejime*, a Japanese method of slaughtering fish, which he says is the fastest and most humane method. All of his activities as an artisan fishmonger stem from his fundamental respect for the ingredient, a principle by which he lives and works.

There are a number of things we as home cooks can do to help protect the oceans. We can eat fish that is sustainably caught. We can avoid wild fish such as bluefin tuna and eel that are on the endangered list. (A bluefin tuna, for example, spawns just once a year and does not reach reproductive maturity until it is between eight and twelve years old. If we overfish bluefin tuna, we essentially stop their reproductive cycle. This makes them more vulnerable to overfishing than other tuna species

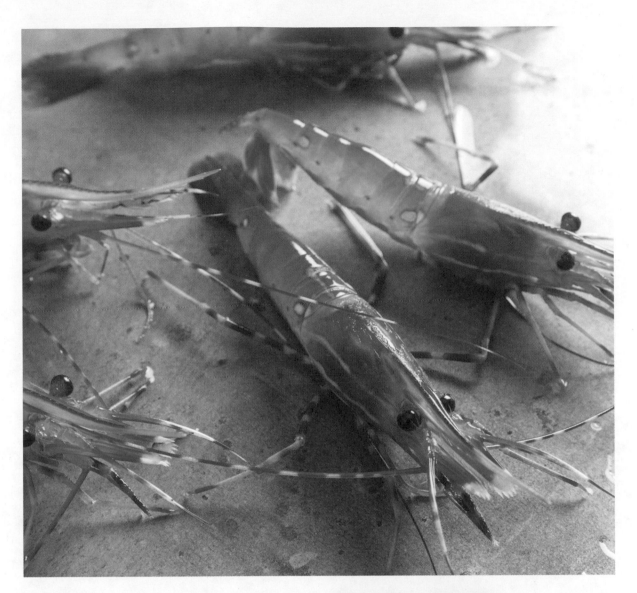

that can spawn several times in a year.) If you live near coastal zones, you can seek out opportunities to meet your local fishermen, get to know your local fish, and use that fish in your cooking. You can also regularly check the Monterey Bay Aquarium's Seafood Watch, which will tell you which fish to eat and which to avoid. If we all take a few steps to protect our oceans and restore their biodiversity in our lifetime, we can still save the ocean, which will ultimately save us.

meat

santa maria–style tri-tip with five *yakumi* (aromatics and herbs)

When entertaining family and friends in the summertime, I like to put a couple of tri-tips on the charcoal grill. I feel very American when I barbecue tri-tip, which I am told originated in the mid-nineteenth century when ranchers of the central California coast would host a feast each spring for their *vaqueros* (cowboys). I marinate the beef a day in advance using a combination of American and Japanese spices, and I serve it with a variety of *yakumi* (Japanese herbs and aromatics including *yuzu kosho* [spicy yuzu paste], julienned daikon radish, *shichimi togarashi* [seven-spice blend], chopped *shiso* leaves, scallions, and ginger). I pass big bowls of steamed rice around so everyone can take some to make their own rice bowls. I also like to serve the tri-tip with Potato *Salada* (page 189). A beautiful accompaniment to this meal is sake from my friends Ken Hirashima and Rumiko Obata, proprietors of Obata Shuzo on Sado Island in Niigata–Manotsuru "Bulzai" ginjo sake–which has fruity aromas and is dry and refreshing with a hint of pepper in the finish.

MAKES 4 SERVINGS

FOR THE TRI-TIP
> 1 teaspoon sea salt
> ½ teaspoon freshly ground black pepper
> 1 teaspoon sweet paprika
> 1 teaspoon *La-Yu* (page 109), or to taste (optional)
> 2 or 3 rosemary sprigs
> 1 clove garlic, smashed
> 1 tri-tip steak, 2 to 2½ pounds (900 to 1100 g)

FOR THE FIVE *YAKUMI* GARNISHES
> 20 *shiso* or basil leaves, thinly sliced
> ¼ cup (30 g) peeled and minced ginger
> 6 scallions, white and light green parts thinly sliced
> 1 cup (100 g) daikon radish sprouts, other sprouts, or microgreens
> 8 ounces (230 g) daikon radish, peeled and julienned

TO SERVE
> *Yuzu Kosho* (page 112)
> 5 sheets nori, cut in half
> 1 lemon, cut into 8 wedges

Combine the salt, pepper, paprika, *la-yu*, the leaves from 1 rosemary sprig, and garlic to make a marinade. Rub it into the tri-tip all over. Cover and marinate in the refrigerator for at least 3 hours or up to overnight.

When you are ready to grill, remove the tri-tip from the refrigerator and bring to room temperature while you prepare a charcoal grill or preheat a gas grill to high. Place the roast on the grill and sear on one side for 7 to 8 minutes. Turn the roast and sear the other side for 7 to 8 minutes, until it is browned.

Move the seared meat to a cooler part of the grill or lower the heat on the gas grill to medium-high. Flip the meat again and cook until the temperature in the center of the meat reaches 135°F (57°C), about 20 minutes. Baste with *la-yu* if you would like to add more spice.

Remove the tri-tip from the grill and let rest on a wire rack or cutting board for about 15 minutes for medium-rare. Resting it will allow the juices to redistribute evenly throughout the meat.

To make the *yakumi* garnishes, combine the *shiso*, ginger, scallions, daikon sprouts, and julienned daikon in a medium bowl set in ice water and let stand for 5 minutes. Store in a container with a lid, lined with paper towels, in the refrigerator until ready for use (they will keep for 2 to 3 days).

Slice the meat ¼ inch (6 mm) thick against the grain. Set the meat on a platter and garnish with the *yakumi*, *yuzu kosho*, nori, and lemon wedges.

grilled lamb chops with spicy miso

When I make grilled lamb chops, I like to serve them with a spicy miso sauce.

MAKES 4 SERVINGS

- 1½ teaspoons chopped rosemary
- ½ teaspoon salt
- ¼ teaspoon freshly ground black pepper
- 1 clove garlic, crushed
- 1½ pounds (680 g) lamb chops with ribs, about 8, trimmed
- 1 tablespoon olive oil

FOR THE SPICY MISO SAUCE

- 3 tablespoons light sesame oil
- 1 serrano chile, seeded and minced, or ¼ teaspoon *Shichimi Togarashi* (page 107)
- 3 tablespoons red miso
- 2 teaspoons cane sugar, or more to taste
- 10 *shiso* leaves, minced
- 2 scallions, green parts minced
- 1 teaspoon lemon zest

Combine the rosemary, salt, pepper, and garlic in a small bowl. Place the lamb chops in a shallow dish and rub the herb mixture and olive oil over the meat, turning the meat over a few times. Cover and marinate in the refrigerator for at least 4 hours or overnight, turning the meat occasionally.

To make the spicy miso sauce, combine the sesame oil, chile, miso, and sugar in a small bowl and mix well. Add the *shiso* leaves, scallions, and lemon zest and stir until just combined. Set aside.

Preheat a grill to very high until almost smoking. Take the meat out of the marinade and pat dry. Place the meat on the grill and sear for about 2 minutes, turning once, and cook for another 3 to 3½ minutes to desired degree of pinkness.

mapo tofu

This is one of my favorite Chinese dishes. I have adapted it by combining Japanese miso with the Chinese fermented beans *doubanjiang* and *dou-chi* to make a spicy meat sauce that wakes up the mild tofu. I like to eat this dish with rice, of course. You can buy the Chinese ingredients at Chinese markets.

MAKES 4 SERVINGS

> Pinch of salt
>
> 2 pounds (910 g) medium-firm tofu (2 blocks), drained and cut into ¾-inch (2 cm) pieces

FOR THE SAUCE

> 2 teaspoons minced garlic
>
> 1 tablespoon finely minced ginger
>
> 1 tablespoon red miso
>
> 1 to 1½ tablespoons *doubanjiang* (fermented broad beans)
>
> 2 teaspoons *dou-chi* (fermented black beans), minced
>
> 1 to 1½ teaspoons minced dried Japanese chile pepper
>
> ½ to 1 teaspoon ground Sichuan peppercorns

FOR THE *MAPO* TOFU

> 1 tablespoon vegetable oil
>
> 8 ounces (230 g) ground pork, chicken, or beef
>
> 2 cups (480 ml) chicken stock
>
> 2 tablespoons cornstarch or potato starch, dissolved in ¼ cup (60 ml) water
>
> 2 tablespoons sake
>
> 2 tablespoons soy sauce

TO SERVE

> 3 scallions, white and light green parts thinly sliced
>
> *La-Yu* (page 109)

Bring a pot of water to a boil in a medium saucepan over medium-high heat and add a pinch of salt. Add the tofu and blanch for 1 minute. Drain. (Blanching firms up the tofu and prevents it from falling apart while cooking).

Combine all the sauce ingredients in a medium bowl and mix well.

Heat the oil in a wok or large skillet over medium-high heat. Add the ground pork and cook, stirring, until cooked through, 5 to 8 minutes. Add the sauce and chicken stock, then decrease the heat to low and simmer for 5 minutes, until the meat sauce cooks in its own juices. Add the cornstarch mixture, increase the heat to medium-high, and cook for 2 to 3 minutes so the meat sauce thickens. Add the tofu, sake, and soy sauce, lower the heat, and simmer for 2 to 3 minutes to heat the tofu. Taste and adjust the seasonings to your liking.

Remove from heat and serve immediately over rice, garnished with the scallions and with *la-yu* on the table for anyone who wants more spice.

okazu, sweets, and beverages

kobumaki (pork kombu roll)

Kombu is used here to wrap meat or fish like a cabbage roll. In this recipe, I use thin slices of *sukiyaki*-style pork as the filling; beef, chicken, and salmon also work well. *Kobumaki* can be added to *oden* or can be served for New Year's as a good luck dish, because kombu rhymes with *yoro-kobu* (happiness).

Kampyo (dried gourd shavings) is used to tie the rolls. If you can't find *kampyo*, use kitchen twine.

MAKES 4 TO 6 SERVINGS

12 ounces (340 g) *sukiyaki*-style
    (thinly cut) pork
4 tablespoons soy sauce, plus more for
    serving (if not serving in *oden*)
3 tablespoons sake
1 tablespoon cane sugar
6 pieces of kombu, about 2¾ x 12 inches
    (7 x 30 cm) each, hydrated in 4 cups (960 ml)
    water for 3 hours, soaking liquid reserved
1 tablespoon mirin
¾ ounce (20 g) *kampyo* (dried gourd shavings),
    rubbed with 1 teaspoon salt and then hydrated
    in 2 cups (480 ml) water for 3 hours, drained
Wasabi

Season the pork with 1 tablespoon soy sauce, 1 tablespoon sake, and the sugar.

Spread one hydrated piece of kombu on a cutting board. Lay several pieces of meat lengthwise across the kombu and then roll it into a pinwheel. Tie the roll with strips of *kampyo* in several places so the roll stays together.

Place the rolled kombu and pork in a large saucepan in a single layer. Add the kombu soaking liquid and bring to a boil over medium-high heat. Lower the heat, add the remaining 3 tablespoons soy sauce, 2 tablespoons sake, and the mirin and stir the liquid with a ladle. Simmer for 20 to 30 minutes, until most of the liquid is absorbed. Leave the kombu rolls whole or cut them in half crosswise if they are large. Add the rolls to your *Oden* (Vegetable, Seafood, and Meat Hot Pot; page 217) or *Nishime* (Dashi-Infused Root Vegetables; page 129), or serve them warm or at room temperature with wasabi and soy sauce.

chikuzen-ni (braised chicken and vegetable stew)

This dish features a few unique ingredients. The first is *konnyaku* (yam cake), a gelatinous, flavorless gray or white block made from the corm (a part of the stem) of the konjac plant, which belongs to the yam family. Its nickname is "broom of the stomach," and it is considered a health food because it aids digestion. Like plain gelatin, *konnyaku* doesn't have much flavor, but in this recipe it takes on the flavor of the seasoned dashi. *Chikuzen-ni* tastes even better a day or two after you make it, as the vegetables have time to soak up even more of the seasoned dashi. You can serve this as a New Year's entry like we do in our family or add it to your bento box.

MAKES 4 TO 6 SERVINGS

- **4 boneless skin-on chicken thighs**
- **One 12-inch (30 cm) piece unpeeled burdock root**
- **2 medium carrots, peeled**
- **4 medium taro roots, peeled**
- **12 ounces (340 g) medium lotus root, peeled**
- **1¼ teaspoons salt**
- **12 snow peas, strings removed, or green beans, trimmed**
- **One 9-ounce (255 g) block *konnyaku* (yam cake)**
- **4 dried shiitake mushrooms, hydrated in 2 cups (480 ml) water overnight, soaking liquid reserved**
- **2 tablespoons grapeseed oil or untoasted sesame oil**
- **6 cups (1.4 L) Kombu Dashi (page 27)**
- **¾ cup (180 ml) *Shoyu Tare* (page 105)**
- **1 teaspoon *kokuto* syrup (page 109) or dark brown sugar**
- **2 tablespoons sake**
- **1 tablespoon ginger juice**

Cut each chicken thigh into 4 to 6 bite-size rectangular pieces.

Slice the burdock crosswise at an angle ¼ inch (6 mm) thick. Slice the carrot into 1¼ x 2-inch (3 x 5 cm) pieces. Rub the taro roots with 1 teaspoon of the salt to remove the sticky surface film. Rinse and drain. Cut the taro in half if large. Slice the lotus root crosswise ¼ inch (6 mm) thick. If the lotus root is large, cut it in half before slicing.

Bring a small pot of water to a boil over medium heat to parboil the ingredients. Add ¼ teaspoon of the remaining salt. Add the snow peas and blanch for 1 minute. Remove from the pot and set aside. Add the taro and blanch for 2 minutes. Remove from the pot and set aside. Add the *konnyaku* and blanch for 1 minute. (This removes the odor from the *konnyaku*.) Drain and set aside. Rinse the *konnyaku* and cut the block into 2-inch (5 cm) rounds using a soup spoon. Fill the same pot with new water and bring to a boil. Add the burdock and cook for 10 minutes, or until it is al dente. Set aside.

In a large saucepan, heat the oil over medium-high heat and sear the chicken pieces skin-side down until they are lightly browned, then add the burdock, carrots, taro roots, lotus root, and *konnyaku*. Add the dashi, *shoyu tare*, *kokuto* syrup, sake, ginger juice, and 1 cup (240 ml) of the reserved mushroom soaking liquid (keep the remaining 1 cup/240 ml mushroom soaking liquid on hand in case you need more dashi to adjust the flavors later), bring to a boil, then lower the heat to medium and cook for 10 minutes. Remove the chicken, taro roots, and carrots so they don't overcook.

Decrease the heat to low and simmer for another 10 to 15 minutes, until about a third of the liquid is gone. Return the chicken, carrots, and taro roots to the pot and simmer for 5 minutes until heated. Garnish with the snow peas and serve warm or at room temperature. This dish tastes better the second day and keeps in the refrigerator for 3 to 4 days.

goya champuru (bitter melon, pork, and tofu scramble)

This is a classic Okinawan stir-fried dish that uses *goya* (bitter melon)—the most bitter fruit in the world. It is so acerbic that it is inedible unless it is blanched in salt water or rubbed with salt. But once that is done, it turns very crisp and its bitterness loses its bite. Bitter melon has been used as an herbal remedy in Asia for hundreds of years. You can find bitter melon at Asian markets. My recipe for *champuru* contains pork, but you can leave it out to turn this into a vegetarian dish. If buying prepared pork, get *sukiyaki*-style or *shabu shabu*-style (thinly sliced) pork.

MAKES 4 SERVINGS

> 1 piece of kombu, 2 x 2 inches (5 x 5 cm)
>
> ½ cup (120 ml) filtered water
>
> 1 medium bitter melon (*goya*)
>
> ½ teaspoon sea salt
>
> 1 block medium-firm tofu (about 14 ounces/ 396 g), drained
>
> 8 ounces (230 g) pork belly, thinly sliced
>
> Freshly ground black pepper
>
> 2 large eggs
>
> 2 tablespoons toasted sesame oil
>
> 1 tablespoon soy sauce

FOR THE GARNISHES

> ½ cup (4 g) bonito flakes
>
> Dried chile flakes
>
> 2 scallions, white and light green parts thinly sliced

Soak the kombu in the filtered water for 1 hour or longer to make dashi. Set aside.

Cut off the ends of the bitter melon and cut it in half lengthwise. Use a spoon to remove the seeds and the pith from the center. Cut the bitter melon diagonally into ¼-inch (6 mm) slices. Sprinkle ½ teaspoon of salt over the slices and lightly massage until water starts to come out, about 2 minutes. Place them in a colander to drain for 15 minutes. Rinse in cool running water and drain. Set aside.

Wrap the tofu in a double layer of paper towels, place on a rimmed plate, lay a cutting board on top, and leave for 20 minutes to press out excess water. Cut the tofu into 1-inch (2.5 cm) cubes.

Season the pork with a few pinches of sea salt and pepper. Beat the eggs in a small bowl and season with a few pinches of salt and pepper.

Heat the oil in a large skillet over medium-high heat. Add the pork and cook, stirring, until it starts to brown a little. Add the bitter melon and tofu and continue to cook, stirring, until the melon is tender, 2 minutes. Add the kombu dashi and soy sauce and mix well. Push the tofu and bitter melon to one side of the pan. Add the eggs to the other side of the pan and scramble them with long cooking chopsticks or a spatula. Mix everything together, remove from heat, and transfer to a serving platter.

Serve immediately, sprinkled with the bonito flakes, chile flakes, and scallions.

pork and vegetable *mizore nabe* (hot pot)

Nabe (hot pot) is an easy and convivial way to enjoy food and conversation with friends and family. It is a dish intended to be cooked and served at the table with a tabletop stove. *Mizore nabe* is named after the minced daikon radish that covers the pork and vegetables; the word *mizore* means "sleet." While the traditional *mizore nabe* is made with grated daikon radish, I prefer the texture of finely minced daikon instead; the choice is yours. There are two options for the dipping sauce: ponzu sauce or sesame *tare*. You can serve both if you like and let your guests decide. The pork is available in Asian markets as *shabu shabu*-style or *sukiyaki*-style cuts. Before you start making this recipe, read my Hot Pot Guidelines (page 218).

After you finish eating all the pork and vegetables, you will have a rich broth left over in the hot pot. You can season it with salt and pepper and enjoy it as is, use it to make *Zosui* (*Nabe* Broth Rice Porridge; page 236), or stick a few pieces of mochi in the toaster oven until they puff up and add them to the hot broth. These finishing dishes will give your diners even more enjoyment. If using a portable butane stove indoors, make sure you have good ventilation and read the manufacturer's instructions.

MAKES 4 SERVINGS

EQUIPMENT

Portable butane stove

Donabe (clay pot) or 4- to 5-quart (4 to 5 L) heavy-bottomed pot

1 pound (455 g) daikon radish, peeled and finely minced

1 piece kombu, about 3 x 3 inches (7.5 x 7.5 cm)

FOR THE TABLE

1 pound (455 g) medium-firm tofu, drained and cut into 1½-inch (4 cm) pieces

1½ pounds (680 g) pork belly or boneless pork shoulder, thinly sliced and cut into 2-inch (5 cm) pieces

12 ounces (340 g) greens (such as spinach or mizuna), ends trimmed; cut the leaves, reserve the stems, about 1 bunch

12 ounces (340 g) Napa cabbage, cut crosswise into thirds

1 bunch scallions, white and light green parts sliced crosswise into 3-inch (12 mm) pieces

8 fresh shiitake mushrooms, stems removed

1 carrot, sliced into ¼-inch (6 mm) rounds (or use a small cookie cutter to make flower shapes)

1 recipe of Ponzu Sauce (page 105)

1 tablespoon toasted sesame oil (optional)

FOR THE SESAME *TARE*

1 cup (240 ml) Kombu Dashi (page 27)

3 tablespoons soy sauce

3 tablespoons mirin

½ cup (4 g) bonito flakes

5 tablespoons *Surigoma* (page 107)

FOR THE GARNISHES

Lemon

Shichimi Togarashi (page 107)

Bring 4 cups of water in a pot to a boil over high heat. Set the minced daikon in a colander and pour the boiling water over it. Rinse the minced daikon under cold running water. Drain. Keep refrigerated in a bowl until ready to use.

To make the sesame *tare*, combine the first three ingredients in a small pot. Bring to a boil over medium heat and turn off the heat. Then add the bonito flakes and let them steep for two minutes. Strain and reserve the sauce. Add the *surigoma* and stir. The sauce is ready. You can make this sauce (as well as the ponzu sauce) the day before and keep refrigerated.

Arrange all the uncooked ingredients for the table on a platter, as appealingly as possible.

To make the *nabe*, bring the platter of uncooked ingredients and the bowl of daikon to the table. Turn on your portable heating unit and set the pot on top. Fill it about two-thirds full with water and drop in the kombu. Bring to a boil and remove the kombu just before a boil. Reduce the heat to low to maintain a simmer.

Set up each diner with a pair of chopsticks, a bowl, and a small dish of ponzu sauce and sesame *tare*. Start with the tofu and cook until warm, a couple of minutes. Add half of the uncooked meat: pick up a slice, dip it in the simmering hot broth, and swish it through until it is cooked. Then dip the tofu and pork into the ponzu sauce, add the garnishes, and eat! (The pork infuses the dashi with umami, before you begin adding the vegetables.) Use the remaining half of the meat and vegetables for the second round of *nabe*.

Add half of the spinach, Napa cabbage, scallions, mushrooms, and carrots to the hot broth, increase the heat to medium, and cover. Cook for 5 minutes then uncover. You are in charge of skimming the surface film with a ladle and keeping the surface of the broth simmering (never boiling). Scoop a cup of the minced daikon radish into the center of the hot pot and cook for 1 minute.

Let everyone continue to pick morsels from the pot and serve the sauces. Keep replenishing the pot until you run out of all the ingredients. It is best to clear the pot before replenishing it with more, so that everything stays freshly cooked.

zosui (*nabe* broth rice porridge)

This porridge makes great use of dashi left over from your hot pot. It pairs well with pickled foods.

MAKES 4 SERVINGS

- 4 cups (960 ml) leftover *nabe* broth (from the hot pot; recipe above) or Kombu Dashi (page 27)
- 1 tablespoon sake
- 1½ tablespoons soy sauce
- 1 tablespoon mirin
- 2 cups (300 g) cooked short- or medium-grain rice
- 2 large eggs, beaten
- ¼ teaspoon salt, or to taste
- 1 scallion, white and light green parts thinly sliced

FOR THE TABLE

One pickle of the following:
- *Nukazuke* (Fermented Rice Bran Pickles; page 94)
- *Umeboshi* (Pickled *Ume* Plums; page 90)
- Quick *Shio Koji*–Cured Napa Cabbage (page 95)

When all the *nabe* ingredients have been eaten, skim the broth, then pour off the remaining broth from the pot until you are left with 4 cups (960 ml). If you have less than that remaining, add more dashi or water to bring it up to 4 cups (960 ml). Add the sake, soy sauce, and mirin and bring the broth to a boil over high heat. Lower the heat to low, add the rice, cover, and cook for 2 to 3 minutes, stirring once. Remove the lid. Quickly pour the beaten eggs over the rice. Cover and cook for about 1 minute. Open and stir the rice once. Cover and turn off the heat. Remove the lid, taste the rice, and adjust the salt as needed. Serve immediately in individual rice bowls garnished with the scallions and pickles on the table.

chicken yakitori on skewers

Yakitori is easy to make. Chicken and a variety of vegetables are cut into bite-size morsels and then threaded on skewers and cooked on the grill (preferably *bichotan*, or charcoal fire). The skewers are basted with *shoyu tare*, a sweet and savory sauce made with soy sauce, sake, mirin, and sugar. I like to alternate pieces of *negi* (onion) with the chicken for best flavor. I also make skewers of seasonal vegetables and boiled quail eggs. They are all in the yakitori family, even though *yakitori* means "grilled chicken." If you don't have a grill, yakitori can also be made in a skillet or in the broiler.

MAKES 4 SERVINGS

EQUIPMENT

Bamboo skewers (soaked in water for 20 minutes) or metal skewers

Bichotan (charcoal fire) grill (optional)

½ cup (120 ml) sake

3 tablespoons mirin

1 tablespoon cane sugar

1 cup (240 ml) *Shoyu Tare* (page 105)

FOR THE SKEWERS

2 pounds (910 g) boneless skin-on chicken thighs, cut into bite-size pieces

4 Tokyo *negi* onions, white parts only, or scallions, white and light green parts cut crosswise into 2-inch (5 cm) slices

½ cup (120 ml) olive oil or untoasted sesame oil

8 fresh shiitake mushrooms, stems trimmed

2 dozen *shishito* peppers, stems trimmed

12 shelled fava beans

12 quail eggs, boiled for 2 to 3 minutes, shocked in cold water, and peeled

TO SERVE

Shichimi Togarashi (page 107)

Sansho pepper

Yuzu Kosho (page 112)

Sea salt

Combine the sake, mirin, and sugar in a small saucepan over medium heat and cook until the sugar is completely dissolved. Stir in the *shoyu tare*. Remove from heat and let cool to room temperature. The *shoyu tare* can be stored in a nonreactive glass or metal container in a cool, dry place or the refrigerator for about 3 months.

Skewer 2 pieces of chicken and 2 pieces of onion, alternating, on each skewer. Start with the larger pieces of meat so they end up at the tip, which will cook more quickly. Make sure there are no gaps between the meat and onions, as bamboo skewers will burn in the gaps. Skewer the vegetables and eggs on their own skewers, about 3 or 4 pieces per skewer, depending on the size of the vegetables.

Heat a *bichotan* (charcoal fire) grill, or heat a gas grill to medium-high, or preheat the broiler.

Lightly baste the chicken with the oil. Grill the chicken and onions for 3 to 4 minutes, turning the skewers several times, until the chicken and onions begin to char. Remove the chicken from the heat and baste with the *shoyu tare*.

Return the chicken to the heat and cook for 2 more minutes, turning the skewers several times. Remove from heat and baste again. Repeat one more time, until the chicken is cooked through and slightly charred, about 8 to 10 minutes total.

Lay the skewered vegetables and quail eggs on the grill and brush them with oil. Grill the vegetables and eggs, turning them over several times, until the vegetables are soft and charred, 5 to 8 minutes (the vegetables have different cooking times, so monitor each type for desired doneness). Brush them with the *shoyu tare* or season them at the table.

Serve the chicken, eggs, and vegetables with *shichimi togarashi*, *sansho* pepper, *yuzu kosho*, and salt.

ranch life in tehachapi, california

My husband and I have a small ranch in Tehachapi, located in the high desert about two hours northeast of Los Angeles. Tehachapi is known as the "Land of Four Seasons." Spring is an especially beautiful time of year, with wild poppies, mustard, and lupines bursting with colors in the fields. Spring—April, to be exact—is also when the horses return to the ranch. They belong to Chris Cummings, a third-generation cowboy and rancher who lives up the road. He brings his horses to graze on our pastures. In exchange, Chris gives us beef, his wife's canned peppers, and local lore. Our valley is named after the Cummings family; they own the mountains behind us and four hundred acres of pastures around us, and they raise three hundred heads of cattle. The valley also has a prison, an apple orchard, an organic carrot farm, and a hydroponic tomato farm. We can see the watchtower of the prison from our ranch.

I didn't know what raising cattle entailed until I went to visit the Cummings ranch early one summer. Kyle, Chris's eighteen-year-old son, offered to take us around in their family jeep. Kyle bears a scar on his right hand, probably from rough bronco riding. He was planning to start college at Cal Poly Pomona to study animal science and join the university's rodeo team in the fall. Kyle took us down to the pond, where his herd of cattle was feeding and napping. All twenty-seven of the cows and calves belong to Kyle, who took out a loan to start his own business as a rancher. There were elegant and healthy-looking longhorns and Black Angus cows. Every cow had a calf, but every calf didn't have a cow. Kyle pointed to two black calves that were on their own. "Their mother died," he said as we passed by, "so I raised them with a bottle."

When the temperature drops in Tehachapi, which has an altitude of four thousand feet, the cattle are moved down to an elevation of one thousand feet, where the temperatures are warmer.

Each animal grazes on about forty acres of pasture. It is a lot of work, but Chris prefers to rotate the animals around rather than keep them grazing in one place. Rotating the cattle gives the grasses a chance to regenerate and the cattle a chance to feed on a variety of grasses. The Cummings' cows have a slower, much better life compared to industrially raised cattle, which are locked up in feed lots, fed antibiotics, and fattened quickly with grains. Most of the Cummings' cows live on the pasture for their entire life span. The oldest cow on the ranch is thirty-three years old and has birthed thirty calves.

As we headed back to the house after our tour, Kyle told us a story from years ago. One night his grandpa was awakened by a noise and the smell of coffee coming from the kitchen. He went to investigate and found a man in a prison uniform sitting at the kitchen counter drinking coffee. Kyle's grandpa asked him, "How can I help you?" The prisoner looked at him and said that he was going to be released from Tehachapi prison the next day but didn't know what to do with his life after prison. So he had run away. He asked Kyle's grandpa if he could have a shot of whiskey before the police were called. So Kyle's grandpa gave him one.

dumplings, noodles, and savory pancakes

ozoni: new year's good luck soup

This is the first soup of the New Year that every Japanese person sips for good luck and good fortune. We drink *ozoni* each day for breakfast, lunch, and dinner for the first five days of the year. I make a big batch of dashi, about 4 quarts (4 L) to last me for the whole week. The featured ingredient in this hearty soup is mochi, which symbolizes flexibility and endurance. In my family, the soup is a simple *suimono* (clear soup) and the mochi is always freshly toasted. The soup also includes bite-size pieces of *kamaboko* (fish cake), chicken, carrots, shiitake mushrooms, some greens (such as spinach, kale, or mizuna), and for garnish, some *mitsuba* leaves and a small bit of lemon or yuzu peel to balance out the colors. Besides this soup, I always make more than a half dozen traditional New Year's good luck *osechi* dishes, which celebrate fertility (eggs, beans), endurance and flexibility (mochi), happiness (kombu), forward motion (lotus wheels), fire (carrots), purity (daikon), and groundedness (root vegetables).

MAKES 4 SERVINGS

- 5 ounces (142 g) spinach or mizuna
- 1 carrot sliced crosswise and cut into flower shape with a cookie cutter
- 1 boneless skinless chicken thigh, cut into ½-inch (12 mm) pieces
- 4 cups (960 ml) Bonito and Kombu Dashi (page 27)
- 1 tablespoon sake
- 1 tablespoon *usukuchi shoyu* (light-colored soy sauce)
- 1 teaspoon sea salt
- Four 1½-ounce (50 g) pieces of mochi
- 4 small fresh shiitake mushrooms, stems removed
- 4 slices *kamaboko* (fish cake), cut crosswise into ¼-inch (6 mm) pieces
- 1 tablespoon julienned lemon or yuzu peel
- 4 sprigs *mitsuba* (Japanese parsley), chervil, or Italian parsley, leaves removed

Fill a medium pot with water and bring to a boil over medium-high heat. Have a bowl of ice water ready. Add the spinach to the boiling water and blanch for 1 minute, or until wilted. Strain into a bowl. Transfer the wilted spinach to the ice water, then drain. Squeeze out excess water. Reserve the cooking water. Bunch the spinach up and cut crosswise into 2-inch (5 cm) pieces.

Return the cooking water to the pot, add the carrots, and blanch for 1 minute. Strain into a bowl, reserving the cooking water. Transfer to the ice water, then drain.

Return the cooking water to the pot once more, add the chicken, and blanch for 1 minute (this removes odor from the chicken). Drain and discard the cooking water.

In a medium saucepan, combine the dashi and the chicken and bring to a boil over medium heat. Lower heat and add the sake, soy sauce, and salt. Taste and make adjustments. You can complete the recipe up to this step up to 3 days in advance.

To serve the soup, bring the seasoned dashi and chicken to a boil over medium-high heat and then bring it down to a simmer while you toast the mochi. Remember, you want to serve the mochi freshly toasted so it tastes soft, not hard.

Preheat the broiler. To toast the mochi, line a baking sheet with aluminum foil. Place the mochi on the pan and broil until the pieces are toasted and puffy, turning them once to toast the other side. Be careful when handling the mochi. When you see one side pop, that is when to make the turn. This will take 3 to 5 minutes, depending on the freshness and thickness of the mochi. Put 1 piece of toasted mochi in each of 4 serving bowls.

Divide the shiitake mushrooms, *kamaboko*, carrots, and spinach among the bowls. Pour the hot soup three quarters of the way up the mochi and add the lemon peel and *mitsuba*. Serve immediately, with chopsticks.

first garden soba salad with lemon–white miso vinaigrette

I visit my recently regenerated vegetable garden every morning to start the day. I pick young lettuce, beet leaves, kale, marigolds, basil, lemon verbena, and nasturtium flowers. The garden benefits from getting thinned out, and I get a basket full of leafy greens to enjoy with my meals. The leaves are so tender and sweet that there is little I need to add to them—just a simple lemon vinaigrette is enough.

Soba noodles pair nicely with these fresh leafy greens. Don't dress the salad until just before serving, and then eat it immediately so the leaves and the soba noodles don't go mushy on you. This is a jewel of a dish.

MAKES 4 LARGE OR 6 SMALL SERVINGS

6 ounces (170 g) fresh baby leafy greens

3 tablespoons fresh lemon juice

1½ tablespoons rice vinegar, or to taste

1 tablespoon soy sauce

1 tablespoon white miso paste (I prefer *saikyo miso*)

1 teaspoon ginger juice (from grated ginger)

½ teaspoon cane sugar (optional)

Freshly ground black pepper

¼ cup (60 ml) extra-virgin olive oil, or as needed

Sea salt

1 pound (455 g) Soba Noodles (page 58)

FOR THE GARNISH

¼ cup (10 g) edible flowers and herbs

Place the greens in a salad bowl.

In a small bowl, whisk together the lemon juice, vinegar, soy sauce, miso paste, ginger juice, and sugar, if using. Grind in some pepper, then slowly whisk in the oil. Taste and make adjustments with more oil, vinegar, or salt as needed.

Cook the noodles following the guidelines on page 58.

To serve, gently combine half the dressing with the noodles and transfer them to a platter. Dress the greens with the remaining dressing. Taste and make adjustments with salt and pepper to your liking. Arrange the greens on top of the noodles and garnish with herbs and flower petals. Serve immediately.

chilled soba noodles with walnut dipping sauce

The classic *zarusoba* (cold soba) is served with a dipping sauce, some grated daikon radish, wasabi, and scallions. Nothing more. It is simple and straightforward. If you visit an artisan soba shop in Japan, such as Hosokawa in Tokyo, that is what the master wants you to eat first. He wants you to taste the soba noodles. When I staged at his restaurant, the staff meal was always *zarusoba*, and nothing more for that reason. When nuts are in season, I add them to the dipping sauce. It so happens that our old English walnut tree in Tehachapi produces the biggest and best walnuts I have ever tasted. Other ground nuts or seeds such as pecans, peanuts, or sesame seeds will work too.

To eat the noodles, dip them in the dipping sauce about a third of the way in with your chopstick and then slurp. This may take a little practice; the idea is not to overwhelm the noodles with the sauce. After you have finished the noodles, you can dilute the dipping sauce with some *sobayu*, the nourishing cooking broth of the noodles, and drink it like a soup. This is a ritual practiced at soba noodle shops.

MAKES 6 SERVINGS

FOR THE DIPPING SAUCE

1 cup (236 ml) *Shoyu Tare* (page 105)

3 cups (700 ml) Bonito and Kombu Dashi
(page 27) or other dashi of your choice

FOR THE NOODLES

1½ pounds (680 g) Soba Noodles (page 58)

FOR THE GARNISH

1 cup toasted finely ground walnuts mixed with
1 tablespoon (18 g) cane sugar

Bring the *shoyu tare* and dashi to boil over medium heat. Lower heat and cook for 2 minutes. Turn off heat. Bring to room temperature. Serve with the noodles. This will keep in the refrigerator for 4 to 5 days.

Cook the noodles following the guidelines on page 58. (Do not make the noodles in advance; cook them as close as possible to serving time, so they are fresh.) Serve the noodles in a *zaru* (Japanese-style bamboo basket), if you have one, or on a large platter with individual serving bowls of dipping sauce and ground walnuts.

Invite diners to mix the ground walnuts into the dipping sauce, dip in the noodles, and slurp. You may also serve a more classic dipping sauce along with the walnut dipping sauce. Simply serve the noodles with grated daikon radish, sliced scallions, and grated wasabi.

spicy duck soba noodles in a hot broth

This is one of my favorite ways to eat soba. It is a rich dish but with only four components: the broth, the noodles, the duck, and the garnishes. The duck breast is seared and then briefly cooked in a spicy dashi so the skin is crispy but it is still pink and tender inside. You can make the broth 2 to 3 days ahead of time and store it in the refrigerator; reheat it when you are ready to serve.

MAKES 4 SERVINGS

FOR THE BROTH

8 cups (1.8 L) Bonito and Kombu Dashi (page 27) or other dashi of your choice

¾ cup (177 ml) *Shoyu Tare* (page 105)

1 tablespoon sake

FOR THE NOODLES

1 pound (455 g) Soba Noodles (page 58)

FOR THE DUCK TOPPING

1 pound (455 g) duck breast (1 whole breast)

¾ cup (180 ml) filtered water

1 piece of kombu, 3 x 3 inches (7.5 x 7.5 cm)

¼ cup (60 ml) *usukuchi shoyu* (light-colored soy sauce)

¼ cup (60 ml) mirin

½ cup (120 ml) rice vinegar

1 dried red chile, seeded and thinly sliced

FOR THE LEEK TOPPING

2 leeks, julienned

2 tablespoons reserved duck fat

FOR THE GARNISHES

Mitsuba leaves or chervil leaves

1 tablespoon julienned lemon, lime, or yuzu peel

2 tablespoons peeled and julienned ginger

Shichimi Togarashi (page 107)

To make the soup base, combine the dashi with the *shoyu tare* and sake in a large saucepan and bring to a boil over medium-high heat. Lower the heat and maintain a low simmer while you prepare the noodles and duck. Or turn off the heat and reheat the soup before serving the noodles and duck. The soup base can be made 1 or 2 days in advance and stored in the refrigerator.

To make the duck, split the breast into two pieces and score the top. In a large skillet over medium-high heat, sear the breast on both sides until it is lightly browned and cooked to medium rare, about 3 to 4 minutes. Reserve the duck fat for cooking the leeks in the same skillet.

While the duck is browning, combine ¾ cup (180 ml) water, kombu, soy sauce, mirin, vinegar, and chile in a large saucepan and bring to a boil over medium heat. Add the seared duck breast and cook for 4 minutes to absorb the broth. Turn off heat. Remove the duck from the cooking liquid and let the duck come to room temperature. When the broth has cooled, return the duck to the broth.

Heat the skillet over medium-high heat with the reserved duck fat and stir-fry the leeks until they are tender, about 5 minutes. Remove from heat and set aside.

You are now ready to assemble the duck noodle soup.

Cook the noodles following the guidelines on page 58. (Do not make the noodles in advance; cook them as close as possible to serving time, so they are fresh.) Divide the noodles among 4 noodle bowls.

Take the duck out of the cooking liquid and slice it crosswise ¼ inch (6 mm) thick.

Bring the broth to a boil over high heat. Pour the hot broth over the noodles, about 1⅔ cups (393 ml) per bowl. Top with slices of duck meat and leeks, and garnish with *mitsuba* leaves, lemon peel, ginger, and *shichimi togarashi*. Serve immediately.

peddler's udon noodles with spicy meat sauce

"Peddler's noodles" are Sichuan Chinese in origin. They are also called *dan dan mein* or *tan tan mein*, names that come from the poles used by street vendors to carry the baskets of noodles and the sauce. Ground meat is flavored here with a spicy bean paste called *doubanjiang* (fermented broad beans), Sichuan peppercorns, and scallions. This spicy meat sauce is also delicious on rice or as a filling in *onigiri*.

MAKES 4 SERVINGS

FOR THE MEAT SAUCE

    2 tablespoons toasted sesame oil

    2 cloves garlic, minced

    2 tablespoons minced ginger

    4 fresh shiitake mushrooms, sliced and minced

    5 ounces (142 g) vacuum-packed or canned bamboo shoots, drained and minced

    8 ounces (230 g) ground pork

    8 ounces (230 g) ground beef

    2 tablespoons *doubanjian* (fermented broad beans)

    2 tablespoons red miso

    ¼ cup (60 ml) sake

    1 tablespoon mirin

    2 tablespoons soy sauce

    4 cups (980 ml) chicken broth

    2 tablespoons kudzu, potato starch, or cornstarch, dissolved in 2 tablespoons water

FOR THE NOODLES

    1 to 1½ pounds (600 to 680 g) Udon Noodles (page 60)

FOR THE GARNISHES

    2 cucumbers (preferably Persian), cut into 3-inch-long (7.5 cm) julienne

    2 cups (100 g) bean sprouts or other sprouts, blanched and drained

    4 scallions, white and light green parts cut into 3-inch-long (7.5 cm) julienne

To make the spicy meat sauce, heat the oil in a large skillet over medium-high heat. Add the garlic and ginger and cook, stirring, for 1 minute. Add the mushrooms, bamboo shoots, and ground meat. Continue cooking for about 5 minutes, until the ingredients absorb the broth.

In a medium bowl, whisk together the *doubanjian*, miso, sake, mirin, soy sauce, and chicken broth. Add the broth mixture to the meat mixture, decrease the heat to medium, and cook for 15 minutes until the ingredients absorb the seasoning. Taste and make adjustments. Add the cornstarch mixture. Stir a few times to incorporate and remove from heat.

While the meat sauce is simmering, bring a large pot of water to a boil over medium-high heat. Drop the noodles into the boiling water and cook for about 10 minutes for fresh noodles, or according to the package instructions (the exact cooking time will depend on their thickness). Strain and rinse the noodles well to remove starch. You may dip the noodles back into the pot of hot water to reheat.

Divide the hot noodles among individual bowls and ladle the hot meat sauce generously on top. Garnish with the cucumber, sprouts, and scallions.

dumplings, noodles, and savory pancakes

yakisoba (stir-fried noodles)

I make this recipe when I have leftover fresh ramen noodles. You can use dried or fresh ramen, udon, or soba noodles to make this versatile recipe.

MAKES 4 SERVINGS

1 recipe Ramen Noodles (page 63)

3 tablespoons light sesame oil or grapeseed oil

2 boneless skin-on chicken thighs, diced into ½-inch (12 mm) cubes

4 Napa cabbage leaves, sliced ¼-inch (6 mm) thick

1 small yellow onion, peeled and sliced ⅛-inch (3 mm) thick

2 cups (100 g) bean sprouts

FOR THE SAUCE

¼ cup (60 ml) sake

2 tablespoons oyster sauce

2 tablespoons Worcestershire sauce

2 tablespoons soy sauce

Sea salt and ground black pepper, to taste

FOR THE TABLE

3 scallions, white and light green parts sliced thinly crosswise

Amazu Shoga (page 87)

Bonito flakes

Flaked nori

To cook the noodles, bring the water to a boil in a large pot over high heat. Add the noodles and cook for 1 minute. Rinse under cool running water and drain.

Heat 1 tablespoon of oil in a large skillet or wok over medium-high heat. Stir-fry the noodles until they are lightly toasted on one side. Turn the noodles over and lightly toast the other side. Transfer the noodles to a large bowl.

In the same skillet or wok, add 2 tablespoons of oil and heat over medium-high heat. Add the chicken. When the color of the meat changes to white, about 5 minutes, add the cabbage and onions. Push to one side of the pan.

Continue cooking on medium-high heat. Add the noodles back into the pan and combine with the other ingredients, except the scallions and bean sprouts. Add the sauce and salt and pepper and stir-fry for 2 minutes. Then add the bean sprouts and stir-fry for 30 seconds. Taste and make adjustments.

Serve on a platter and garnish with scallions, *amazu shoga*, bonito flakes, and flaked nori.

okazu, sweets, and beverages

ramen bowls

What makes a good ramen? Many Japanese people say the ramen soup makes the ramen. I care about both the soup and the quality of the noodles, so I make my own, whenever I have time to crank them out on my pasta machine. What makes this easy is that ramen is an "assembly" dish with only three basic components: the soup, the noodles, and the toppings. I make my soup a week to two in advance and freeze it, and then I make the *yakibuta* topping and noodles a day or two in advance. That way I only have to pay attention to assembling the ramen on the day I'm planning to serve the dish. To assemble, you simply heat the soup, cook the noodles, and put your proteins and garnishes on top.

Ramen is touted for its rich dashi, which comes from using the right kind of bones and being attentive to the stock. *Tonkotsu* ramen is the classic flavor, made with the fat and marrow of pork trotters and leg bones to produce the creamiest collagen-rich stock. I like to make mine with pork trotters, pork leg bones, chicken backs, necks, and wings, dried shiitake mushrooms, kombu, and vegetable scraps, the synergy of which deepens the umami. If you prefer a vegetarian version, try the noodle soup I use with soba and udon noodles (see *Shoyu Tare*, page 105). It is a *wafu*-style (Japanese) ramen that tastes light and clean and not greasy at all, but there are all kinds of ramen in the ramen kingdom.

The three classic seasonings for ramen are salt, soy sauce, and miso. If you go to a ramen shop, the ramen master will ask for your preference for salt, soy sauce, and miso and will season the broth accordingly. You can season your own ramen stock with plain salt, *shio koji*, or miso, if you like. Season gradually and taste as you go. Again, if you prefer a lighter vegetarian *tare*, use the *shoyu tare*, using the ratio for noodle soup, which is 9 parts broth to 1 part *tare*.

I make ramen noodles by hand and crank the noodles out in an Italian pasta machine to get the required thin, long noodles. It works pretty well, and they taste better than industrial noodles. You can make your noodles more flavorful by blending in some ancient grains such as spelt, Sonora wheat, or Pasaytan wheat.

MAKES 4 TO 6 SERVINGS

- 1 recipe fresh Ramen Noodles (page 63)
- 6 cups (1.4 L) Ramen Broth (recipe follows) or 6 cups (1.4 L) Bonito and Kombu Dashi (page 27)
- 1 cup fat reserved from Ramen Broth
- 2 cups (480 ml) filtered water
- 1 recipe *Yakibuta* Pork (page 258), sliced crosswise ¼ inch (6 mm) thick
- ⅔ cup (156 ml) sauce from *Yakibuta* Pork or *Shoyu Tare* (page 105)
- 1 teaspoon sea salt
- 2 tablespoons mirin, or to taste (optional)
- 2 tablespoons sake, or to taste (optional)
- 6 scallions, white and light green parts thinly sliced
- 6 *Nitamago* (page 83) or soft-boiled eggs, peeled and cut in half lengthwise
- 1 recipe *Memma* (page 259)
- ½ cup (64 g) toasted sesame seeds
- 1 piece nori, cut into 4 pieces
- *Shichimi Togarashi* (page 107) or *Yuzu Kosho* (page 112)

Pour the 6 cups (1.4 L) concentrated ramen broth into a 3-quart (3 L) pot and add 2 cups (480 ml) filtered water. Each serving will consist of 2 cups (480 ml) seasoned ramen broth. Bring the broth to a boil over medium-high heat. Lower the heat to a simmer. Now begin seasoning the broth with the sauce from the *yakibuta* pork or the *shoyu tare*. Add 1 teaspoon salt to start. Stir and taste. Start building flavor by adding 1 tablespoon *yakibuta*

pork sauce or *shoyu tare* at a time. If you'd like to sweeten and round out the broth, you can add mirin or sake. Stir and taste again. You will probably need to add a couple more tablespoons of the salty seasonings and a few teaspoons of the fat (reserved from the broth) to get to the flavor you like. Once you have reached the desired flavor, raise the heat to bring the broth to a second boil and then lower the heat to keep it at a simmer while you cook the noodles.

Bring a large pot of unsalted water to a boil over high heat. Add 2 servings of the noodles and cook for about 1 minute. Take one noodle out of the water and taste. The cooked noodle should be chewy and springy. Repeat with the remaining noodles.

While the noodles are cooking, bring the seasoned broth back to a rolling boil. Put a tablespoon or more of the reserved pork fat in each. When the noodles are ready, scoop the noodles out with a strainer or ramen basket. Drain the noodles and divide them among six bowls. Then pour the boiling broth into bowls. Stir the broth to incorporate the fat and pour it over the noodles. Top with the pork, scallions, egg slices, sesame seeds, bamboo shoots, nori, and *shichimi togarashi*. Eat immediately with chopsticks and soup spoons.

ramen broth

This recipe makes a concentrated broth, which you will then dilute and season for your ramen bowls. For the pork trotters and bones, ask your butcher to cut them in half so that you can get the most flavor out of them.

MAKES ABOUT 3 QUARTS (3 L)

2 pounds (910 g) pork trotters (*see headnote*)
3 pounds (1.4 kg) pork bones (*see headnote*)
2 chicken backs
5 quarts (5 L) filtered water
1 piece of kombu, about 5 x 5 inches (13 x 13 cm)

5 dried shiitake mushrooms, hydrated in 4 cups (960 ml) water for 1 hour to overnight, soaking liquid reserved
2 leeks, cut lengthwise in half, and then into thirds
1 onion, cut in half
1 medium carrot, peeled and cut into chunks
1 tablespoon peeled and sliced ginger
2 dried Japanese or Mexican chile peppers
5 cloves garlic, peeled
1 teaspoon black peppercorns

Place the pork trotters and pork bones in a large saucepan with enough water to cover. Bring to a boil over medium heat, then lower the heat and simmer for 15 minutes. Remove the bones to a bowl, then repeat with the chicken backs in the same water. Transfer the chicken backs to the bowl with the pork bones. Discard the blanching water and wash the pot. Scrub the bones with a brush to remove any blood clots.

Return all the bones to the same pot and add 5 quarts (5 L) fresh water and the kombu and mushrooms and their soaking liquid. Bring to a boil, then turn the heat down to maintain a very low simmer. Add the leeks, onion, carrot, ginger, chile peppers, garlic, and peppercorns and cook for 8 to 10 hours, until the liquid is reduced by nearly half. Remove the bones and cooked vegetables. Clear any surface scum and discard. Strain the stock through a not-too-fine strainer and then return it to the pot. Let cool, then refrigerate overnight. Skim the fat from the broth the next day if you wish to have a lighter soup; reserve the fat in a small bowl and add it back to the broth if you want a richer broth.

Your broth is now ready for use in making Ramen Bowls (page 255). You can store the broth in the freezer for up to 1 month. Keep the fat in the fridge for up to 1 month.

yakibuta pork (braised pork belly)

The hidden flavor of this fragrant *yakibuta* pork is in the dashi. You can use any dashi you like; I use kombu dashi but have also made this dish with other types of dashi. This recipe was given to me by my friend Mamiko Nishiyama of Yagicho Honten, the three-hundred-year-old dashi shop in Tokyo. The *shio koji* tenderizes and adds a miso-like flavor to the pork belly. This pork can also be enjoyed with rice.

MAKES 8 SERVINGS

3 pounds (1.8 kg) pork belly

4 tablespoons *Shio Koji* (page 95) or 2 tablespoons sea salt

2 tablespoons vegetable oil

1 piece kombu, 3 x 6 inches (7.5 x 15 cm), hydrated in 4 cups (960 ml) water overnight, soaking liquid reserved

4 dried shiitake mushrooms, hydrated with the kombu

2 scallions, white and light green parts cut into 2-inch (5 cm) pieces

2 ounces (57 g) ginger, peeled and sliced ¼ inch (6 mm) thick

4 cloves garlic, sliced

3 Japanese dried red chiles, seeded

½ teaspoon freshly ground black pepper

1½ cups (360 ml) sake

¾ cup (180 ml) soy sauce

2 tablespoons *kokuto* sugar, or other dark brown sugar

Tie up the pork belly into a roll with kitchen twine or ask your butcher to do it for you.

Puncture the skin of pork in several places with a knife. Rub with *shio koji* and let stand in the fridge for 2 to 3 days. Bring the pork belly to room temperature, rinse off the *shio koji*, and dry the pork belly with a paper towel before cooking.

Heat the oil in a large skillet and sear the pork belly until browned on all sides, about 15 minutes. Remove and discard the fat.

Transfer the seared pork belly to a large saucepan and add the kombu and mushrooms and their reserved soaking water, then add the scallions, ginger, garlic, chiles, pepper, sake, soy sauce, and *kokuto* sugar. Bring to a boil over medium heat. Skim any surface scum and discard.

Lower the heat and simmer for 3½ to 4 hours, turning the meat every 15 minutes, until half the sauce is evaporated and the meat is thoroughly cooked. The internal temperature should be around 165°F (73°C). Turn off the heat and let the pork rest in the sauce until it comes to room temperature, preferably overnight to make slicing easier.

Alternatively, put the pork, soaking water, and the seasonings in a pressure cooker. This method actually produces a more tender pork. Make sure that the volume of the liquid doesn't go more than one-third of the way up the pot. Bring to a boil over high heat, close the lid, and bring to full pressure. Then lower the heat to medium and pressure cook for 35 minutes. Turn off the heat and let the pressure come down to normal. Open the lid and check for doneness by slicing off the end piece. Turn the meat to coat it in the sauce. Pressure cook for an additional 5 to 10 minutes, or until the meat is tender and thoroughly cooked. Always follow the manufacturer's instructions for pressure cooking.

Allow the meat to come to room temperature, then slice ¼ inch (6 mm) thick and serve with your Ramen Bowls (page 255). Reserve the sauce as a seasoning for the ramen broth.

memma (braised bamboo shoots)

Braised bamboo shoots are a classic accompaniment to ramen.

MAKES 1 CUP

> 8 ounces (230 g) vacuum-packed or canned bamboo shoots
> 1 tablespoon sesame oil
> 1 cup (240 ml) Ramen Broth (page 257) or Bonito and Kombu Dashi (page 27)
> ¼ cup (60 ml) *Shoyu Tare* (page 105)
> 1 tablespoon mirin
> 1 teaspoon *La-Yu* (page 109)

Cut the bamboo shoots into ½-inch-wide (12 mm) rectangles about ¼ inch (6 mm) thick.

Heat the oil in a large skillet, add the bamboo shoots, and cook for 1 minute. Add the ramen broth, *shoyu tare*, and mirin, and cook until the liquid is mostly absorbed in the bamboo, about 20 minutes. Finish with the *la-yu*. Add to your Ramen Bowls (page 255), or cool and store in the refrigerator for up to 1 week.

okonomiyaki ("as you like it") pancakes with bonito flakes

The Japanese version of a savory pancake is called *okonomiyaki*. It is made with fresh eggs, flour, and water and seasoned with soy sauce and *tonkatsu* sauce. Shredded cabbage is also part of the equation; it gives the pancake its soft texture and subtly sweet flavor. Protein toppings include combinations of meat, shrimp, and vegetables. When the pancake is cooked, it is topped with mayonnaise and *tonkatsu* sauce and garnished with bonito flakes and *aonori* (dried green seaweed flakes) or crumbled nori. *Aonori* is available at Japanese markets. I prefer the "naked" flavor of the *okonomiyaki*, so I usually skip the mayo and go easy on the *tonkatsu* sauce or eat it with soy sauce.

MAKES 8 PANCAKES (2 CUPS/480 ML BATTER)

1½ cups (180 g) all-purpose flour

1 teaspoon baking powder

¼ teaspoon sea salt

1 large egg, beaten

1¼ cups (296 ml) whole milk or milk of your choice

8 ounces (230 g) cabbage, thinly sliced

2 scallions, white and light green parts chopped

½ yellow, green, or red bell pepper, thinly sliced

4 tablespoons vegetable oil

8 ounces (230 g) boneless chicken, shrimp, crab, or *sukiyaki*-style beef or pork, cut into ½-inch (12 mm) pieces

2 tablespoons Japanese Mayonnaise (page 189)

2 tablespoon or more *Tonkatsu* Sauce (page 156)

½ cup (4 g) bonito flakes

½ cup (4 g) crumbled nori or *aonori* flakes

Amazu Shoga (page 87)

Whisk together the flour, baking powder, and salt in a small bowl.

In a medium bowl, whisk the egg and milk. Add the flour mixture and mix until just blended. The batter should be quite thin. Add the chopped vegetables to the batter and mix well.

Heat 1 tablespoon of the oil in a medium non-stick skillet over medium-high heat. Pour ¼ cup (60 ml) of the batter to make a 6-inch (15 cm) pancake. Cook until medium brown, about 1 minute. Place ¼ of the meat on top of the pancake and then flip the meat side down. Turn heat to low and cook until the bottom of the pancake is browned, the meat is thoroughly cooked, and the vegetables are tender—about 10 minutes. Repeat until the batter is used up.

To serve, brush the pancake with mayonnaise and *tonkatsu* sauce, or soy sauce. Sprinkle with the bonito flakes and crumbled nori. Eat while piping hot. Serve with *amazu shoga* on the side.

pork and shrimp *shumai* (steamed dumplings)

Shumai is a convenient *okazu* (dish) found in the frozen section in Japanese markets that often ends up on the breakfast table or in bento boxes. Like *gyoza*, this is another crowd-pleasing dumpling that is easy to put together.

MAKES 24 DUMPLINGS

EQUIPMENT
Stackable steamer or wok with a steamer rack

4 ounces (110 g) shrimp, peeled, deveined, and coarsely chopped

¼ teaspoon salt

1 egg white

1½ tablespoons potato starch or cornstarch

8 ounces (230 g) ground pork

4 ounces (110 g) vacuum-packed or canned bamboo shoots, drained and minced

¼ teaspoon ground white pepper

2 teaspoons ginger juice (from grated ginger)

1 tablespoon sake

1 tablespoon toasted sesame oil, plus more for brushing the cabbage or parchment

1 teaspoon cane sugar

1 tablespoon soy sauce, plus more for serving

24 fresh or frozen green peas

24 Dumpling Wrappers (page 65)

Napa cabbage leaves (optional)

TO SERVE
Soy sauce
Ponzu Sauce (page 105)
La-Yu (page 109)
Japanese or Dijon mustard

Place the shrimp in a medium bowl and rub it with the salt. Let stand for 5 minutes (the salt removes the odor of the shrimp). Rinse off the salt under running water and drain.

Combine the egg white and potato starch in a small bowl and mix well.

In a large bowl, combine the shrimp, pork, bamboo shoots, potato starch mixture, pepper, ginger juice, sake, sesame oil, sugar, and soy sauce. Mix well, turning and massaging the mixture with your hands, until it is smooth, about 3 minutes. Cover and let rest in the refrigerator overnight.

To wrap the *shumai*, take 1 dumpling wrapper in the palm of your hand and place 1 to 1½ tablespoons of the filling in the middle of the wrapper. Bring the edges toward each other by closing your palm loosely and gently gluing the wrapper to the filling. Flatten the bottom by gently tapping the *shumai* on the cutting board. Make a small indentation in the middle of each *shumai* using the tip of a chopstick and garnish with a pea. Continue wrapping the remaining *shumai*.

Line a steamer tray with parchment paper or sliced Napa cabbage leaves, about ½-inch (6 mm) wide, and brush lightly with oil. Pour enough water into the wok or steamer so the water level reaches about 1 inch (2.5 cm) below the steamer tray.

Arrange the *shumai* in the steamer tray, making sure they don't touch one another (steam in batches if your steamer tray is small). Then bring the water to a boil over medium-high heat. Cover and steam the *shumai* for 10 to 12 minutes, until the filling is firm to the touch and cooked through. Take one out of the steamer and cut it in half to check for doneness. Serve straight from the steamer at the table with soy sauce, ponzu sauce, and *la-yu*. You can also eat the steamed cabbage, if using.

sweets

anko (sweetened adzuki bean paste) ice pops

This is a simple ice pop made of *anko* (sweetened adzuki bean paste), milk, and cream. The beans will sink to the bottom of the mold and give you a two-tone ice pop. You can make the adzuki bean paste or buy it at a Japanese market or online.

MAKES 12 ICE POPS

EQUIPMENT
  12-hold ice pop mold and sticks

8 ounces (230 g) *Anko* (page 79)
2 cups (480 ml) whole milk
⅔ cup (156 ml) heavy cream
¼ teaspoon sea salt
3 tablespoons cane sugar or honey (optional)

In a medium bowl, combine the adzuki bean paste, milk, cream, and salt. Whisk until the mixture is well combined. Taste. If the liquid needs more sweetness, add the sugar or honey. Strain the liquid through a strainer. Reserve the beans.

Pour the liquid into ice pop molds. Freeze for 2 hours until the liquid is set halfway. Add the reserved beans evenly into each individual mold. Freeze for another hour and then insert the sticks into each individual mold and freeze overnight.

To remove the ice pops from the molds, run each under warm water for about 5 seconds, and gently pull on the stick. Serve immediately, or store the pops wrapped in waxed paper in the freezer for 2 weeks.

strawberry *daifuku* mochi

Daifuku ("big luck") mochi is a kind of dumpling made by stuffing steamed mochi with *anko* (sweetened adzuki bean paste). My grandmother made it for us often. This *daifuku* recipe is made with plain mochi and is enhanced by wrapping fruit in a layer of bean paste and then wrapping it all with mochi. Popular stuffed *daifuku* are strawberry, kiwi, fig, mango, and ice cream. I like strawberry *daifuku* because it brings fresh flavors and textures to the dessert and offers the contrasting colors of red, white, and brown. You can make the adzuki bean paste or buy it at a Japanese market or online.

MAKES 6 TO 8 *DAIFUKU*

EQUIPMENT
Stackable steamer

¾ cup (100 g) *shiratamako* or *mochiko* (glutinous/sweet rice flour)
½ cup plus 2 tablespoons (150 ml) filtered water
¾ cup (80 g) cane sugar
1½ cups (300 g) *Anko* (page 79)
½ cup (70 g) cornstarch
8 small strawberries, hulled

Combine the *shiratamako* and filtered water in a medium heat-resistant bowl and mix until smooth. Add the sugar and liquid rice mixture. Make sure there are no lumps of flour in the rice mixture.

Preheat a two-tier steamer over medium-high heat.

Cover the bowl with a dish towel and place it in the heated steamer. Steam over high heat for 5 minutes, until the rice mixture thickens. Prepare a small bowl of water. Take the bowl out of the steamer, dunk a spatula into the bowl of water and then stir the mixture about 20 times vigorously. Cover the bowl and return to the steamer and steam for another 5 minutes until the mixture begins to turn sticky in texture and opaque in color. Take the bowl out of the steamer, dunk a spatula in the bowl of water and stir again, about 20 times vigorously. Return to the steamer and steam for another 5 minutes until the mixture is sticky and stretchy.

Meanwhile, divide the *anko* into 8 balls. Flatten 1 ball into a disk and wrap it around 1 strawberry. Tuck the seam of the *anko* under the stem side of the strawberry. Repeat with the remaining strawberries.

Sift about ¼ cup of the cornstarch onto a small baking sheet. Transfer the hot mochi to the sheet using a wet spatula and lightly coat the top of the hot mochi with more cornstarch (for easy handling). Flatten the mochi while it is warm, using your hands, and gently fold it in half. Let cool for 15 minutes.

Shape the mochi into eight round disks, about 3 inches (7.5 cm) in diameter. Brush off excess cornstarch. While the mochi is still warm and elastic, envelop each bean paste–covered strawberry with a mochi disk, pulling and lifting the edge of the disk and tucking it under the strawberry. Shape the bundle so that the mochi stands up. Repeat 7 more times.

Eat within a day, at room temperature (but do not refrigerate). Serve with tea.

amazake (fermented rice drink) ice pops with pickled cherry blossoms

Amazake is an ancient Japanese beverage made by inoculating rice with a mold called koji, or *Aspergillus oryzae*, which is also used for making miso, sake, soy sauce, and rice vinegar. *Amazake* is sweet without any additional sugar, is an incredibly nourishing food for the intestinal flora, and is easy to make. *Amazake* looks like rice pudding, but you can dilute it with water, milk, or cream and puree it to the consistency of cream.

These ice pops are subtly spiced with ginger and garnished with pickled cherry blossoms, which add a pretty color, a salty taste, and a floral fragrance. I like to pop these ice pops in my mouth when I need an energy boost. You can also sprinkle *amazake* with any topping that you would use on ice cream or sorbet.

MAKES 12 SERVINGS

EQUIPMENT
Food processor
Silicone ice cube tray (for 1-inch/2.5 cm) cubes

1 cup (240 ml) whole milk (or ½ cup/120 ml whole milk and ½ cup/120 ml heavy cream)
1 cup (240 ml) *Amazake* (page 289), pureed with a food processor
1 teaspoon ginger juice (from grated ginger)
Pickled Cherry Blossoms (optional; recipe follows)

To make the *amazake* ice pops, combine the milk, *amazake*, and ginger juice in a pitcher. Mix well. Pour the liquid into an ice cube tray. Cover and freeze overnight.

To serve, remove the *amazake* from the ice cube tray and serve with the pickled cherry blossoms on top, if using.

pickled cherry blossoms

Cherry blossoms are the messenger of spring in Japan. Starting in March, you will notice that Japanese take their time to enjoy their pink cloud–like beauty. They even pickle the cherry blossoms and put them in tea, bread, and cakes and use them as a garnish for various dishes. Use the multilayered petal type of cherry blossoms for pickling.

8 ounces (230 g) fresh cherry blossoms (clustered, multilayered petals, half opened) with stems attached, leaves discarded
2½ tablespoons (55 g) sea salt
1 cup (240 ml) plum vinegar (*umezu*) or apple cider vinegar

Rinse the blossoms and pat dry with a paper towel. Weigh the blossoms and measure enough salt to equal 25 percent of the weight of the blossoms. (If the blossoms weigh 8 ounces/230 g, use 2½ tablespoons/55 g salt.)

Lay half of the salt evenly out on a baking sheet. Place the blossoms on top of the salt in a single layer and cover the blossoms with the remaining salt. Put a cutting board on top of the blossoms to press them down and leave for 3 days. The blossoms will release water; drain the water daily.

After 3 days, transfer the pickled blossoms to a small bowl. Pour the plum vinegar on top and marinate for 3 more days.

Drain the blossoms and set them in the sun to dry for 3 days. Cover with a mesh screen to keep out insects. Beautiful salt crystals will form on the surface of the blossoms. Transfer the pickled blossoms into a glass container with a tight-fitting lid and store in the refrigerator for up to 3 months.

kinugoshi dofu to kuromame-no-amani (homemade tofu custard with sweetened black soybeans)

This is a custard made from fresh soy milk that is light and creamy. The custard is essentially a silken tofu, or *kinugoshi* tofu. Here we use gypsum, a naturally occurring mineral, to coagulate the soy milk; the gypsum creates a tofu that is creamier than tofu made with *nigari* coagulant. You can order the coagulant online from GEM Cultures (see Resources, page 291). You can also serve the tofu custard with Ginger Syrup (page 274) or *kokuto* syrup (page 109).

This tofu is also good served as a savory dish. Skip the *kuromame-no-amani*. Instead garnish the tofu with grated ginger, chopped scallions, and sprinkles of bonito flakes and serve with soy sauce.

MAKES 8 SERVINGS

EQUIPMENT
> Eight 5-ounce (142 g) ramekins
> Stackable steamer
>
> 3½ cups (830 ml) Soy Milk (page 74)
> 2 teaspoons gypsum coagulant diluted in 2 teaspoons filtered water
> 1 recipe *Kuromame-no-Amani* (page 78)

Refrigerate the soy milk overnight to prepare for making the tofu custard.

To make the tofu custard, add water to a stackable steamer and bring it to a boil over high heat. When the water reaches the boiling point, lower the heat to a simmer to steady the flow of steam.

Place the chilled soy milk in a bowl and add the diluted gypsum. Mix well. Divide the mixture equally among the 8 ramekins. Cover each ramekin with plastic wrap or foil.

Place the covered ramekins in the heated steamer. Steam on high heat for 1 minute, then bring the heat down to a simmer and steam until the soy milk mixture is set and a toothpick inserted comes out clean, about 7 to 10 minutes. Check to see if the custard is set by gently wiggling the ramekin. If there is no wiggle, then the custard is set. If it is runny, you will need to continue steaming for another 2 to 3 minutes.

Separate the steamer trays and cool for a few minutes before removing the ramekins, then cool the custard completely while still covered. Refrigerate overnight. The custard will keep in the refrigerator for 3 to 4 days.

Serve each chilled tofu custard with a teaspoon of *kuromame-no-amani*.

butter mochi with adzuki beans and walnuts

Butter mochi is a Hawaiian cake that is gooey, sweet, and very addictive. You might think that butter and mochi are an odd pair of ingredients for a cake, but of course there is a story behind that. Apparently the early Japanese immigrants in Hawaii did not have steamers to make rice cakes, so they baked their mochi in ovens instead, discovering along the way that adding butter gave the mochi a nice brown crust and richer flavor. Butter mochi can also be filled with slices of mango, peaches, coconut flakes, almonds, *matcha* (green tea) powder, or cocoa powder. I have adapted this recipe from Peggy Wang's version.

MAKES 4 TO 6 SERVINGS

- ¾ cup (1½ sticks/170 g) butter, melted, plus 2 tablespoons softened butter for greasing
- One 13.5-ounce (400 ml) can unsweetened coconut milk
- 14 ounces (414 ml) sweetened condensed milk
- 4 large eggs
- 1 pound (455 g) *mochiko* (glutinous/sweet rice flour)
- 1 tablespoon baking powder
- ½ teaspoon sea salt
- 8 ounces (230 g) *Anko* (page 79) (optional)
- ½ cup (58 g) roughly chopped walnuts or pecans

Preheat the oven to 350°F (175°C). Grease a 9 x 13-inch (23 x 33 cm) glass or ceramic baking dish with the 2 tablespoons butter.

In a medium bowl, whisk the coconut milk, condensed milk, eggs, and melted butter. In a large bowl, whisk the *mochiko*, baking powder, and salt. Pour the wet mixture into the dry mixture and whisk until smooth to form a batter.

Spoon half of the *anko*, if using, on the bottom of the prepared baking dish and spread it out evenly. Pour half of the batter over to cover. Spread another layer of *anko*, if using, over the batter. Spoon the remaining batter on top, covering evenly. Top with the walnuts.

Bake for 30 to 45 minutes, until set. Use a knife or toothpick to test for doneness; there should be no batter on the knife or toothpick when you pull it out. For a browner crust, preheat the broiler and broil for up to 30 seconds.

Using a spatula, take the butter mochi out of the pan, then cut it into desired pieces. Serve warm or at room temperature.

berry *kanten–yose* and *shiratama* mochi with ginger syrup

This is a Japanese version of a fresh fruit cocktail with many interesting textures and flavors. The dish is made with *kanten* (agar) jelly, accompanied by sweetened beans, *shiratama* mochi (rice dumplings made with sweet rice flour), and fruit. *Kanten* is similar to gelatin but hardens at room temperature and is delightfully refreshing for dessert. There are many variations. The classic *kanten* jelly dish is called *mitsumame* if the dish contains cooked beans, and *anmitsu* if the dish contains *anko* (sweetened adzuki bean paste). This recipe deviates a bit; because it is made without the beans it gets another name, *kanten-yose*. I made this *kanten-yose* with fresh strawberry juice; you can use any fruit juice to make *kanten*. I have used apple, plum, grape, and persimmon juices and purees. If the juice or puree is sweet enough, you can omit the sugar. You can prepare the *kanten* a couple of days in advance and keep in the fridge. For the *shiratama* mochi, use *shiratamako* (glutinous rice flour), which yields a very smooth mochi; for a more rustic mochi, use *mochiko* (another glutinous rice flour). You'll want to make the mochi dumplings as close as you can to the time you want to serve the *kanten* so they remain as soft and fresh as possible. If you add *Kuromame-no-Amani* (Sweetened Black Soybeans; page 78) in this dish, you can call it *mitsumame*.

MAKES 4 TO 6 SERVINGS

FOR THE FRUIT *KANTEN* (AGAR)
- 10 ounces (284 g) hulled strawberries
- ¼ cup (50 g) cane sugar, or to taste
- 2 cups (480 ml) filtered water
- 2 teaspoons *kanten* (agar) powder or 2 tablespoons agar flakes

FOR THE GINGER SYRUP
- 1 ounce (30 g) unpeeled ginger, cut into ⅛-inch (3 mm) slices, about ¼ cup
- 1 cup (240 ml) filtered water
- 1 cup (200 g) *kokuto* syrup (page 109) or dark brown or cane sugar
- Pinch of salt

FOR THE MOCHI DUMPLINGS
- ¼ cup (60 g) *shiratamako* or *mochiko* (glutinous/ sweet rice flour, preferably Blue Star Mochiko)
- 2 tablespoons filtered water, or more as needed

FOR THE GARNISHES
- 8 ounces (230 g) stone fruit, such as plums, peaches, or nectarines, pitted and cut into ¼-inch-thick (6 mm) wedges
- 6 ounces (170 g) blueberries, blackberries, strawberries, or boysenberries
- Mint leaves

To make the fruit *kanten*, combine the berries, sugar, and 1 cup (240 ml) water in a medium saucepan and cook over medium-low heat, stirring frequently, until the fruit releases its juices and starts to break down. Lower the heat and continue simmering for 10 minutes. Let cool for about 20 minutes, then strain the mixture through a fine-mesh strainer. For the recipe, you will need 1 cup (240 ml) of juice. If you are short, add water to make 1 cup (240 ml). Taste the juice. If it is too tart, add more sugar to taste. Set aside and enjoy the fruit solids with yogurt or ice cream at another time.

Combine the *kanten* powder with the remaining 1 cup (240 ml) water in a small saucepan and bring to a boil over medium heat, whisking vigorously. Lower the heat and simmer for 2 to 3 minutes, until the powder are completely dissolved.

Gently reheat the juice until it is lukewarm, about 104°F (40°C). Add the *kanten* mixture to the warm juice and blend with a whisk. Pour the mixture into a rectangular container, 5 x 4 x 2 inches (13 x 10 x 5 cm). Cover and refrigerate until set, about 3 hours or up to overnight.

To make the ginger syrup, combine the ginger, water, *kokuto* syrup, and salt in a small saucepan. Bring to a boil over medium heat, then lower the heat to maintain a simmer and cook for 20 minutes, skimming any foam from the top, until darkened and syrupy. Remove from heat and let cool. You can strain the syrup through a fine-mesh strainer and discard the ginger or leave the ginger intact. You will have about ¾ cup of syrup. Store the syrup in a glass container, covered, in the refrigerator until ready to use. It will keep for up to 3 weeks.

To make the mochi dumplings, in a small bowl, mix the *shiratamako* with the water. The flour will be crumbly and will pulverize easily with a fork or spoon. Knead with your fingers until a soft white dough, almost the texture of your earlobe, is formed. You may need to add an additional 1 to 2 teaspoons of water to achieve a pliable paste that is neither crumbly nor creamy and that can be formed into small dumplings. Form about 24 small dumplings using a ½ teaspoon measuring spoon, then flatten the dumplings into disks.

Bring a medium saucepan of water to a boil over medium-high heat and have a bowl of ice water ready. Drop in the dumplings 8 at a time and cook until they begin to float to the surface. Continue cooking for 2 minutes more. Remove from the water using a slotted spoon and drain, then chill in ice water for 2 minutes and drain. Repeat with the remaining dumplings, adding them to a small bowl as they are done.

To serve the *kanten*, cut it into ¾-inch (2 cm) dice; you can use a ruler as a guide to keep the line straight. Put the kanten dice into one medium glass bowl or individual bowls or plates. Add the stone fruit, berries, and then the mochi dumplings. Garnish with the mint and serve with the ginger syrup, using 1 to 2 tablespoons per serving.

hoshigaki (dried persimmons)

Every December, for more than fifty years, my parents would receive a package of *hoshigaki* (dried Hachiya persimmons) in the mail from my old Japanese language tutor who lives in Ogaki, in Gifu Prefecture in the center of Japan. In the box would be eight pieces of acorn-shaped *hoshigaki*—all perfectly uniform in size, their skin soft and smooth with an earthy orange hue and dusted in a powdery white sugar—set in a bed of straw. As a girl, each time I opened the package I was astonished by their beautiful presentation and their floral scent. These *hoshigaki*, produced by the Tsuchiya family for more than 250 years, are called *Gozen Shirogaki*, or imperial white persimmons, named in honor of Emperor Meiji, who loved them.

I never imagined that I could get *hoshigaki* locally in Los Angeles. But several years ago, I was at the Santa Monica Farmers Market and came upon boxes of *hoshigaki*. Their earthy orange hue, dusty white surface, and aesthetic presentation immediately brought me back to Japan. Jeff Rieger and his partner, Laurence Hauben, of Penryn Orchards, based in Placer County at the foothills of the Sierras, make *hoshigaki* following the traditional Japanese method. As the story goes, Jeff was a builder who had bought the orchard from a retired Japanese American farmer with the idea of developing the land and selling it, but he fell in love with the fruit trees and became a farmer himself. He couldn't just cut down thirty years of someone else's life. I took a *hoshigaki* class from Laurence several years ago, and ever since I have turned *hoshigaki* making into a fall tradition. Nowadays, my friends Nancy Nelms in Topanga Canyon, Karen Hillenburg in Pasadena, Jason Kaplan in Silverlake, and more offer me their persimmons when the season arrives, before the birds get to them.

EQUIPMENT

Bucket (metal or plastic)

Box of noncorrosive stainless-steel screws (24 screws)

Kitchen string

Laundry rack or rod to hang the persimmons

Small fan

Newspaper to line the floor

24 red Hachiya persimmons, firm or slightly soft to the touch and dark orange in color, with ½ inch (12 mm) of the branches attached

Wash the fruit in a bucket of water and dry with a towel. Sort them by size—large, medium, and small. It is best to use larger persimmons, which will allow for more shrinkage.

To trim the calyx (the fruit cap that protects the bud and to which the stem is attached), hold the fruit with one hand and a paring knife with the other. Insert the tip of the knife at an angle so it comes out in front of the stem. Using the hand that is not holding the knife, rotate the fruit and cut all around the calyx to remove the peel. If a stem is missing from a persimmon, use a stainless-steel screw; simply screw it gently into the top of the fruit where the stem was.

Cut lengths of kitchen string to about 18 inches (46 cm) long; you'll be attaching one persimmon to each end of the string. Aim to have a pair of persimmons of similar size on each string.

Using a slip knot, tie the ends of the strings to the stem (or stainless-steel screw) of each fruit. Trim the short ends with scissors so they don't touch the fruit.

Bring a medium pot of water to a boil and dip the fruit in it for 3 seconds. This will sterilize and kill any bacteria—an important step before you dry the fruit.

Hang the tied fruit on a rack, making sure the persimmons are not touching one another. Put the rack close to a sunny window. The rack can be placed outside during the day but must be brought inside at night. Put a newspaper underneath the fruit to catch any dripping juice or fallen fruit. Place a small rotating fan in the room near the persimmons to speed up the drying process and maintain good air circulation; the fan will also keep fruit flies away.

After a week, check to see if the fruit is dry. If it is dry to the touch, start massaging it. Begin with just a gentle touch once a day—do not squeeze— and work your way up to a gentle massage, but no squeezing. The fruit will start to soften and shrivel. If you see any mold (white or black spores) forming, scrape it away and dab a bit of vodka or other clear liquor in the area. Tie the remaining fruit to the rack and allow it to dry.

Repeat this daily massage for 3 to 4 weeks, until the fruit feels firm but with some softness remaining inside. Cut a piece and taste it. If it is raisin-like in chewiness and sweet, the persimmon is ready. A white coating forming on the surface of the fruit is the natural sugar crystalizing, so don't confuse this coating with mold. The coating is a sign that the fruit is drying properly.

Remove from the rack and store in a plastic container or bag in the refrigerator or freezer. It will keep for up to 1 year. You can enjoy it straight—it is great with blue cheese—or steeped as tea with some cinnamon sticks, sliced ginger, and honey.

beverages

everyday teas

Japanese people have enjoyed tea for centuries not only as a soothing beverage but also for its restorative and relaxing value. Tea was introduced to Japan by the Chinese in the eighth century and made popular by Zen Buddhist monks who drank tea to stay awake during the long hours of meditation. Later, tea drinking was turned into an artistic and philosophical practice that evolved into the tea ceremony. In my grandmother's house in Kamakura, there was a formal tea room where the tea ceremony was performed on a weekly basis. I recall my grandmother spending a good amount of time preparing the tea room for the tea ceremony, arranging the flowers in a vase, changing a single scroll painting to suit the seasons, and heating the charcoal to boil the water. The tea master and ladies who lived in the neighborhood would gather in the tea room, prepare the tea, and engage in stylized conversation. The tea ceremony took a couple of hours, sometimes even longer if a small meal was served to whet the appetite for tea. My grandmother would invite me to join the tea ceremony, usually when the little tea cakes were served with the *matcha* tea. I always enjoyed the rituals of the ceremony.

While Japanese appreciate the essence of the rituals of the tea ceremony, you will find more "everyday" or informal tea drinking in Japan today.

There are two categories of Japanese tea: leaf tea and powdered tea. Leaf tea is the most popular type. For leaf tea, leaves are steamed and then shaped, dried, and separated by quality. Powdered tea comes from leaf tea; the steamed leaves are laid flat to dry and then stone milled into a fine green powder.

When making tea, it is best to use spring water. I use filtered water for my everyday tea.

matcha

Matcha is a bright jade-green tea that is served at formal tea ceremonies but also has many other preparations these days: as a popular drink taken casually with milk, as a seasoning to make green tea ice cream, or even as a fragrance for cosmetics. *Matcha* is made from the budding leaves of the tea plant, dried and crushed to a fine powder in a mill. *Matcha* is not steeped in hot water, as most Westerners prepare tea, but simply added to hot water and then whipped to a creamy froth. The initial taste is slightly bitter but then it settles into a mellow flavor.

To make 1 serving, sift 1 to 2 teaspoons *matcha* into a small bowl using a small sifter. Add ¼ cup (60 ml) hot (not boiling) water. Holding the bowl with one hand, whisk vigorously in a zigzag pattern using a bamboo tea whisk held in your other hand. Avoid scratching the bottom of the tea bowl with the whisk because it will hurt the tip of the whisk. Fine froth is preferred over big, frothy bubbles on the surface of the tea. Serve immediately, sipping straight from the bowl.

sencha

Sencha is green tea of the highest quality, made from the first harvest in May. Freshly picked leaves are steamed, quickly cooled, and then rolled by hand or machine. It is appreciated not so much as a thirst quencher as for its beautiful fragrance; it also has a pleasant bitter flavor and a lovely light-green color. *Shincha,* or new crop *sencha,* is available in Japan in April and is fragrant and full of umami flavors.

To make 4 servings of *sencha,* bring 1 cup (240 ml) water to a boil, let it stand for 2 minutes, and then pour into a pot with 2 teaspoons of tea leaves. Let stand for 1 minute and then pour the tea bit by bit, alternating among 4 cups so that everyone gets an equal amount of tea of equal strength.

bancha

Bancha is the lowest grade of tea, made from mature tough tea leaves and twigs; it has a grassy straw smell that I love, perhaps because it was the only kind of tea that my paternal grandmother in Toyko would drink. *Bancha* is a good basic tea with a toasty, nonbitter taste that suits all occasions. A few twigs and stems at the bottom of your cup are considered attractive. And if a twig or stem is seen afloat in your tea cup in a vertical position—which is very rare—it is regarded as a sign that good luck is coming your way. As a child, I always wished for a standing twig in my tea cup.

To make 4 servings of *bancha*, put 2 to 3 tablespoons of tea leaves into a tea pot. Add 2 cups (480 ml) boiling water and steep for 1½ minutes. Pour into tea cups to serve.

hojicha

Hojicha came out in Kyoto in the 1920s, when tea merchants started roasting *bancha* tea leaves over charcoal—possibly as an economical way to make use of mature tough tea leaves and twigs that got mixed in with the tea leaves. The roasted mixture produced an appealing, strong aroma, and the process of toasting or roasting *bancha* became popular enough to create a new style of green tea.

To make 4 servings of *hojicha*, put 2 to 3 tablespoons of tea leaves into a pot. Add 2 cups (480 ml) boiling water and steep for 1½ minutes. Pour into tea cups to serve.

genmaicha

Genmaicha is *bancha* blended with toasted and popped sweet or glutinous rice. It is less astringent than regular green tea and is aromatic with a robust flavor. This tea was "discovered" when a tea merchant tried to repurpose *kagami mochi*, the ceremonial New Year's pounded rice. He cracked and toasted the mochi and then added it to tea.

To make 4 servings of *genmaicha*, put 2 to 3 tablespoons of tea leaves into a pot. Add 2 cups (480 ml) boiling water and steep for 1½ minutes. Pour into tea cups to serve. Do not let the tea steep for too long or the tannins will be released and make it bitter.

sake

Even though my mother drank beer and my father didn't drink very much at all, sake was brought out on festive occasions and for ceremonial purposes to serve the household gods or pay respects to our ancestors. Sake is the most iconic drink of Japan. I have always associated sake with a kind of elixir. When my father became old, he bought himself a beautiful sake jug and a pair of cups so he could have a few sips of the fragrant drink with every meal, like a potion for longevity. When I was back in Tokyo, we would enjoy sips of sake together. My father lived to the ripe age of ninety-three. I find sake to be a particularly elegant and versatile drink. Try it on its own, paired with food (both Japanese and Western), or, like my father did, as a fountain of youth.

Sake is made by fermenting rice, water, yeast, and koji (*Aspergillus oryzae*). It is produced by a brewing process similar to beer. Flavorwise, sake is as complex as wine. It can be dry, sweet, crisp, fruity, mellow, and acidic; it is less acidic than wine and pairs well with almost any food. There are so many styles of sake to choose from. *Tokutei meisho-shu*, premium-grade sake, makes up 25 percent; and *futsu-shu*, ordinary table sake, makes up 75 percent.

There are a number of factors that distinguish premium-grade sake from ordinary-grade sake. Within the premium-grade sake, there are two categories: *junmai-shu* and *honjozo-shu*. *Junmai-shu* is made with pure rice, koji, yeast, and water. *Honjozo-shu* is made when a small amount of distilled alcohol is added near the end of the fermentation process; the added alcohol brings out the aroma. It is lighter than *junmai-shu*. It's a matter of taste.

To make sake, rice grains are polished away, leaving mostly the starch that is used by the brewer. The starch percentages range from 35 to 65 percent. The higher the polishing ratio, the cleaner and fruitier the sake becomes; the sake made from less polished rice tends to have an earthier, fuller, slightly more acidic flavor than other sakes. The word *ginjo* indicates a higher polishing ratio of 40 percent (with 60 percent of the rice grain remaining); *daiginjo* indicates an even higher polishing ratio of 50 percent or more (with 50 percent of the grain remaining). So if you see a sake labeled *junmai ginjo*, it means it is pure rice sake with a polishing ratio of 40 percent. If it has added alcohol, it will be labeled as *ginjo*. *Namazake*, which is unpasteurized fresh sake, is bolder and more refreshing in taste than pasteurized sake but must be kept refrigerated. *Nigorizake*, which is milky and cloudy because it contains the sake lees—these are filtered out in other kinds of sake—is sweet and can be served with spicy foods or as a dessert sake. I suggest you try the premium-grade sake, starting with *junmai-shu*. You can work your way into the variations of *junmai-shu*, *junmai ginjo-shu*, and *junmai daiginjo-shu*, and other types of sake.

HOW TO SERVE SAKE

There are a number of ways to enjoy sake. Let's consider temperature. You can drink sake slightly heated, at room temperature, or chilled. The optimum temperature for serving sake, according to sake experts, can vary depending on several factors: dryness, acidity, mellowness, and fragrance, similar to wine. Do not serve sake too cold or too hot—never higher than 105°F (40°C). Warm sake should be warm to the touch. Cold sake should never be icy cold. Extreme temperatures overwhelm the subtle fragrance or flavors. Premium-grade sake should never be heated but enjoyed chilled. Sake can also be served on the rocks or like a cocktail with fruit juice or club soda.

SHELF LIFE OF SAKE

A good thing to know is that sake is usually consumed within a year (within six months is even better) and stored in a cool place or refrigerated. Regular sake, however, loses its crispness and vitality after a year. I use old sake for cooking. There is also a type of sake that is aged. At Obata Brewery, they age sake in the old gold mines of the Sado Island where the temperatures remain low. I tasted their ten-year-old-plus aged *ginjo-shu* sake. It took on a pleasant amber color, medium texture, and rich and subtly spicy flavors. Proper care is needed to age sake.

SAKE RITUAL

If you are at someone's home or at a restaurant and the host offers you sake, hold up the cup to make pouring easier. You will take a sip, then reciprocate by serving the host. A few polite exchanges will happen until you can say, "Don't worry, I can pour myself." If you are not a drinker and someone offers you sake, it is better to receive a little and pretend to take a small sip than to say no thank you. Repeated toasts of good luck, friendship, or love happen throughout the course of the meal.

OTSUMAMI (NIBBLES WITH ALCOHOLIC BEVERAGES)

Niboshi (dried sardines, page 28) makes a crunchy, calcium-rich, tasty *otsumami*. I would keep them in a tin box for my son to snack on when he was a boy. For a quick recipe, simply toast the *niboshi* in a dry pan for a few minutes, until they turn crispy. Then, you can add some peanuts or sesame seeds and chopped dried chile peppers in the mix for extra crunch and spice.

okazu, sweets, and beverages

other japanese alcoholic beverages

Japanese craft beer, *shochu*, and whiskey are gaining fans around the world, becoming available in many stores in the United States. In Japan, dining often begins with a ritual of toasting with beer. You will hear people say *"Mazu biru de kampai!"* which means "Let's toast with beer first!" and then you can either stay with beer or move onto sake or other alcoholic beverages. *Shochu* is a distilled beverage with a 25-40 percent alcohol. While sake is more well known outside of Japan, *shochu* is the more popular alcoholic beverage in Japan. It is made of *imo* (sweet potato), *kome* (rice), *mugi* (barley), *soba* (buckwheat), *goma* (sesame seed), and more than a dozen other ingredients. Flavors can range from light to earthy, peppery to grain-like, and dry to subtly sweet in taste. Then there are the Japanese whiskeys, which are highly sought after and get super high marks by critics. Japanese whiskey is known for its distinctly smooth and silky texture. Besides whiskey, the Japanese are also producing wines. In fact, my paternal grandfather, Rihei Kondo, and wine maker Denbei Kamiya of Hachibudo-shu were pioneer producers of wine in Japan in the early 1900s. They were successful in marketing the wine, but the task to convert Japanese was not easy. Kamiya added honey and Chinese herbs to make the beverage sweeter to suit the Japanese palate. Before the war, my grandmother opened a restaurant in Tokyo that served wine with Japanese food. I still have remnants of the cotton cloths used by the servers with the company logo of bees and grapes. I treasure the piece of Hachibudo-shu's history. Today there are more than two hundred Japanese wineries. Their endeavor continues. The thing to do when you visit Japan is to try a variety of beverages.

umeshu (plum wine)

Umeshu (plum wine) is a liquor made with *ume* plums. I make plum wine with *shochu*, a distilled Japanese liquor made from sweet potato or grains such as barley, rice, and buckwheat. Plum wine is enjoyed on the rocks or with club soda, or as a little shot to boost your energy. *Shochu* and rock sugar are available at Japanese markets. If you have trouble finding *shochu*, use vodka instead.

During *ume* season, I also make *Ume* Syrup (page 288). It is a versatile, mild, and fruity syrup that can be used like a simple syrup; I baste my *Tonkatsu* (Pork Cutlet; page 155) with it. And although they are called plums, *ume* plums belong to the family of apricots, so don't try to substitute other plums for *ume* plums. Look for *ume* plums between May to June in Asian markets.

MAKES ABOUT 2 QUARTS (2 L)

EQUIPMENT
    4-quart (4 L) glass jar, sterilized

2¼ pounds (1 kg) green *ume* plums
4 cups (794 g) white rock sugar
7½ cups (1.8 L) *shochu* or vodka

Remove the stems from the plums and discard any bruised ones. Wash the plums and drain. Dry with paper towels.

Put the plums in a 4-quart (4 L) glass jar in a single layer. Add enough rock sugar to cover the plums. Then make another layer, followed by more sugar. Repeat this step until you use up all the plums and sugar.

Pour the liquor over the plums and keep the jar loosely closed. Store in a cool, shady place for a year to ferment, giving the container a shake to stir the sugar on the bottom after 1 month. The liquor can be enjoyed on the rocks or diluted with club soda or water. The plums also can be eaten.

ume syrup

This is a fragrant syrup that my Korean friends showed me how to make and cook with. In Korean, it is called *maesil chung*. Follow the same recipe as *umeshu* but omit the liquor. After a week in the jar, the liquid will start to emerge from the plums. Turn the jar upside-down and mix the liquid with the sugar by gently shaking the container several times. The sugar will dissolve on its own accord and turn into syrup. After 3 months, the syrup will be golden in color and ready to use. Drain the syrup through a strainer and transfer it to a bottle.

The syrup makes a very refreshing and fragrant beverage. Dilute it with water or club soda and serve it over ice. You can also use the syrup as a substitute for cane sugar. I use it to make an *ume shiso* paste for my *Tonkatsu* Sauce (page 156).

amazake (fermented rice drink)

During New Year's or Girls' Day in Japan, people drink *amazake* as part of the festive rituals held at Shinto shrines. *Amazake* is one of the oldest fermented rice beverages in Japan. It is sweet without having any added sugar and has a pleasant grassy aroma. It is also considered an energy booster.

Though it sounds a bit like sake, most *amazake* is alcohol-free, so children can drink it too; in fact, Japanese people call *amazake* "mother's milk" and even give it to their babies. *Amazake* is currently enjoying a comeback in Japan because of its nutritious probiotic qualities and its versatility as a seasoning. It is loaded with enzymes and bacteria that aid digestion.

The consistency of *amazake* is like a rice porridge. When pureed, it turns into cream; when it is diluted with water, it behaves like milk. I like *amazake* straight, by the spoonful like a porridge. You can serve the *amazake* seasoned with grated ginger, yuzu, or lemon zest. You can also drink it like Mexican *horchata* (made with rice, cinnamon, and vanilla). Or you can make *Amazake* Ice Pops (page 271). You can also baste meat or seafood with *amazake* because it acts as a marinade and tenderizer. In this it is similar to *shio koji* (fermented koji salt), except that *amazake* is salt-free.

Amazake is made by inoculating steamed rice with the fungus *Aspergillus oryzae*, just like miso, soy sauce, sake, and rice vinegar. While prepared *amazake* is available at Japanese markets, making it yourself is easy. All you need is rice, koji, and filtered water. For this recipe, I use short or medium grain white rice or *haiga* rice. To ferment the rice, you will need a way to keep it warm (at around 140°F/60°C) for at least 8 hours. For this you can use an electric rice cooker, yogurt maker, dehydrator, or even a thermos. You can buy dried koji at Japanese markets or online. I use Cold Mountain Dry White Rice Koji.

MAKES ABOUT 3½ CUPS (830 ML)

EQUIPMENT
> Digital thermometer
> Rice cooker, yogurt maker, dehydrator, or large thermos (*see note*)

> ¾ cup (180 g) uncooked short- or medium-grain white rice or *haiga* rice
> 2½ cups (600 ml) filtered water
> 1 pound (455 g) dry white rice koji

Rinse the rice and soak it in 1¼ cups (300 ml) filtered water for 30 minutes. Then cook the rice as you would Basic White Rice (page 46).

Combine the hot rice with the remaining 1¼ cups (300 ml) filtered water, stirring with a wooden paddle or spatula to lower the temperature to 140°F (60°C). It is important to maintain this temperature for the rice to ferment. Mix in the dried koji and transfer to an electric rice cooker on the "keep warm" setting with the lid open and covered with a kitchen towel for 8 hours; or use a yogurt maker or dehydrator set at 140°F (60°C) for the same amount of time. After 8 hours, stir well. When the mixture is creamy and sweet, it is ready.

Cool the *amazake* to room temperature and store it in the refrigerator in a loosely covered container.

Note: If using a thermos to make *amazake*, preheat the container with hot water. Discard the hot water and then add the warm inoculated rice mixture. Wrap the thermos in a towel and leave it in a warm room. After 8 hours, give the rice mixture a stir and taste.

acknowledgments

In memory of Ana (2000–2017),
our beloved dog who loved my *onigiri*.

There are so many people who encouraged me to write this book, which represents years of meals, kitchen sessions, writings, conversations, food preparations, research, recipe testing, pop-ups, seminars, workshops, camping, grain-growing experiments, and sleepovers. These experiences and people inspired me to think about the quality of food we grow, cook, and eat; they helped convince me that home cooking is essential to a sustainable and healthy society. I learned so much from all of them, and I hope they see themselves reflected in this book.

I would first like to thank those who guided me in making this book: To my publisher, Sara Bercholz, and everyone at Roost Books who believed in Japanese Home Cooking from the start. To my wonderful editor, Jennifer Brown, for her vision and careful pruning of my culinary ramblings. To those on the team at Roost: Audra Figgins, Kara Plikaitis, Claire Kelley, Jess Townsend, Laura Shaw, Leda Scheintaub, Emily Wichland, and Victoria Jones.

To my agent, Danielle Svetkov, for her great instincts and wisdom.

To Juliette Bellocq, for her lovely illustrations and creativity.

To Erin Hogan, who helped me structure my thoughts early on and to whom I owe more gyoza.

To the brilliant photographer Rick Poon, who was with me on this project from start to finish, capturing the light and laughter from kitchen to rice farm.

To Mamiko Nishiyama for being my dashi maestra and longtime friend.

To Niki Nakayama and Carole Iida-Nakayama for sharing their talent and support.

To Robin Koda for letting me use her vintage Japanese tableware for the shoot, laughter, and making sure I never ran out of rice.

To Karen Hillenburg for her generous and kind spirit.

To Laiko Bahrs for helping me navigate the food world and for the love of baked eggs.

For their inspiration and support, my sincere thanks to Francesco Allegro, Yoshitomo Arakawa, Sean and Renee Baker, Nick Balla and Courtney Burns, Yolanda Burrell, Sonya Chun, Caroline Forbes, Cindy and Doug Daniels, Tara Duggan, Lydia Esparza and Nick Lessins, Gillian Ferguson, Harriet Fukushima, Paul Gamba, Angelo Garro, Teri Gelber, Ingrid Goesnar, Clemence Gossett, Jeffrey Hammelman, John Hammond, Ben Hunter, Dr. Stephen Jones, Flora Ito, Roxana Jullapat, Sandor Katz, Bill and Miriam Keener, Bora Kim, Christina Kim, Ji Hey Kim, Evan Kleiman, Jessica Koslow, John Lewallen and Barbara Stephens, Jodi Liano, Takashi Hosokawa, Rachel Khong, Francis Lam, Travis Lett, Cecilia Leung, Ramsey Naito, Sherry Mandell, Deborah Madison, Na Young Ma, Peggy Marks, Nanna Meyer, Tim Michael, Veronica Miller and David Motta, Naoko Moore, Christine Moore, Diane Plaskow, Mihn Pham, Russ Parsons, Chad Robertson, Nicole Rucker, Mary Pult and Mitch Rosenthal, Marisa Roth, Glenn Roberts, Keiko and Tak Shinomoto, Agnes and Richard Thaler, Hannah Tierney, Katheryn Doi Todd, Fred Seidman and S. Irene Virbila, Mutsuko Soma, Kwang Uh and Mina Park, Marta Teegan and Robert Stelzner, Alice Waters, Alex Weiser, Kirsten West, Kelly Whitaker, Seiichi Yokota, Kuniko Yagi, Shiho Yoshikawa, Angie Meung and Ted Vadakan, Jeff and Emma Zimmerman, and Lora Zarubin.

I am grateful to all my students who offered to test my recipes and provide me with insight.

My gratitude goes to all my friends. It is impossible to list everyone that has helped me along this journey. Ultimately, I want to acknowledge and express my deepest appreciation for the entire community that has supported my pursuit of food and culture.

Last, but certainly not least, warmest thanks to my family. Domo arigato to my sisters, Fuyuko and Sachiko, and my niece, Miki. To my son and daughter-in-law, Sakae and Binah. To my stepson, Tyler, and his family, Emmalina, Masa, and Mai. To my husband, Katsuhisa Sakai—always.

resources

FOR FOOD

ANSON MILLS
(803) 467-4122
ansonmills.com
Heirloom grains and flours, including *sobakoh* (soba-grade flour)

COOKBOOK
(213) 250-1900
cookbookla.com
Grocery store in Los Angeles

THE JAPANESE PANTRY
thejapanesepantry.com
Japanese artisan foods

KAI GOURMET
(310) 988-4345
kaigourmet.com
Premium-quality seafood

KANDARIAN ORGANIC FARMS
(805) 528-4007
kandarianorganics.com
Heirloom grains, legumes, and flours

KING ARTHUR FLOUR
(802) 649-3361
kingarthurflour.com
Flours and bakeware

KODA FARMS
(209) 392-2191
kodafarms.com
Superior Japanese-style rice

LAURA SOYBEANS
(515) 583-2198
laurasoybeans.com
Non-GMO soybeans

MENDICINO SEA VEGETABLE COMPANY
www.seaweed.net
(707) 895-2996
Wildcraft seaweed and seaweed workshops

MEIJI TOFU
(310) 538-0403
meijitofu.com
Artisanal tofu

MITSUWA MARKETPLACE
(310) 398-2113
mitsuwa.com
Japanese groceries

NIJIYA MARKET
(310) 575-3300
nijiya.com
Japanese groceries

TOKYO FISH MARKET
(510) 524-7243
tokyofish.net
Japanese groceries

UWAJIMAYA
(206) 624-6248
uwajimaya.com
Japanese groceries

WEISER FAMILY FARMS
(213) 748-9300
weiserfamilyfarms.com
Vegetables, fruits, and heirloom grains in California

YAGICHO HONTEN
+81-3-3241-1211
yagicho-honten.tokyo
Premium-grade bonito flakes, seaweed, dried shiitake mushrooms

YOKOSE SEAFOOD
(310) 766-0316
yokoseseafood.com
Premium seafood, local (Southern California) and imported from Japan

FOR JAPANESE BEVERAGES

JOTO SAKE
(919) 253-7700
www.jotosake.com
Artisanal sake imported into the US

OBATA SAKE BREWERY
obata-shuzo.com
Premium sake brewery on Sado Island, Niigata Prefecture

SAKAYA
(212) 505-7253
sakayanyc.com
Japanese premium sakes from artisanal, small-production breweries

UMAMI MART
(510) 250-9559
umamimart.com
Japanese sake, *shochu*, whiskey, and barware

FOR CERAMICS, POTTERY AND KITCHEN EQUIPMENT

COLLEEN HENNESSEY CLAYWORKS
colleenhennessey.net
Simple, functional ceramics

HITACHIYA USA
(310) 534-3136
hitachiyausa.com
Japanese cutlery (including soba-making tools), cookware, tableware, and workshops

MITSUKO SIEGRIST
mitsukosiegrist.com
Handmade ceramics

MT. WASHINGTON POTTERY
mtwashingtonpottery.com
Handmade pottery and ceramics

SHED
(707) 413-7433
healdsburgshed.com
Japanese cookware, tableware, and artisan food products

TIGER
(866) 558-4437
tiger-corporation-us.com/support/service-centers/
Electric rice cookers

TOIRO KITCHEN & SUPPLY
(323) 380-5052
toirokitchen.com
Donabe (clay pots)

TORTOISE GENERAL STORE
(310) 314-8448
tortoisegeneralstore.com
Japanese ceramics, tableware, and workshops

index

about the author

SONOKO SAKAI is a cooking teacher, noodle maker, food writer, and grain activist. She was born in New York and raised in Tokyo, Kamakura, Mexico City, San Francisco, and Los Angeles. She is the author of two other Japanese cookbooks, *The Poetical Pursuit of Food: Japanese Recipes for American Cooks* and *Rice Craft*. Her stories and recipes have been featured in the *Los Angeles Times*, *San Francisco Chronicle*, *Chicago Tribune*, *Saveur*, and *Lucky Peach*. Today, along with teaching cooking workshops around the world, she devotes her time to the restoration and preservation of food traditions and culture, soba noodles being among one of her pursuits. She lives in Los Angeles and on a ranch in Tehachapi with her husband, the sculptor Katsuhisa Sakai, their dog, Q, and two cats, Kinchan and Chapi.

for my students

The artist Seiho Takeuchi (1864–1942) once told his students that they should first learn to draw from life as carefully as possible, then do so using their brush as little as possible; and that after that it was all *satori*, enlightenment. Cooking is the same: enlightenment.

—KITAOJI ROSANJIN, artist and epicure (1883–1959)

Roost Books
An imprint of Shambhala Publications, Inc.
4720 Walnut Street
Boulder, Colorado 80301
roostbooks.com

©2019 by Sonoko Sakai
Photographs ©2019 by Rick Poon

9 8 7 6 5 4 3 2 1

FIRST EDITION

Printed in the United States of America
⊗ This edition is printed on acid-free paper
that meets the American National Standards Institute
Z39.48 Standard.

♻ Shambhala Publications makes every effort to print on recycled paper. For more information please visit www.shambhala.com.

Roost Books is distributed worldwide by Penguin Random House, Inc., and its subsidiaries.

Designed by Laura Shaw Design

LIBRARY OF CONGRESS CATALOGING-IN-PUBLICATION DATA

Names: Sakai, Sonoko, 1955– author.
Title: Japanese home cooking: simple meals, authentic flavors / Sonoko Sakai; photographs by Rick Poon; illustrations by Juliette Bellocq.
Description: First edition. | Boulder: Roost Books, 2019. | Includes index.
Identifiers: LCCN 2018041562 | ISBN 9781611806168 (hardback: alk. paper)
Subjects: LCSH: Cooking, Japanese. | LCGFT: Cookbooks.
Classification: LCC TX724.5.J3 S24 2019 | DDC 641.5952–dc23
LC record available at https://lccn.loc.gov/2018041562